I0484417

PHENOMENA

Horror off the screen... And into your lap

Phil Russell

PHENOMENA

A Bad News Press book

First published by Bad News Press in 2015

PHENOMENA

Text copyright © Phil Russell

This volume copyright © Phil Russell 2015

Cover image courtesy of S.N. Prodis

<phil.russell81@hotmail.com>

A CIP catalogue record of this book is available at the British library.

ISBN-13: 978-1508717003

ISBN-10: 1508717001

Introduction

Hello and welcome to another volume of movie reviews. This latest volume is a little different from the previous books as this time I explore the horror genre as a whole rather than concentrating on the most controversial and disturbing titles. That's not to say that this book doesn't contain its fair share of twisted pics; I have included reviews of Olaf Ittenbach's extremely violent *Beyond the Limits* (2003), William Friedkin's highly controversial serial killer opus, *Cruising* (1980), Harmony Korine's insane *Gummo* (1997), *Julien Donkey-Boy* (1999) and *Trash Humpers* (2009), the Australian vigilante shocker, *The Horseman* (2008), and Marian Dora's extremely distasteful art-trash, *Melancholie der Engel* (2009), among others.

In the following pages you'll find entries for all kinds of horror – and horror-related – films, from past and present. From mainstream hits like *Critters* (1986), *The Blob* (1958, 1988), *Misery* (1990) and *Evil Dead* (2013), to lesser-known titles like *Carver* (2008), *The Farm House* (2008) and *American Mary* (2012). The idea behind the book was to watch and write about whatever genre movies came my way in the last twelve months The aim was to sift through as much crap as I could, and hopefully uncover a few gems along the way. Among the pleasant surprises were the interloper nightmare of *Devil's Pond* (2003), the Heaven's Gate-related, destructive cult epic, *Mysterious Two* (1982), the assorted monster-mash of *Curse of the Blue Lights* (1988), the unintentionally hilarious *Seven In Darkness* (1969), the 'mad doctor' movie turned on its head in *The Rejuvenator* (1988), the garbage-munching zombie beach bums of *Surf II* (1984), and Bernard Rose's postmodern kill-a-thon, *Snuff-Movie* (2005).

PHENOMENA

Another film that bowled me over was *V/H/S 2*, especially as the original was such an over-hyped piece of shit. For me, the sequel ranks in the top 3 greatest anthology horrors of all time. If you enjoyed the alarming, hand-held chaotic likes of *[Rec]* and *Cloverfield* then *V/H/S 2* is a must-see movie. I also attempt to defend Ridley Scott's nightmarish and misunderstood *The Counselor* (2013), a film which – I promise – will be a cult classic in years to come. But for all the goodies to be found in this book, there is also a lot of crap to wade through, which, if you're a horror fan like me, you'll know it comes with the territory.

Do you ever stay up half the night watching shit movies? If you do, you're not alone. I do it more than I care to admit. Your senses are much more alert at night, it's an evolutionary trait we inherited as human animals. Back in the caveman days, those who didn't pay attention to the bumps in the night were often torn to shreds by wild animals. But we descended from the jittery ones; the paranoid, shifty scaredy-cats who were looking over their shoulders every two minutes. Hence, that's probably one of the reasons why movies – particularly *horror* movies – are much easier to appreciate at night in a darkened theatre or in your darkened living room at home. Our ancestor's genes live on within us when we see some stupid jock take a hatchet to the face – that primordial part of our DNA still loves to poke a stick at the corpse of that bloated, brave caveman who was simply too fucking stupid to pay attention to the bumps in the night.

But it's not all bad. Towards the back of the book, I struggle to express my love for *The Walking Dead* (2010-) while kicking myself for having ignored the series for so long. Other TV series' covered include the little seen *Darkroom* (1981-82), the classic *Tales From the Crypt* (1989-96), and the mediocre *Nightmares and Dreamscapes* (2006), based on the stories of Stephen King.

Anyway, thanks to everyone who has stuck around and read my mumblings. As always, feel free to get in touch with suggestions and recommendations. But please don't ask me to follow you on Tweetbook or any of that stuff. It's not my thing. I know, I'm a caveman, so leave me alone. I think I've managed to zap all the typos this time, but if you notice any, please keep them to yourself. I don't want to know. Typos tend to breed like rabbits when I'm not looking, I get it now – keep them as pets or something.

I'm also proud to say that all of the reviews in this book are my real opinions; unlike some other books and horror review websites, where every movie they see is 'awesome!', no matter how appallingly bad they are, just so they can continue to receive free DVD screeners and be invited to press screenings, while actively misinforming their 150,000 or so Facebook 'likers.' Not so here. I don't accept free screeners, I don't have any filmmaker friends, I don't owe any favours, and I don't feel obliged to be kind to any film I review. That's not to say that I'm overly critical, either. I like to think I'm fair.

Oh, and by the way, if you're offended by any word in the English language, you shouldn't be reading this book. Just put it down and go away. What are you even doing here? Piss off! Go on, and close the door behind you, you squeaky little cunt fart.

I hope the rest of you enjoy the book.

Phil Russell
March, 2015

Abducted (1973)

(aka *Schoolgirls In Chains*; *Girls in Chains*; *Let's Play Dead*)

Dir: Don Jones /USA

Two retarded brothers are 'instructed' by their twisted, domineering mother to abduct young women and bring them back to their underground lair in the backyard. There, the unfortunate girls are subjected to rape and other 'games' like doctor and hide and seek, while they are restrained with collars and chains around their necks. However, one day the simple brains kidnap a feisty blonde who isn't in the mood for their shit... *Abducted* is an underrated backwoods horror of the post-*Psycho* (1960) variety that nonetheless absorbs its inspiration to successfully ring a few changes on the familiar theme. It isn't often that you'll find realistic acting abilities in grindhouse exploitation movies, but this film boasts impressive performances all round. There are no hammy psychos here; from the retarded games of the brothers to the fearful, captive women desperate to escape, all of the performances ring true. John Stoglin's role as the frustrated child in a man's body is superb, and all the more creepy as viewers are subjected to his rape fantasies from his own childish perspective. Gary Kent – an exploitation regular who also crops up in the works of Al Adamson and Ray Dennis Stekler – offers a more subtle form of madness inflicted by the monstrous mother who sexually abused him, even into adulthood. The result is a film which, despite all the leering, grindhouse sleaze, is actually an emotionally-driven film rather than one built purely on visceral shocks. Similarly-themed movies include *Deranged* (1974), *Mother's Day* (1980) and *Barn of the Naked Dead* (1974).

The Abominable Dr Phibes (1971)

Dir: Robert Fuest /USA

"Nine killed her. Nine shall die. Nine eternities in doom!" After a team of physicians fail to save a woman's life following a car crash, her husband, the horribly disfigured Dr Anton Phibes, engineers an elaborate scheme of revenge, murdering each of them in the style of Old Testament biblical plagues of Egypt: hence rabid rats, frogs, bees, locust's blood, hail, etc. Phibes sees Vincent Price's third term as the horror anti-hero of choice after doomy 50s fare like *House On Haunted Hill* and *House of Wax*, and the 60s flamboyance of *The Fall of the House of Usher* and *Masque of the Red Death*. By this time in the early 70s, Price had embraced the gothic roots of horror with this Hammer-esque madcap caper which mixes slick art deco stylings with a British-style gallows humour. The detectives on the case constantly hit a brick wall due to their belief that Phibes is dead, but the avenging doctor is still very much alive and communicates through a victrola via a cord, and drinks wine through a hole in his throat. It was followed by the sequel, *Dr Phibes Rises Again* (1972).

The Abominable Snowman (1957)

(aka *The Abominable Snowman of the Himalayas*)
Dir: Val Guest /UK
Not long after the success of *The Curse of Frankenstein* (1957), Hammer produced this film based on Nigel Kneale's 1955 TV play, '*The Creature*', starring Peter Cushing. Shot in atmospheric black and white, and avoiding the colourful excesses of *Curse*, this film nonetheless offers up a certain degree of tension and unease, and is still worth a watch on a cold winter's night. The story centres on a Himalayan expedition headed by an American entrepreneur (Forrest Tucker) and an English doctor (Cushing), who are out to discover evidence of the Yeti's existence. And it isn't long before their party is being picked off, one by one. Though it was largely shot on the backlots at Bray Studios and Pinewood, the film also has the added benefit of location shots in the Pyrenees, managing to convince viewers of its Himalayan setting. There's also a Tibetan monastery set designed by Bernard Robinson which offers acute details, and a wise old Llama who seems to know more than he lets on about the elusive Yeti. Audiences at the time who were expecting a typical 'monsters-on-the-rampage' type of horror show were largely disappointed by the film's thoughtful, character-driven, philosophical approach, but the film's overall message – basically, a rumination on the destructive nature of mankind – was a refreshing one for its time, as noted in the Sunday Times; "For once an engaging monster is neither bombed, roasted nor

electrocuted. For this welcome courtesy, as well as its thrills and nonsense, I salute *The Abominable Snowman*."

The Abomination (1986)
Dir: Max Raven /USA
A bizarre, home-brewed horror in which a mother coughs up her lung tumour. It then mutates, enlarges, takes control of her son and terrorises a small Texas community. Hmm, I wonder if there could be a message here about the ravages of cancer... This film marks a rare attempt by a low-budget filmmaker to tackle Cronenbergian body horror, and if the results are far from successful, this flick does at least have a vicious toothy cancer creature in the mix which looks similar to the critters in *The Deadly Spawn* (1982). Perhaps director Max Raven will return to filmmaking one day with a movie about gonorrhea in which a town full of dicks and pussies suddenly ooze a thick green slime that dribbles out from the bottom of their hems and leaves trails on the ground. The local virgin follows the tracks while stopping his dog from licking up the gloop, and the trail leads to a Texas barn where unprotected demonic orgies are going on... You know, something with a very subtle social message like *The Abomination*.

Affliction (1997)
Dir: Paul Schrader /USA
Wade Whitehouse is a small town traffic cop trying to gain custody of his daughter. He also bears the scars of being raised by a monstrous father. And after a visitor to the town dies in a hunting accident, Wade begins to piece together a murder conspiracy which seems to involve corruption in high places. But his attempts to get to grips with the mystery are thwarted by an incessant tooth-ache. Tensions reach boiling point after the death of his mother, when he and his girlfriend are forced to move back into his vicious father's house. The brilliant Paul Schrader wrote and directed this icy gem that delves into the dark heart of masculinity. And with the film based on Russell Bank's novel, and with the much underrated Nick Nolte in the lead role, this tripple-whammy of talent only raised the question of why these three had never teamed

up before (or since). The accumulation of abuse suffered over the years since birth is slowly transforming Wade into a monstrous mirror reflection of his drunken, wretched father. But the real tragedy is that Wade can foresee exactly what a monster he is becoming, and yet is helpless to do anything about it.

Aftershock (2012)
Dir: Nicolas Lopez /USA /Chile

Set in Chile, this two-sided film starts out by forcing viewers to sit through 45 gruelling minutes of 'party' footage wherein a trio of dribbling numb-skulls go from club to club in their efforts to get laid. Mercifully, an earthquake comes along and crushes, maims and impales most of the revellers in falling debris, which leaves Eli Roth and his bearded shitbag buddies no choice but to put their vacation on hold while they scramble for their lives. Yeah, you're not having fun *now*, *are you*, you fat little cunt. Things pick up by the hour mark with the arrival of a mini tsunami, along with looters, street riots and escaped prisoners to make the situation even better. Shortly after this, my hatred for this movie was soon curtailed when Roth gets his hips crushed under a fallen chunk of marble, and is tortured and burned to death by dangerous convicts... The first half of *Aftershock* is bloody awful, but it picks up greatly towards the end with lots of twists and turns, and characters you expect to make it to the end are casually killed off until the film no longer resembles what it was at the start in any way, shape or form. It starts out as a *Hangover*-type party movie, turns into a disaster movie, and finally strays off into catacombs horror in the last reel. Skip the first 40 minutes and you may find a fun little flick hiding behind a piss-poor party movie.

Aileen: Life and Death of a Serial Killer (2003)
Dir: Nick Broomfield & Joan Churchill /UK /USA

This charts the final days of Aileen Wuornos, America's most notorious female serial killer, as she sabotages her own appeal on the eve of her execution. The second of Nick Broomfield's documentaries about Wuornos, and one of his strongest and most moving films of his long career. It's stark and upsetting as an intimate portrait which raises some serious doubts about the quality of psychiatric assessment for those on death row.

Alien Beach Party Massacre (1996)
Dir: Andy Gizzarelli /USA
An alien spacecraft crash-lands near a California beach community. The only survivor is a pasty-faced dweeb who befriends a group of beach bums who are organising a party. Meanwhile, a group of evil aliens with large piggish snouts land in the area to track down the pale one because he is in possession of some kind of gadget they want to get their evil mits on... It's a micro-budget production with some well-observed humour and a surf guitar soundtrack, but there's no massacre here, folks.

Alien Trespass (2009)
Dir: R. W. Goodwin /USA /Canada
An affectionate homage to 50s invasion movies like *The Day the Earth Stood Still* (1951) and *Invaders From Mars* (1953). Here we get another small American town populated with the usual residents – teenage love birds, an eccentric hillbilly, a naïve diner waitress and a sceptical Sheriff. Their town comes under siege when a spacecraft from a distant planet crash-lands in the rocky desert, unleashing a one-eyed tentacled creature that zaps the wholesome humans and transforms them into steaming 'puddles of mud.' On its trail is Urp, a kindly alien that usurps the body of a local astronomer, Ted (Eric McCormack), *Invasion of the Body Snatchers*-style, and whose mission is to subdue the destructive creature and escort it to some far-flung prison colony at the other side of the galaxy... *Alien Trespass* is a fun little film that perfectly encapsulates invasion movies of old. McCormack's performance is great as Urp, as he manages to convey the 'alienated' nature of being stuck on distant earth while at the same time subtlely poking fun at stilted, wooden actors from the 50s era, with his awkward posture, swivelly eyes and slightly robotic line delivery. The menacing 'Ghota' creature looks similar to the space aliens in *It Came From Outer Space*

(1953) and *The Trollenberg Terror* (1958). And the movie culminates in a tribute to *The Blob* (1958) when a movie theatre showing the film comes under attack from the alien cyclops.

Alligator (1980)
Dir: Lewis Teague /USA
This formulaically-plotted creature feature manages to rise above its lesser rivals thanks to a witty and engaging script by monster movie maven, John Sayles. Set mostly in downtown Chicago, this film pits a beleaguered cop (Robert Forster) against a gigantic, rampaging 'gator that has been living in the sewers since it was flushed down the toilet in the late 60s. For more than a decade it has been feeding on dead animals that were experimented on with illegal growth hormones, and now it has emerged from underground to terrorise the city... Of course, in Sayles' eyes, the monster here is one that gains viewer sympathy for devouring an assortment of shady characters; a pet thief (Sidney Lassick), who sells animals for illegal experiments, is taken out in the sewers while he tries to discard some dead dogs, a smug hunter (Henry Silva) is eaten whole in a darkened backstreet, and in the finale, the 'gator (dubbed 'Ramon') emerges at a pool-side wedding reception and gloriously devours the tuxedoed guests who represent the city's corrupt side, from bad cops and self-serving politicians to members of the evil chemical corporation responsible for Ramon's condition.

Alligator II: The Mutation (1991)
Dir: Jon Hess /USA
A sequel that bears very little connection to the original film other than the alligator-running-amok basis. We get another mutated alligator, this time lurking in a large city pond where a greedy land developer (Steve Railsback) has dumped toxic waste chemicals, and intends on running a carnival in the area. However, when humans fall prey to the beastie, he hires Richard Lynch and Kane Hodder and co as big game hunters to get rid of the problem. And meanwhile, detective Hodges (Joseph Bologna) fails to convince people of the 'gator problem until it's too late... An uninspired, uninvolving film that follows formula in

predictable ways, and lacks the wit, satire and pace of the original. Some may want to give it a watch if only for the ridiculous carnival attack at the end, however.

Amateur Porn Star Killer (2006)
Dir: Shane Ryan /USA
Pseudo-snuff garbage about a young man who lures girls into making porn, but then murders them on camera. Dull, pretentious and boring beyond belief, at least they got the 'amateur' part right. A little character development for the victim could have worked wonders in improving the dramatic arc, but no, it never happens. Two equally crappy sequels followed in 2008 and 2009.

American Horror House (2012)
Dir: Darin Scott /USA
TV movie made for the Syfy Channel in which college girls in a haunted house are murdered by Miss Margo, the twisted sorority mom. And meanwhile, a party is attacked by demons. This is fairly bloody and gruesome for a TV movie, but there's really nothing else to commend it. In fact, it's nonsensical in large parts. The filmmakers throw everything they can at the screen in the hope that something will stick – blood, guts, ghosts, ghouls, killers, urban legends, teens, parties, booze, pervs, etc – but the result is a total mess that has all the subtlety of MTV. No one involved in the production had any idea what horror movies are about, and tried to remedy this by treating it as kind of Halloween party scary movie 'greatest hits' package. And to make matters worse, the characters here are extremely annoying; we get the usual adolescent drinking games with the 'wooing' and cheering as if they've never had a drink before. There's no one to root for; these morons are either loud-mouthed frat pricks or spoilt brat chimpettes. So it's a bit of a mystery as to why the filmmakers would attempt to create moments of suspense and tension. If this is just a silly party movie, why would you even try to make an audience feel uneasy? It doesn't work, stupid. What, am I supposed to feel scared for these morons in their perilous situations? They can all fucking die for all I care.

American Mary (2012)
Dir: Jen & Sylvia Soska /Canada

Poor med student, Mary Mason (*Ginger Snaps*' Katherine Isabelle) visits a strip joint to find work, and ends up earning five grand for a backroom surgical repair on a badly injured man. Word of her services spreads underground, and she is soon contacted by members of a body modification cult who want to turn themselves into 'dolls.' Thus, Mary finds herself earning thousands of dollars to remove a woman's nipples and sew up her snatch. She has to balance her studies with her nocturnal profession, and is constantly fucking pestered by her fucking professor who says the word 'fuck' in every sentence because he's so fucking modern and down with the brats, maaaan. And after he drugs and rapes her, Mary becomes an all-out monster, with a ruthless revenge in which she takes an active, sadistic pleasure in torture. *American Mary* is a decent debut feature, but it could have been so much better. The film never quite reaches the disturbing depths it promises, perhaps because the filmmakers wanted their flick to appeal to a mainstream audience (which is understandable, considering that the Soska sister's parents re-mortgaged their house to fund it. That's *a lot* of pressure to secure a hit). On the positive side, the film is at least more engaging than that other body cult movie, *Quid Pro Quo* (2008), and it has its roots in an assortment of horror-related sub-genres, such as mad doctor flicks, torture porn, rape/revenge, Cronenbergian body horror, and good old *femme fatale* flicks.

American Movie: The Making of Northwestern (1999)
Dir: Chris Smith /USA

"I'm thirty-years-old and I'm about to start cleaning up somebody's shit, man." Hilarious documentary about a horror fan, Mark Borchardt, who attempts to complete his first feature film, *Northwestern*. The budding filmmaker, along with his friend, Mike Schank, have to pass a seemingly endless amount of hurdles, and encounter numerous eccentrics in their efforts to get Mark's movie completed and up on the big screen. However, the lack of funds forces Mark to put his feature on the back-burner, and instead he puts his time and efforts into completing his short film, *Coven*, a semi-autobiographical black and white horror short. What Mark lacks in funds is made up for in his unstoppable tenacity and 'never-say-die' attitude. He sort of reminds me of other 90s indie filmmakers like Scooter McCrae and Jim VanBebber in the way he insists on shooting with 16mm film (among many 90s indies, shooting on video was frowned upon much more than nowadays). He uses aggressive tactics to get what he wants, and seems to be driven by mad obsession. During an afternoon shoot, most of his actors don't show up, so Mark simply orders his parents to play the roles instead ("But Mark, I have to go shopping"). Other characters we meet along the way include the aforementioned Mike Schank, a pleasant but dim-witted man whose brain has been frazzled by years of LSD use (he also contributes to the soundtrack with an acoustic version of Metallica's *Fight Fire With Fire*). Also, Mark's parents, who don't share his enthusiasm for filmmaking, an assortment of unknown actors, and Mark's uncle Bill, an 82-year-old man who lives in a trailer park despite having hundreds of thousands of dollars in the bank, and who also delivers one of the funniest lines ("...It's alright... it's okay... uuuhhhh..."). I cannot stress how great this film is; whether you're a budding filmmaker yourself, or a horror fan, or just someone interested in the quirkier side of film, *American Movie* is one of those precision-perfect documentaries – the sheer fluke of capturing those people in that time and place, and immortalising them on film, was a million-to-one shot. Audiences and critics agreed, as the film has become a cult favourite. It even picked up the Grand Jury Prize at Sundance in 1999. Mark Borchardt has since made several appearances on *Letterman*, as well as other TV shows and films, including *Family Guy*, along with Schank. *Coven* was released on VHS in the late 90s, but *Northwestern* (along with another 'in production' feature, *Scare Me*) still haven't been completed.

American Psycho 2 (2002)
(aka *American Psycho 2: All American Girl*)
Dir: Morgan J. Freeman /USA
This supposed sequel to Mary Harron's *American Psycho* (2000) drops

the social satire and dark humour of the original in favour of lukewarm, bloodless banality. It stars Mila Kunis as Rachel, a psycho college student who claims to have bumped off Patrick Bateman. She applies for a job as teaching assistant for a professor who had worked on the Bateman case in the 80s. However, the tough competition from the other hopeful candidates provokes her into killing off her rivals... Even if this film wasn't passed off as a sequel to *American Psycho*, it would still be seen as a bland and pointless film. It blends post-*Scream* bogus cool nonsense with art house pretentiousness, and falls flat on it face.

The Amityville Asylum (2013)
Dir: Andrew Jones /UK

This astoundingly dull movie – which is not part of the official *Amityville* series – is about a student who gets a cleaning job at a psychiatric unit, even though she sneezed and snotted on the interviewer's hand. Not only does she have to put up with arsehole co-workers and threats from the criminally insane, but she is also targeted by malignant supernatural forces. And when she learns that the asylum was built on Amityville grounds (the infamous house at 112 Ocean Avenue had been demolished to make way for the institution), she also uncovers a sacrificial witchcraft cult... This is a painfully slow, borderline amateur feature that would have worked much better as a 40-minute short. However, horror freaks will spot references to other movies and true crime ghouls, such as Ronald DeFeo, the man who shot dead his family in 1974 (as fictionalised in *Amityville 2: The Possession* (1982)), and Mansonite Sadie Krenwinkel as a delirious inmate from a witch cult. There's also an inmate called 'John Doe,' in reference to the twisted serial killer in David Fincher's *Se7en* (1995), and the 'Long Island Cannibal,' Dennis Palmer, in reference to Nathan Schiff's gory cult movie, *The Long Island Cannibal Massacre* (1980), whose namesake here – bizarrely enough - serves as a polite psychopath with an English accent. And of course, the ending strays into territory well-trodden by the likes of *Mansion of Madness* (1973), *Silent Night, Bloody Night* (1972), and *Shutter Island* (2010).

And Soon the Darkness (2009)
Dir: Marcos Efron /USA /Argentina /France

And Soon the Darkness is a dismal remake of Robert Fuest's 1970 classic. This time the story is set in rural Argentina with the two American girls on a cycling trip. They stop by at a bar, and Ellie makes a total twat of herself with a karaoke mic. Ooh, look, she's a fun-loving girl! Oh dear, she's fucking annoying. Kill the idiot! Like many modern horror movies, we can't have nice, decent characters anymore; oh no, they must be obnoxious drunken buffoons nowadays. This time the story mostly stays away from the peace and tranquility of the original set in France, and instead opts for the *Hostel*-like approach of young Americans getting themselves entangled in a culture that is alien to them. Oh, you gonna ride your likkle bikey around Argentina? You gonna get all cultured, eh? Well, in Argentina, you're going to learn about rape and imprisonment: Bettcha can't wait to put *those* holiday snaps on your Facebook and Instagram, can you? Besides which, there's very little mystery here; viewers have a very good idea from the get-go of who has abducted Ellie. And interestingly, the locals seem to reject the American ideals out of sheer resentment rather than 'morality.' This remake also drops the fairly downbeat denouement of the original in favour of a 'can do' exercise in viewer empowerment; see girls, if you ever find yourself in a situation where three ruthless men have you held in captivity with the intention of selling you on to a prostitution racket, just simply beat 'em up and shoot 'em! It's easy! You go, girl, you can do it. You only weigh 100lbs and have never shot a gun in your life, but hey, it's the 21st Century, get with the programme sister.

The Andromeda Strain (1970)
Dir: Robert Wise /USA

A satellite falls out of orbit and crashes in the desert town on Piedmont in New Mexico, killing everyone. The U.S. Airforce calls an emergency as the satellite was part of project Scoop, created to gather alien micro-organisms from outer space. Mankind now faces extinction as an alien virus is unleashed, and to combat this, a team of expert scientists are hastily assembled to try and contain the outbreak before it's too late...

PHENOMENA

Based on Michael Crichton's great novel about the dangers and accomplishments of science, this atypical invasion movie posits the idea of aliens posing an unseen, microscopic threat. The film works wonders at wringing dramatic tension, both as a conventional thriller and also as an intellectual puzzle for the characters to solve. The action kicks off in the devastated town of Piedmont, where the local's blood has turned into powder; it then moves along to the enormous underground research lab where the decontamination process is explored in detail; and the final act reverts to more conventional means as the virus – dubbed the Andromeda Strain – breaks out of the facility. What separates this film from most of its kind is the way it depicts scientists; they are presented as what they are – intelligent, rational people faced with a crisis. And the casting of unknowns instead of the usual Hollywood stars also helps. Director Robert Wise, who also brought us such classics as *The Body Snatcher* (1945), *The Day the Earth Stood Still* (1951) and *The Haunting* (1963), presents his film as a possible reality rather than mere escapism - as often befell most disaster movies as they flourished in the 70s. And Crichton's moral message about how science should always be subservient to mankind – as echoed in many of his books – is delivered here in full.

Angel (1984)
Dir: Robert Vincent O'Neill /USA

A demented necrophiliac serial killer targets L.A.'s street hookers. Donna Wilkes plays the title character, a 14-year-old student who moonlights as a street walker to fund her education. She has seen several of her friends fall victim to the killer, and the only people looking out for her are a no-nonsense transvestite (Cliff Gorman) and a detective concerned for her well being who urges her to stay away from the streets. But instead, Angel arms herself with a pistol and confronts the maniac, who has by now disguised himself in Hare Krishna garb. This is a routine, join-the-dots killer movie that nonetheless outshines most others of its like thanks to some decent production values, a well-observed grim humour, and a roster of unforgettable characters, including Susan Tyrell's ludicrous lesbian who has the best line: "You can't die. You still owe me $147, you fucking faggot."

Apocalypto (2006)
Dir: Mel Gibson /USA

You can always rely on Mel Gibson to pile on the insanity, that bug-eyed, fly-eating, crazy fucking lunatic. And *Apocalypto* (2006) is certainly no let down. Set in the final days of the ancient Mayan civilisation where a young warrior manages to escape his fate of bloody sacrifice, he heads back to his village to rescue his wife and baby who are trapped down a well. This is an audacious historical epic, subtitled entirely in Yucatec and is as brutal and graphically violent as we have come to expect from Gibson, especially the scenes of the ancient Mayans cutting out human hearts. But for all its supposed historical details and unflinching gruesomeness, *Apocalypto* is just an overwrought chase movie at heart. And not a bad one, either. Gibson is probably doomed to spend eternity languishing in the depths of hell, shrieking in excruciating agony as giggling demons slowly turn his sphincter inside out over and over again, whilst using his tears as lubricant to jerk off – but *Apocalypto* is pretty good. Perhaps the servants of hell will allow him a brief, five-minute respite from his punishment every hundred years or so out of a begrudging respect. Fingers crossed, eh Mel?

April Fools Day (1986)
Dir: Fred Walton /USA

College kids head for a house on an island where they are picked off by an escaped lunatic... This film offers a novel twist on slasher movie conventions, but this doesn't make things any less tedious to sit through. We get a hackneyed script which is heavily influenced by Agatha Christie's *Ten Little Indians*, a lack of suspense (save for a spooky basement scene near the end), and the most irritating cast of characters this side of *The Burning* (1981); a bunch of 'hark-at-us' show-offs whom you can't wait to see the backs of. In its favour, this does have some good production values for an 80s 'slasher' movie, but of course, the whole film turns out to be a waste of time once we get to the revelation at the end. Check out David Fincher's much superior *The Game* (1997) instead.

Apt Pupil (1997)
Dir: Bryan Singer /USA /Canada /France
An unusual relationship develops between a high school kid and an ageing Nazi war criminal. After the success of *The Usual Suspects* (1995), director Bryan Singer could have easily followed in the footsteps of Quentin Tarantino with a big-budget crime drama, but instead he took on a more intimate, claustrophobic story with just two main characters. Based on the novel by Stephen King, *Apt Pupil* stars Brad Renfo as Todd, a school kid who approaches a retired immigrant (Ian McKellen) with accusations that he was Kurt Dussander, an extermination camp commandant back in the 1940s. Todd basically threatens to expose the old man to the authorities unless he agrees to help him with a school project by telling him stories about his involvement in the holocaust. Of course, Dussander is initially reluctant to divulge his secrets, but gradually begins to exert a predatory interest in the kid, and enjoys boasting of his past crimes while attempting to seduce the youthful mind and create a new monster. This film is held together by fantastic performances from McKellen and Renfo, but is ultimately content to be a watered-down version of the book.

Arachnophobia (1990)
Dir: Frank Marshall /USA
Tagline: 'Eight legs. Two fangs. And an attitude.' Poisonous spiders from South America attempt to take over the world in this family-friendly movie that is only scary to those who are afraid of creepy crawlies. The film is perhaps most memorable for the role of the almighty human arse cheek, John Goodman, who here plays 'the exterminator.' Sometimes the humour is a little over the top, as in the 'love' scene between two spiders in a barn. But the 'spider cam' shots are well done.

The Astronaut's Wife (1999)
Dir: Rand Ravich /USA

Johnny Depp plays an astronaut who returns to earth after a space mission. And, after a mishap, his wife (Charlize Theron) suspects she may have been impregnated by an alien... This is basically a re-working of Roman Polanski's *Rosemary's Baby* (1968), with two major differences: 1) Here, the heroine is impregnated by an alien rather than the Devil, and 2): *Rosemary's Baby* is actually a decent film. Actress Charlize Theron even gets to sport a similar short hairdo as Mia Farrow had in Polanski's film.. Her character also has a history of mental instability, which throws up the usual question of whether she is correct in her fears, or whether she's just losing her mind. And by the time the truth is revealed, most audiences couldn't care less either way. Depp's performance is pretty good, but overall the film is completely devoid of suspense and atmosphere.

Asylum (2008)
Dir: David R. Ellis /USA

Irritating college kids discover that their dorm was once an insane asylum in the 1930s, and the mad doc who ran the place is now out to kill them all. But, wait a minute, wouldn't that make the doctor around 100-years-old or more? Oh dear... *Asylum* is a patchwork of horror movie cliches; from the building with the sinister past, the sensible girl who is determined to uncover the truth, and the usual *de rigueur* irritating college cunts. It tries to be like *A Nightmare On Elm Street 3: Dream Warriors* (1987), but it actually owes a greater debt to the remake of *House On Haunted Hill* (1999) and *Session 9* (2001). But, while those aforementioned movies are good for a giggle, this is just bloody awful in every conceivable way. Hey, how does one utilise character development in a movie script? Why, you simply have your characters sitting around telling boring stories about their pasts – that seems to do the trick.

Attack of the 50ft. Woman (1993)
Dir: Christopher Guest /USA

"The world is my dollhouse." Aliens zap Daryl Hannah with a laser beam which somehow causes her to grow in size every time she gets angry. She then strides across town in search of her cheating husband (played by one of the Baldwin brothers, the fat one), increasingly upset and growing to enormous size. This HBO remake of the classic 50s B-movie does a decent job of replicating that 50s drive-in vibe of a small town under attack, much like John Carpenter's remake of *Village of the Damned* (1995) and Chuck Russell's update of *The Blob* (1988). The film is clearly played for laughs, but it doesn't go far enough. How many little people could she carry around in her cleavage? How many could she bowl over with a well-aimed blast of flatulence?

Unfortunately, we never get the answers to those questions. It's a fun film if you're in the right mood, but Hannah's 'rampage' through the desert town is a bit of a let down, probably because the town miniature sets were too expensive to have them destroyed. Boo. This film is crying out for some lewd scene, something to give it some extra oomph. A scene where a giant Hannah sits back on a hill while masturbating with a bus would have been great. There could have been a fun 'interior' shot of the passengers and their disarray, tumbling back and forth down the bus aisle as she sloshed the vehicle in and out of her giant crack, with the little people stranded on some kind of pinky-pubey-foamy car wash ride.

Attack of the Killer Tomatoes (1978)
Dir: John De Bello /USA
In a cynical attempt at gaining some cult appeal, *Attack of the Killer Tomatoes* deliberately goes for broke with cheesy special effects, ridiculous acting and knucklehead dialogue. If anything, the filmmakers achieved their aim, but this is a boring, charmless film. It tries too hard to be ridiculous, and though the idea of homicidal vegetables rolling around and splattering innocents may sound amusing, actually sitting down to watch this shit for 90 minutes is enough to make anyone long for Edward D. Wood's *Plan Nine From Outer Space*. The song parodies are okay but Troma's *Poultrygeist* beats this film in every department. Sequels followed: *Return of the Killer Tomatoes* (1988), *Killer*

Tomatoes Strike Back (1990) and *Killer Tomatoes Eat France!* (1991). All are thoroughly terrible.

ATM (2012)
Dir: David Brooks /USA /Canada

A trio of young yuppies stop by at an ATM booth on their way home from a party and are attacked by a mysterious figure in a parker and brandishing sharp implements. I watched this on a large projector screen, and the non-horror movie fans I watched it with foretold every little horror movie cliché it threw at us, even though they – like me – hadn't actually seen it before. And that should give you some idea of how worthless and derivative this film is. On the subtextual front, the ATM booth could represent the American corporate world of banking and commerce, the safe bubble of power; and the killer out in the surrounding darkness represents the anger of the masses, furious and vengeful about the recklessness of the bankers and the failing economy. Indeed, one of the characters early on tries to buy off the killer by offering him a wad of cash, but the confrontation has gone way beyond anything money can buy. Of course, this kind of thing had been done previously to much better effect in *The Mist* (2009), in which the residents of a small American town find themselves trapped in a large supermarket which represented America itself, the land of plenty, while outside in the post-9/11 world, the Americans' eyes were opened to the outside world for the first time; a murky, hostile world full of monsters out to get them. As for *ATM*, another of the film's stumbling points – aside from it's lack of originality or likeable characters – is that the film's makers side with the corporate scum when most of us want those yuppie cunts to die.

AVN: Alien vs Ninja (2010)
Dir: Seiji Chiba /Japan

The Japanese shitter, *AVN: Alien vs Ninja* (2010), sees a team of modern-day ninjas being picked off in the woods by an alien predator that hunts humans for sport. It's a goofy *Predator* rip-off that boasts some spectacularly gruesome deaths, spectacularly awful CGI effects, slapstick humour and a camp army commander. If the original *Predator* (1987) boasted a 10 foot tall, fanny-faced alien, the biggest curiosity here is an equally unlikely creature: a schoolboy's re-creation of a xenomorph, complete with go-go-gadget pink dicks that shoot out of its body to wrap around throats and throttle the ninjas to death, and a dolphin's head with bowling ball-type holes in which it carries its young. The surviving ninjas set up their own 'jungle traps' as a way of putting an end to the beast, but it seems to be immortal.

Babadook (2014)
Dir: Jennifer Kent /Australia /Canada

A widow, Amelia (Essie Davis) whose husband died in a car crash, raises her six-year-old boy, Samuel (Noah Wiseman), on her own. The boy is troubled; he won't go to school, he puts broken glass in mummy's custard, defaces photos of mum and dad, and is obsessed with 'Babadook,' a spooky character from a pop-up book. Amelia becomes increasingly concerned about Sam's behaviour, so much so that she tears up the book and throws it in the bin. However, it later shows up on the doorstep, glued back together. The situation gets even worse; Amelia takes Sam to see a doctor, and he says the boy could have an anxiety disorder. She then suspects that someone in the neighbourhood is stalking her. She contacts the police, but they don't take her claims seriously. And meanwhile, the kitchen is infested with cockroaches, and she hasn't been showing up to work....

Babadook is the type of film I was hoping *Sinister* (2012) would be, an extremely creepy parable steeped in the dark heart of cautionary fairy tales. But whereas *Sinister* felt compelled to turn its creepy premise into just another fairytale boogeyman movie, *Babadook* instead keeps things subtle, preferring to stick to its guns rather than pandering to audience expectations. And the result is extremely effective at getting under the skin. *Babadook* began life as a short film by writer/director Jennifer Kent entitled *Monster* (2005), in which her skin-crawling tale was first road-tested on screen. After almost a decade of fund-raising, Kent was at last able to expand her startling short into a full-on feature. Thematically, the film has much in common with Stanley Kubrick's

The Shining (1980) and Mario Bava's *Shock* (1977), while visually it owes much to German expressionism by way of Hideo Nakata and Sam Raimi. The Babadook itself resembles a Victorian-era boogeyman, like how people would imagine Jack the Ripper to look. In fact, the creature looks almost identical to Lon Chaney in the lost film, *London After Midnight* (1927), with its top hat and bared teeth. Go to Google Images and see for yourself. Even more impressive is the performance by Essie Davis; a truly astonishing turn as the mother whose world is falling apart. The way the film flits between horror and heartbreak is largely down to how effective she is at dishing out terror and tenderness to her son. Her performance is one of the most hair-raising since Isabelle Adjani in *Possession* (1981). Noah Wiseman as the tormented boy isn't bad, either. Whether you see the Babadook as a metaphor for madness or guilt or grief, or any other underlying anxieties, it can't be denied that this is one of the finest horror movies of the century so far.

Watching the film again a second and third time, you may notice several clues as to Amelia's crumbling mental state. For instance, in one scene she mentions that she used to write children's books. And later, at the police station, her hands are covered in what looks like smudged black ink. Also, her deceased husband's clothes and hat are pinned to the wall in the basement – an outfit similar to the one worn by the Babadook. Most disturbingly, in the scene after she takes the bowl of dirt and worms down to the basement, she returns to the garden, and when she smiles you can see dirt on her teeth as she smiles. Spooky.

The Babysitter (1980)
Dir: Peter Medak /USA
A much-ado-about-nothing TV movie about an interloper child minder who drives a family apart. We know she's a little fucked in the head when she moans in orgasmic pleasure while clubbing a fish to death. She flirts with the husband (William Shatner) while wearing his wife's little black dress; she encourages mom to relapse into alcoholism; and when her concerned doctor investigates her past, he discovers she may have been responsible for the death of a baby. And when the family learn of her ways and try to oust her from the house, she figures if she

can't be part of the family, then they all must DIE HORRIBLY. But fortunately, the Loomis-like Dr. Linquist shows up to save the day. Bloodless and derivative but watchable on a slow afternoon.

Back From the Dead (1957)
Dir: Charles Marquis Warren /USA

An architect's wife suffers some kind of seizure and has a change of personality, convinced that she is her husband's deceased ex-wife. This is the kind of old skool movie where it's perfectly acceptable for men to slap hysterical women across the face until they come to their senses, grateful that the hero is there to knock some sense into them. Whether the woman is possessed by the evil spirit, or just mentally ill is not made clear until the very end, but the dead girl's mother has been practising the black arts and is convinced.

Badlands (1973)
Dir: Terrence Malick /USA

A teenage girl (Sissy Spacek) and a garbage collector (Martin Sheen) take to the road together and travel across America on a vengeful murder spree. This cult classic has been hugely influential over the years, with the template of 'young lovers on the run' used by subsequent filmmakers who have made use of its engaging power. The story is told mainly through the eyes of Spacek's Holly, who sees Kit's actions as endearingly romantic; she's blinded by her unquestioning, adolescent crush on him, and the stark dislocation between her dreamy, 'head in the clouds' acquiescence and the downbeat horror of the couple's actions gives the film a deftly disturbing power, which flits between feeble fantasy and earth-shattering reality. The film is based on the crimes of Charles Starkweather and Caril Fugate's killing spree in the Dakota badlands in the 1950s.

Bag of Bones (2011)
Dir: Mick Garris /USA

Originally broadcast on television in two feature-length instalments, but has also been shown in its entirety of three hours (including ad breaks).

Novelist Michael Noonan (Pierce Brosnan) sees his wife getting hit by a vehicle in the street during a book signing. After the funeral, he decides to deal with the loss by heading out to his country cabin to write a new book. And there he meets Mattie (Melissa George), a young mother in the middle of a custody battle with her evil rich father-in-law. And meanwhile, Michael's dead wife's spirit is trying to communicate something important to him from beyond the grave.

Stephen King fans will notice many casual references to him and his work, including *Misery*, Kubrick's *The Shining* ("Lie still Bag of Bones"), and his Bachman pseudonym. Pierce Brosnan's performance here is pretty good – I'd always had an aversion to him, probably since my mind was scarred by *Mamma Mia!* (2008), the godawful Abba musical in which Brosnan, in all seriousness, attempts to sing *SOS*: his grunt-like, off-key yelping of the chorus sounds like a dog getting its testicles caught in barbed wire. Watch a clip on YouTube if you don't believe me. Just don't say I didn't warn you. For such a low-scale project with just a handful of key characters, the story dawdles and meanders much more than necessary. The film would have been much better had it focused on the essentials and kept things tight. The biggest criticism, though, is that *Bag of Bones* never delivers on the horrific which it seems to be constantly building up to. We don't actually see the rape and drowning scenes until after two hours, and though far from pleasant, the sequence is short and no way as emotionally effective as it should have been. By this point, viewer interest tends to fall behind, and the flashy, strobe-lit ending kills off any hardened viewers who are still tuned in. All in all, the film is way too sketchy for it to work, like a 'bare bones' idea, or if you will, a 'bag of bones' in need of flesh and form.

Basket Case 2 (1990)
Dir: Frank Henenlotter /USA
Basket Case 2 picks up right where the original left off, as Duane and Belial are whisked off into the protective custody of their aunt, a 'freak's rights' activist whose remote country house serves as a safe haven for a variety of genetic oddities. However, when a prying

reporter gets too close, all hell breaks loose once again. Not in the same league as part one, this sequel concentrates more on the satirical aspects of the genre, from political correctness and the increasingly tabloid-centric American culture, and the battle for social justice in a post-Regan, conservative climate.

The Basketball Diaries (1995)
Dir: Scott Kalvert /USA

A rebellious Catholic schoolboy gets hooked on heroin and turns to theft and prostitution to feed his habit. Based on the diaries of Jim Carroll, which were published and caused a bit of a sensation at the time, this film version doesn't really have anywhere to go beyond wallowing in junky cliches. However, the film also serves as a showcase for Leonardo DiCaprio's acting talent. Sure, the guy's about 40-years-old now and still hasn't started puberty yet, but this - along with his astonishing turn in *What's Eating Gilbert Grape?* - shows that he is indeed a superb actor when he has a decent role to sink his teeth into.

Battle Heater (1989)
(aka *Electric Kotatsu Horror*; Orig title: *Batoru Hita*)
Dir: Joji Iida /Japan

Another in the line of homicidal appliance movies which includes deadly fridges in *The Refrigerator* (1991) and *Attack of the Killer Refridgerator* (1990), a homicidal vacuum cleaner in *Tabloid* (1985), a deadly lawn-mower in *Blades* (1989), deadly electrical sockets in *Pulse* (1988), an evil elevator in *Down* (2001), and even deadly mobile phones in *One Missed Call* (2003). From Japan we have *Battle Heater*, a fun film about an electric heater possessed by a demon. It eventually to sprouts creepy arms and devours people in an apartment building with plenty of assorted weirdos and killers in residence to keep it well fed for an entire running time. Goofy fun with a touch of satire.

Beaks – The Movie (1987)
Dir: Rene Cardona Jr /USA

Written, produced and directed by Rene Cardona Jr (the man behind such exploitation classics as *Survive* and *Guyana: Crime of the Century*), this film pays homage to the eye-gouging scene in Hitchcock's *The Birds* within the first ten minutes. *Beaks* stars Michelle Johnson as an ambitious young news reporter who is given the shitty assignment of reporting on a spate of deaths caused by killer birds. Her scepticism on the subject is soon banished, however, when it becomes clear that the murderous pests have indeed declared war on the human race. Owing just as much to Spielberg's *Jaws* as it does to *The Birds*, *Beaks* is played surprisingly straight considering its amusing title, but can't avoid the inevitable tongue-in-cheek style which is the obvious way to go when dealing with a human bird-feed scenario.

Beast Cops (1998)
(Orig title: *Ye shou xing jing*)
Dir: Dante Lam & Gordon Chan /Hong Kong
Winner of Best Film at the Hong Kong Film Awards in 1999, *Beast Cops* stars Anthony Wong as a detective who is teamed up with Michael Fitzgerald Wong (no relation), and becomes entangled with girls and gangsters when a triad boss heads out of town. It's basically a routine cop actioner with the added bonus of an extremely violent finale with the use of guns, swords and meat cleavers, which earned the film a CAT III rating in its native land. The wardrobe department had a field day dressing Anthony Wong in an assortment of suede jackets, black shades and white turtle necks, making him look like he has just stepped out of a 70s crime thriller. It's only toward the end of the film when things take on a traditional CAT III flavour; Wong's character has no intentions of getting out alive when he enters the triad's hideout for revenge; but he sure is hard to kill – even with knives protruding from his neck and torso, Wong picks up a machete and stalks the corridors of the building, hacking and slashing the scumbags to death while bleeding heavily from his mortal wounds.

The Bell Witch Haunting (2013)
Dir: Glenn Miller /USA

PHENOMENA

The details of how a family came to be brutally murdered are pieced together with video footage taken from the victim's phones and video cameras. Of course, this being a 'found footage' film, it means viewers are forced to sit through endless scenes of shaky birthday party footage with snarky teens and other imbeciles drinking from red plastic dixie cups. And it isn't long before supernatural goings on are captured on tape... This is a desperate, half-arsed mixture of *The Amityville Horror* (1979), *The Blair Witch Project* (1998) and *Paranormal Activity* (2007), as a series of ghost movie clichés are fired at the audience with very little rhyme or reason. None of the characters are likeable, and this just makes it even more difficult to care about what's going on. The sibling rivalry and bitchiness between the teens, Brandon and Dana, is so pathetically juvenile you'll be praying for their gruesome deaths within the first ten minutes. And the parents aren't much better; they're basically a pair of useless, doddering numb-skulls. The father seems to only exist so that he can run into Dana's bedroom to console her when she has screaming fits and night terrors, which, in this film, happens EVERY FIVE FUCKING MINUTES! And the mother serves absolutely no purpose except to remind us that she's the one responsible for spawning those infuriating brats from her 'tard-launcher cunt. In a word: Abysmal.

Benny's Video (1992)
Dir: Michael Haneke /Austria /Switzerland

A video-obsessed teen lures home a girl from a video rental store and kills her on camera. In typical Haneke form, *Benny's Video* is about alienation and the questioning of the purpose of video violence in society. Haneke has said that the film is a statement "about the American sensational cinema and its power to rob viewers of their ability to form their own opinions." Like his other films, such as *Funny Games* (1997) and *Code Unknown* (2000), this is a very cold and clinical look at the modern world which, ironically, is sure to alienate many horror fans.

Beware! The Blob (1971)

(aka *Son of Blob*)

Dir: Larry Hagman /USA

In this sequel, a frozen chunk of blob is brought back from the North Pole where it was dumped at the end of the original film. The wife of a lab technician accidentally defrosts the thing and before long the gloopy monster is swallowing kittens, bald guys in bathtubs, and stoned hippies while growing to enormous size. This time the horror is ignored in favour of laughs, but this film is rarely funny. *Beware! The Blob* has become a cult item on home video among those who enjoy delirious, wrong-headed movies.

Beyond the Limits (2003)

Dir: Olaf Ittanbach /Germany

A diptych of dipshittery which serves as a gruesome treat for fans of extremely violent movies. Here we have a double-bill of dark tales from German splatter king, Olaf Ittenbach. The first story sees a young journalist interview a cemetery keeper, and he tells her the story of high-stakes gangsterism and stolen cocaine shenanigans. Gangsters invade the home of an associate who is accused of treachery. The gang is headed by a sadistic brute who has a Mike Tyson-type facial tattoo and refers to himself as 'God.' He subjects the dinner guests to much brutality: They are tied to chairs, some are beaten, others suffocated, and garrotted; others are shot in the head numerous times, or smashed in the head with a sledgehammer, or butchered with meat cleavers. A brave woman fights back and stabs the lunatic in the face as he attempts to rape her. And for her trouble, she is summarily executed by another lunatic whose girlfriend has been thrown out of a tower block window. This story really doesn't have much of a point to it, but is incredibly violent. The sadist is a cliché arch-villain; he speaks in faux-cultured tones, is calm even when dishing out extreme torture, and says things like, "I'm sorry, it's nothing personal," after he has just blown someone's brains out with a shotgun. All this trouble over a poxy bag of cocaine. What losers.

The second story deals with the Church's persecution of 'heretics' in

England in the Middle Ages, and kicks off with a brutal massacre at a church where men, women and children are slaughtered. The Priest of this illegal gathering is kept alive so that he can be slowly tortured on a stretching rack. The Priest is butchered and burned and has his eyeball gouged out. The man conducting the torture in the name of the Church is actually a closet Satanist who keeps a human heart which he believes is his ticket to immortality. And when the 'heretic' finally 'confesses,' he is burned at the stake in a public square. The man and his assistant discover that the more true believers they sacrifice to the heart, the more it comes to life. So they go around deliberately scooping up anyone they can lay trump blasphemy charges on in their quest for eternal life. This tale takes all the most gruesome bits from heretics and witch persecution movies, and ups the gore quotient a tenfold. It's a film which adds nothing to the horror genre, or cinema as a whole, but is a must for violence and gore fans.

Bits and Pieces (1985)
Dir: Leland Thomas /USA
At the bottom of the 80s slasher movie barrel you'll find *Bits and Pieces*, another micro-budget, 'damaged-by-mummy' schizo killer movie. Like Joe Spinell in *Maniac* (1980), this maniac keeps a collection of mannequins which serve as clothes props for dressing in the souvenirs he has taken from his victims. And like Norman Bates in *Psycho* (1960) and Dan Grimaldi in *Don't Go in the House* (1979), he is still tormented by his mother by way of the ghostly voices in his head. When he was a child, his mother would make him watch her have sex with random guys (a form of abuse experienced by the real life serial killer, Henry Lee Lucas), and the killer takes out his frustrations by kidnapping women, torturing them in his basement, and dumping their dismembered remains in dumpster bins for anyone to find. But for all the film's attempts to create a serious character study, the amateur feel of the production is a major let down.

Black Book (2006)
Dir: Paul Verhoeven /Holland /Germany /UK /Belgium

Dutch-Jewish cabaret singer Rachel Steinn aims to survive the Nazi occupation of Holland during the war by joining the Resistance movement and fraternising with Nazi officers to gain information. When her plans backfire, however, she finds herself ostracised by both sides. This was Paul Verhoeven's first film made in his native Holland after 20 years in Hollywood, and touches on many sore points about the Dutch Resistance. He sets out to de-mythologise legends about heroism and accuses most of collaborating with the occupiers (similar to the situation in France where, after the war, *everyone* claimed to have been part of the Resistance, but in reality the opposite was probably much closer to the truth). In Verhoeven's eyes, no one emerges from the story untarnished, not even his resourceful heroine. For her, moral ambiguity and treachery were vital for her chances of survival. It's a film which is just as hard on the Dutch Resistance as it is on the Nazis. Packed full of grim details and vulgarity, Verhoeven and his scriptwriter, Gerard Soetman, claim they spent 20 years working on the script, and insist that Rachel's character is a composite of several real people.

Black Cadilac (2003)
Dir: John Murlowski /USA
A direct-to-video creepy road movie. A group of youngsters pick up a hitch-hiker Sheriff (Randy Quaid), who is surprisingly laid back and just wants "to go home." Not long after, their Saab is menaced on the deserted snowy roads by the title black Cadilac. The fact that this film is derivative and lacks a solid punchline doesn't spoil the overall unsettling build-up and decent character development, with some interesting revelations. The explanation at the end is disappointing but this is a better-than-average video release.

Blair Witch 2: Book of Shadows (1999)
Dir: Joe Berlinger /USA
Myrick and Sanchez returned with a narrative-based sequel to *The Blair Witch Project* while handing over directorial duties to Joe Berlinger, the man famous for his bold and disturbing *Paradise Lost* documentaries. A group of youngsters sign up to spend the night in the

woods near Burkitsville, Maryland, where the film crew of the original movie disappeared (it has now become a ghoulish kind of tourist trap). But when they return to town they realise that they have no memory of the previous night. Gradually it becomes apparent that they have brought something horrible back from the woods with them. Like the first film, this features a cast of unknowns and has a documentary feel in some places, with the bigger budget adding a professional sheen. But even with some creepy scenes and a decent soundtrack – which includes the great Queens of the Stone Age – much of the impact of the original is lost here. Overall, it feels like a quick cash-in.

Blindness (2008)
Dir: Fernando Meirelles /Canada
Based on the novel by Jose Saramago, an author who seems to have no idea how diseases really work, *Blindness* takes its literary cue from John Wyndham's sci-fi novel, *Day of The Triffids,* whilst at the same time making sure to distance itself from the genre while pilfering its dramatic power. The film version by Fernando Meirelles sees a nightmare scenario unfold where everyone goes blind and society falls apart. The disturbing power of the film comes from the details as things become increasingly dark and dangerous as groups form and degradation sets in. Shot on digi video which seems to drain all shots of their colour.

Blitzkrieg: Escape From Stalag 69 (2009)
Dir: Keith J. Crocker /USA
An attempt to revitalise the long-dead Nazisploitation sub-genre, *Blitzkrieg* is a surprisingly tasteful approach to the subject (unlike many of the notorious 70s counterparts), and borrows just as many elements form neorealists like Rossellini as well as exploitative shockers like *Love Camp 7* and *The Beast In Heat*. The story takes place in a POW camp, Stalag 69, run by a despised SS commandant, a man so nasty and sadistic even his fellow Nazis hate his guts. And when a group of female American prisoners are brought to the camp, it leads to his inevitable downfall.

The Blob (1958)
Dir: Irvin S. Yeaworth /USA

Jack H. Harris, the cheapjack producer who went on to make the forgettable 'comedy', *Mother Goose a Go-Go* (1965), struck it rich with this film that gave Steve McQueen his first lead role after a few supporting stints in *Somebody Up There Likes Me* (1956) and *Never Love a Stranger* (1958). This is a classic teen terror movie with McQueen and Aneta Corsaut trying to convince the folks in their small Pennsylvania community that they've seen a huge reddish-purple intergalactic gloop eating people alive. And of course, just like in countless other creature features over the years, no one believes them until it's too late. Boasting a classic theme tune by Hal David and Burt Bacharach, and one of the greatest moments in 50s horror when the blob invades a packed movie theatre, this film also gets away with many eccentricities of the time (such as the casting of leads in their late-twenties as teens, repressed authority figures, etc), but *The Blob* remains one of the most memorable B-movies of its time. It was followed by a sequel, *Beware! The Blob* (aka *Son of Blob*) (1971).

The Blob (1988)
Dir: Chuck Russell /USA

A faithful remake of the classic 50s B-movie which sticks to the original theme of small-town American teenagers trying to convince the sceptical populace of the arrival of a blob-like invader from another world. This time the blob serves as a genuinely menacing threat, thanks to the vast improvement in budget and special effects since the original was made. The opening scenes of the homeless guy losing his hand, to the *Alligator*-like action in the sewers is tightly constructed and moves at a fair old clip. Director Chuck Russell (the man behind *A Nightmare On Elm Street 3: Dream Warriors*, made in the previous year) pays homage to the first film without crossing over the 'fanboy' threshold, which may well have happened if Rob Zombie got to work on his own remake which he eventually decided against.

Blood Feast (1963)

Dir: Herschell Gordon Lewis /USA

Peoria, Illinois, 1963. It was a Friday night at the local drive-in theatre. Dozens of cars were lined up facing the huge whitewashed wall which suddenly burst into life as the projector light beamed upon it from across the parking lot. The audience, usually made up of courting couples and boys fingering the girls in the back seats, were immediately distracted from their semi-private activities by events playing out on screen; within moments of the film starting, a blonde woman taking a bath is attacked by an intruder with dark, blueish hair, and he proceeds to hack off her leg in full-bloodied colour. The drive-in patrons were stunned. It was the first time in movie history that an audience had witnessed graphic gore on a cinema screen, and it wouldn't be the last.

The film they were watching was *Blood Feast*, a low-budget horror quickie produced and directed by Herschell Gordon Lewis and David F. Friedman. The pair had previously churned out nudie cuties like *Living Venus* (1961), *Daughters of The Sun* (1961) and *Nature's Playmates* (1962), but decided out of sheer boredom to try something new. They had noticed that horror movies had always shied away from showing gruesome death; characters either died cleanly and quietly with their eyes closed, or the screen would fade to black just at the moment the killing started. And having noticed this strange discrepancy, they decided to shatter the taboo in full-on *grand guignol* style. With a budget of $24,000 and a Playboy pin-up girl (Connie Mason) for their lead actress, this bloody-minded duo set to work.

The plot of *Blood Feast* concerns a young woman, Suzette (Mason), who dates the local shit-for-brains cop, Pete. They attend a lecture on Egyptian cults. Meanwhile, young women are being butchered by the local caterer, Faud Ramses (Mal Arnold), who sets his eye on Suzette becoming the latest sacrifice to the Egyptian god, Ishtar.

Lewis and Friedman decided to premiere their blood-drenched movie in Peoria, where, according to Lewis, "If the film dropped dead, no one would know." *Blood Feast* opened on a Friday, and the filmmakers deliberately stayed behind in Chicago unaware of how their pic was being received by audiences. The following day, anticipation got the better of them and they decided to take a drive to see for themselves, and what greeted them was a spectacle of unprecedented chaos. Speaking to John McCarty (author of the book *The Sleaze Merchants*), Lewis revealed, "Even though there was a major fair in town, theatre traffic was backed up so far the State Police were directing it. We were still about a quarter mile from the theatre when I turned to Dave, held out my hand, and said 'I guess we've started something.'" People were so grossed-out by the film that they went and told their friends about it and returned the following night, *en masse*, with those who wanted to see what all the fuss was about. Local residents complained that 60 foot images of women being mutilated were visible from their bedroom windows and giving them nightmares.

Blood Feast is at once funny and revolting, the acting terrible, the lighting flat, the camera almost completely static throughout. Lewis described the film as an 'experiment' project, and admitted to directing it in four days in a rushed, careless manner, aware that the finished product could easily sink without trace in its opening weekend. However, despite its many faults, this film will always have its place in horror history for daring to try something new, and for its defiantly in your face, gore-for-gore's-sake attitude. Tongues are ripped out, legs cut off (see the newspaper headline!). We also get to witness tabletop eviscerations, skulls ripped open and entrails fondled in loving close-up. John Waters later used bloody clips from *Blood Feast* in his suburban satire, *Serial Mom* (1994). He also claims to have used binoculars to spy on screenings of *Blood Feast* at the drive-in near his home in Baltimore as a child, to which Lewis commented, "If John did that, he's a bigger masochist than I thought!" Lewis and Friedman became exploitation legends overnight, and their film enjoyed a huge success in the American underground and the drive-in circuits, with Lewis later christened as 'the Godfather of gore'. The pair returned the following year with *Two Thousand Maniacs!*

Blood Frenzy (1987)
Dir: Hal Freeman /USA
This film opens with a prologue in which a young boy slashes the

throat of his father. It then starts proper with a group of head-cases driven out to the desert in a camper van to undergo 'confrontational therapy' with their doctor. We know that one of the group is the now-grown-up psycho killer, but we – supposedly – don't know who it is until the bodies have piled up. *Blood Frenzy* is the kind of 80s video fare that completely bypassed the DVD boom of the 00s, and it isn't difficult to see why; almost everything about it is wretched, save for a bloody table-top torture scene in an old mine shaft that evokes *The Last House on Dead End Street* (1977). Even among such neurotic patients, the killer here stands out like a clown at a funeral. At first I thought he was a blatant red herring, but no, he's the culprit. A similar concept was explored almost a decade later in the vastly superior *Color of Night* (1994), an American giallo which includes a similar bunch of neurotics (the prude, the 'Nam vet, the alcoholic, the nympho, the lesbo, the chauvanist, etc) who are being picked off by one of the fellow patients. And Bruce Willis tries to nail the culprit while donning an ill-fitting hairpiece. As for *Blood Frenzy*, I read somewhere that the film was intended to be a cross between H.G. Lewis' *Blood Feast* and Alfred Hitchcock's *Frenzy* (1972), but frankly, those comparisons are lost on me.

Blood Games (1990)
(aka *Baseball Bimbos in Hillbilly Hell*)
Dir: Tanya Rosenberg /USA
A 'pro-feminist' horror movie about a baseball game between two teams of the opposite sex. Things get nasty when the men lose, and they wave confederate flags, set up road blocks and even commit murder to get even with the women.

Blood Lake (1987)
Dir: Tim Boggs /USA
More 80s video trash in which a group of wise-cracking youngsters head out on a weekend trip to a lake. And after much lame innuendo and endless footage of piss-poor water-skiing, a killer finally shows up around the 47-minute mark. The slayings are all of the 'rolling-eyes-

and-smeared-ketchup' variety, and the killer's motivation doesn't stem from any deep-seated resentment or childhood trauma. Oh no. He's simply getting even for a bunch of unpaid cabin rental fees!

Bloodline (1979)
Dir: Terence Young /USA

Bloodline sees Aubrey Hepburn inherit a multi-national corporation when her father dies. It later turns out that her father's death was no accident. Numerous shareholders within the company are suspected of the murder, and when prostitutes are brutally murdered in a series of snuff clips, Hepburn realises her own life is in danger. *Bloodline* was a shoddy production; underfunded and brimming with hilarious gaffs, underwhelming performances, terrible FX sequences and studio interference. The film was made during the breakdown of Hepburn's second marriage. She accepted the role of Elizabeth on a whim, and became very upset when she learned about the film's murky snuff movie sub-plot. She initially washed her hands of the project, only to return in a bid to honour her contract with Paramount. Many of her fans never forgave her for appearing in such R-rated filth. Television prints of *Bloodline* include an extra 40 minutes of footage which helps to clear up some of the more confusing loose ends of the theatrical version. But that extra footage has never been included on any of its home video or DVD releases.

Blood Rage (1983)
(aka *Nightmare at Shadow Woods*)
Dir: John M. Grissmer /USA

A pair of twins, one of whom is an axe murderer, blame each other for a series of brutal slayings. The evil twin's psychosis seems to stem from the mother's promiscuous behaviour, in the way they would see her fucking random guys at a drive-in movie theatre. Memorable killings include a guy having his beer-holding hand lopped off, a woman in the woods chopped in half at the waist, and the axe-to-the-face murder in the prologue. Add to this a synth-heavy soundtrack, big hair and scream queens, *Blood Rage* is the perfect item for those looking for some early

80s slasher nostalgia. But beware, an edited bloodless version is doing the rounds under the title *Nightmare at Shadow Woods*.

Blood Tracks (1985)
Dir: Mike Jackson [Hal Elge] /Sweden
A mother escapes an abusive relationship by stabbing her husband and taking her large brood of children to hide out at a snowed-in abandoned factory. The family survive by picking off travellers and intruders. And when the famous rock band, Solid Gold (real name Easy Action), stop by to shoot a music video, the group and their entourage are attacked. *Blood Tracks* is a Swedish take on the Sawney Beane legend by way of Wes Craven. It has a wonderful 80s synth score, clumsy dubbing, atrocious fashions and ugly, mutant-like creatures. A more accurate title for the film would have been *The Snow Has Eyes*.

Bloodtide (1982)
Dir: Richard Jeffries /UK /Greece
A bog-standard monster movie in which James Earl Jones uses a chunk of semtex to blow up a cave. It turns out to be a silly move as he uncovers an ancient sea-dwelling demon. Not only does he have to fend off the bald, diseased dog of a beast, but he also has to appease the locals on a Greek island who are prone to offing outsiders in sacrificial rituals to keep the demon's hunger sated. The only good thing I can say about this film is that it's better than *Demon of Paradise* (1987). But that isn't saying much.

The Bloody Exorcism of Coffin Joe (1974)
(Orig title: *Exorcismo negro*)
Dir: Jose Mojica Marins /Brazil
Marins finds himself under threat from his fictional alter-ego in this blatant cash-in on William Friedkin's *The Exorcist* (1973), which at least has the distinction of pre-dating such postmodern horrors as *Wes Craven's New Nightmare* (1994) and Lucio Fulci's *A Cat in the Brain* (1990) by almost two decades. Marins spends Christmas with friends working on the script for his latest horror film, '*O Exorcismo negro*,' (or

'The Black Exorcism'), and soon uncovers strange demonic possessions, treachery, sacrificial rituals, murder and witchcraft in their midst. Who could be behind all this skullduggery? Why, it's the one in the top hat with the long, curly finger nails, of course.

The Brazilian media had vilified Marins for years, accusing him of desecrating gravestones, sleeping in graveyards, abusing his actresses, being a drug addict (he was heavily into amphetamines at one point), and even necrophilia. Perhaps with this film, Marins was attempting to balance the issue by drawing the very distinct separation between his real identity and his fictional persona. But it made no difference. Upon the release of *The Bloody Exorcism*, the media accused him of being insane, and the censors banned his film for years. Highlights include a crying girl holding a dead fox while the adults stand around gawping at each other; the zombie-like possessed ones who look like they've just stepped in from George Romero's *The Crazies* (1973); and the bloody axe dismemberments and group tortures in the finale.

Book of Blood (2009)
Dir: John Harrison /UK
Paranormal investigators stay in a house that sits in the middle of a 'highway' of the dead, the route that the spirits of the dead have to take. Based on Clive Barker's story (*Books of Blood Vol. 1*), the film shares similarities with *Hellraiser* (1987) in that it has a strange, transatlantic feel, a sinister attic, and things back from the dead. However, unlike *Hellraiser*, it is horribly miscast and dull beyond belief.

The Book of Zombie (2010)
Dir: Erik Van Sant, Paul Cranfield & Scott Kragelund /USA
Mormon zombies attack non-believers in a small town in Utah. A bickering husband and wife team up with an assortment of dorky Darwinists and hold up in a local convenience store and a bar called The Drunken Dragon. Originally intended as a short clip to be uploaded onto YouTube, the filmmakers re-wrote the script and made this hour-long offering, which, though it contains flashes of well-observed humour here and there - and also the concept of Mormon zombies

heading door to door is a good one – this is painfully amateur in all areas. The $16,000 budget looks to have been blown on the bizarre stop-motion title credits sequence, which is perhaps the most impressive part of the film. In this film, the ghouls are easily dissolved with 'sinful' substances such as caffeine, nicotine and fizzy drinks, so one character straps himself up with cans of cola, and heads outside to dispatch a few zombies as a 'suicide bomber,' but even this good idea fizzles out into nothing.

The Borrower (1991)
Dir: John McNaughton /USA

A criminal alien is 'genetically devolved' into humanoid form and dumped on planet earth as punishment for some unspecified crime. However, the culprit's head explodes on arrival, and so it resorts to ripping off fresh human heads and wearing them like a series of hats while it causes havoc in downtown Chicago. A tough female cop (Rae Dawn Chong) is assigned the task of tracking down the elusive alien while her sceptical superiors thwart her every move... *The Borrower* is typical monster alien nonsense that is played for laughs. Director John McNaughton brought over much of the same cast and crew that worked with him on his previous film, *Henry-Portrait of a Serial Killer* (1986), most notably script writer Richard Fire, actress Tracy Arnold, and Tom Towles who here plays a hick whose head is stolen early on in the woods. See also *The Hidden* (1987).

The Boy Who Cried Werewolf (1973)
Dir: Nathan H. Juran /USA

Kerwin Matthews is attacked by a werewolf while strolling in the woods with his son one night. Matthews becomes infected and transforms into a lycanthrope himself. Of course, no one believes the son's claims that there is a werewolf on the loose. And when daddy takes chunks out of a nearby Christian hippy camp, the boy is torn between wanting to help his father and slaying the beast. This is typical furry nonsense with a hackneyed plot and transformation sequences that date back to Lon Chaney Jr in the 1940s. There still hasn't been a completely satisfying werewolf movie.

Bodycount (1987)
Dir: Ruggero Deodato /Italy
By the late 80s and early 90s, Italian horror production was winding down with lame, half-arsed Fulci efforts (*Aenigma, Demonia*) and crude, Bruno Mattei cine-tranquilizers (*Zombi 3, Shocking Dark*). Spaghetti horror had turned lukewarm, and things were never the same. *Bodycount* is one of the better Italian horror movies of that era, directed by Ruggero '*Cannibal Holocaust*' Deodato. And though it's a far cry from the best of pasta-land efforts, there is still much to be impressed by here if you accept it for what it is: a routine slasher movie made for the American market. The film pits an all-American cast – which includes Mimsy Farmer and David Hess – against an 'Indian Shaman,' a hulking great Worzel Gummidge on steroids. Cue lots of mayhem as the merry campers are picked off, one by one. *Bodycount* is worth watching if only for the prank scene – which is one of the funniest in slasher movie history – as the gullible fat kid is told that there is an orgy going on in one of the cabins. He immediately strips off his clothes and runs inside with a smile on his face and tiny cock jiggling about, only to be met by a girls' parents who are having a quiet lunch together. He screeches to a halt, apologises and then gets the hell outta there.

Brain Dead (1990)
Dir: Adam Simon /USA
Not to be confused with Peter Jackson's zombie bloodbath, this *Brain Dead* is an intelligent mind-bender that shares similarities with both *Lost Highway* (1997) and *Jacob's Ladder* (1990). Bill Pullman stars as Dr. Rex Martin, a paranoid loner whose life changes irrevocably when he is assigned the task of restoring the mind of a genius who had killed his family and went insane. Penned by *The Twilight Zone* producer, Charles Beaumont, it's a film which reminds us that perspective is all, and that a damaged brain brings on a damaged 'reality.'

Brainscan (1994)

Dir:John Flynn /Canada /USA /UK

A young Edward Furlong enters a virtual reality game and commits a murder. He later learns on the news that the murder happened for real. He then finds himself in a panic, having to dispose of body parts while the 'Trickster,' a ghoulish emissary from the VR world (who looks like Flea from Red Hot Chilli Peppers in a red hot wig), tries to convince the kid about the virtues of killing. This is typical early 90s horror fare with its grungy soundtrack and Furlong still sporting his baby face and floppy mange fresh off of *Terminator 2: Judgement Day* (1991). His then-revolutionary home computer set-up looks horribly dated by today's standards, and T. Ryder Smith as the Trickster is overtly pantomime-ish for it to be much of a cult success. Ultimately, this film stands as a conservative critique of the rise of violent video games and horror movies; strongly implying that this kind of thing inevitably leads to real-life violence. If that is so, then what are we to make of *Brainscan*? Surely this is a dangerous film that no one should see lest it were to cause imitative violence in its viewers? Oh yeah, great marketing strategy!

The Brave (1997)

Dir: Johnny Depp /USA

Produced, directed, co-scripted and starring Johnny Depp, *The Brave* centres on Raphael (Depp), a native-American recently released from prison. He accepts a large payment of up-front cash in order to be tortured and killed by underground smut dealers in a snuff movie. Raphael hopes to treat his family and get them out of the shanty town where they live. But he only has a short amount of time before he must step up to meet his dreadful fate. This is a competently made, well acted drama, but the film's central premise is not altogether convincing; Raphael never once even considers the possibility of doing a runner with the money – he accepts everything that will happen to him, no questions asked. The snuff theme hangs over the film like a dark cloud, but nothing is explicitly shown. Depp refused to release the film in America because he was infuriated by the way the critics savaged it after its screening at Cannes. But, to be fair, the American criticisms aren't entirely unfounded; the film has a sickly sweet romanticized view of shanty town life; everyone in the community is lovely! They have regular get-togethers and barbeques! In reality, shanty towns are full of druggies and dealers and gang-bangers and other criminal scumbags. The film has a very old-fashioned, rose-tinted view of the poor, like some 19th Century communist pamphlet, and was directed by a man who has clearly never known hardship in his life.

Bride of Re-Animator (1990)
Dir: Brian Yuzna /USA
For the sequel, Brian Yuzna took on directorial duties and crafted a wickedly funny tribute to Universal's *Bride of Frankenstein* (1935). Herbert West and Dan Cain resume their activities by creating a new life-prolonging agent from the amniotic fluid of an iguana. This time around the ingenuity is gone, and the sick humour and gruesome special effects take centre stage.

Broken (1993)
Dir: Peter Christopherson /USA
Four years after the controversy that surrounded *Down In It*, another Nine Inch Nails video/short, *Broken* caused much controversy due to its extreme content. Directed by the late Peter 'Sleazy' Christopherson, *Broken* consists of four music videos and a framing scenario of snuff death and torture. The video is perhaps most notable for its jarring and abrasive sounds and visual style. Supermasochist, Bob Flanagan, makes an appearance as himself sitting in an S&M chair having his nads groped by sharp metallic claws (taken from the much banned *Happiness Is Slavery* video). And though *Down In It* was banned from playing on MTV, *Broken* proved to be too outrageous to be released at all. Copies were leaked and bootlegged on VHS in the 90s, and exchanged via the internet in the 00s. Some bootleggers even added extra footage, including Robert 'Bud' Dwyer's infamous suicide. More recently, *Broken* was officially made available uncut by Reznor himself for streaming on Vimeo, but it was immediately removed. The website

released a statement saying "Vimeo does not allow videos that harass, incite hatred or depict excessive violence."

The Brown Bunny (2003)
Dir: Vincent Gallo /USA
Starring Vincent Gallo's cock and Chloe Sevigny's mouth, *The Brown Bunny* is a dismal, agonisingly slow road movie about a motorcyclist who drives around in his car, while his hair gets stragglier by the minute. He also rides his motorbike in the desert. And, to wrap things up, Sevigny smokes a crack pipe and then smokes his cock in a hotel room. Those who are curious as to whether Sevigny is any good at giving head will be disappointed as Gallo doesn't let her perform properly. He only lets her suckle the bell-end while he jerks off into her mouth, the fucking ego-maniac, coked-up control freak. That was her chance to shine! He made sure he controlled every millisecond of fun while going 'hey, look at me and my cock art!' Is it art? Kind of. It's the kind of art a supermarket trolley collector would come up with if he was trying to tackle French new wave. Both Kirsten Dunst and Winona Ryder were fired from the set during the shoot, presumably because they refused to give him a blowy on camera. *The Brown Bunny* was also subjected to a memorable put down from Roger Ebert who commented, "I had a colonoscopy once, and they let me watch it on TV. It was more entertaining."

Bunnyman (2010)
Dir: Carl Lindbergh /USA
After the lame snuff-based *Carver* (2008), which fumbled with its supposed 'based on a true story' theme, *Bunnyman* even went as far as basing its title character on a real-life urban legend; in Fairfax County, Virginia in 1970, a man in a bunny suit is said to have murdered several people with an axe. Like *Carver, Bunnyman* bases its plot on a group of young Americans heading out into the wilderness on a camping trip and falling foul of the local maniacs, one of whom wears a bunny suit and carries a chainsaw. Heavily derivative, the opening reel reprises such classic maniac-on-the-road movies as *Duel*, *The Hitcher* and *Joy*

Ride/Road Kill. It then goes on to riff on *Blair Witch* with the bags of bones hanging from trees in the woods; *Grotesque*, with the evildoer listening to Ludwig Van during the torture ceremonies; any number of stranded-teens-being-offed-in-the-woods slasher movies (*Friday The 13th* and its sequels, for example); a whole bunch of 70s backwoods shockers (*Deliverance*, *The Texas Chain Saw Massacre*, *Motel Hell*, etc). It even recycles the foot-hobbling scene from *Misery*. For a change, the characters are somewhat likeable here but the constant wrong-headed decisions they make becomes irksome very quickly and leads to disaster for all. The snuff element is played up heavily during the opening and closing credits, but there's actually very little snuff play during the film, save for the torture scenes which are recorded on video.

Burned at the Stake (1981)
(aka *The Coming*)
Dir: Bert I. Gordon /USA
By Bert I. Gordon's usual standards, *Burned at the Stake* is not a bad movie at all, despite the fact that no witches were ever burned at Salem. After a prologue set during the height of the witch trials in 1692, we cut to modern-day Salem where a morbid teenage girl – who looks a lot like one of the accusers in the prologue – is harassed by the ghostly father of an accused woman. And the girl, who could be the reincarnation of the accuser, is captured and somehow hypnotised into committing evil deeds. According to this film, it wasn't necessarily superstition that was to blame for the tortures and executions of those times, but rather malicious accusations that got out of hand. The bureaucracy of the Church-sanctioned laws were exploited by deviant folks with petty grievances, and the authorities had no choice but to act on the accusations as instructed in the law books. That's not to say that those holding the trials were entirely reasonable or logical; while one man pleads his innocence while heavy boulders are crushing his chest, the man conducting the torture says, "If you were innocent, why would God allow you to be treated in this way?" Chilling. How can you argue with such lop-sided thinking? Such twisted 'logic' runs through many witch-themed movies, such as *Witchfinder General* (1968), *Mark of the*

Devil (1969), and *The Bloody Judge* (1970). Bert I. Gordon, known affectionately as the 'Notorious B.I.G.' to his fans, may not have been the greatest filmmaker around, but when he had interesting material to work with, the results were often quite enjoyable.

Bus 174 (2002)
Dir: Jose Padilha /Brazil
Documentary centering on the hijacking of a bus by Sandro do Nascimento, a Rio street kid, and the nightmarish five-hour stand-off with the police before the tragic finale. A troubling film which exposes the gulf between the rich and poor in a country where society pays no heed to the social problems until the dispossessed stand up and take violent action against those who are better off. Writer/director Jose Padilha shows great compassion, and *Bus 174* isn't just an unforgettable film, but a masterclass in how to present an argument on screen.

By the Devil's Hand: The 666 Killer (2009)
Dir: Christopher Abram /USA
For those of you looking for a film that has has a bit of style and competence, don't go anywhere near *By the Devil's Hand: The 666 Killer* (2009). This is a bottom of the barrel, low-budget 'torture porn' shitter in which we're made to suffer the usual cliches – sets decorated with polythene sheets hung up on the walls, overblown credits sequences, appallingly generic movie 'score,' etc. It's a film which rides on the coattails of whatever is popular at the time, which happens to be evil killer movies set in dingy lairs where young women are tortured. The gimmick here is the '666 killer,' a sadistic lunatic who subjects six victims to die in six days using six different murder methods. There is also an overblown sub-plot with a boring drama about a boring woman with a boring job and a boring fucking life. The killer allows a 'lucky' victim to choose how she would like to die. I know what *my* answer would be in that situation: "Hmm, I think I'll choose dying of old age, please, Mr. 666 Killer. So if you'd kindly untie me and let me go, I'll be on my way..."

Calvaire (2004)

(aka *The Ordeal*)

Dir: Fabrice Du Welz /Belgium

For those interested in the 'new French extremity' films, there's *Calvaire*. Although this film is actually Belgian, it is in the French language and features Phillipe Nahon, French cinema's go-to guy for the unhinged maniac role. Coming on like a Gallic take on *The Old Dark House* (1933) by way of *The Texas Chain Saw Massacre* (1974), *Calvaire* takes viewers right inside the mouth of madness as a travelling singer's car breaks down in a remote area, and he soon finds himself at a run-down guest house and at the mercy of some very unstable creeps. Offering tonnes of black humour and bizarre non sequiturs, this film plays like a twisted ballad of broken men. Look out for the 'dance' scene.

Cannibal Ferox 2 (1985)

(aka *Massacre in Dinosaur Valley*; Orig title: *Amazonas*)

Dir: Michael E. Lemick [Michele Massimo Tarantini] /Italy /Brazil

A paleontologist visits Brazil with a group of tourists. They're heading for 'The Valley of the Dinosaurs' to collect pre-historic fossils. However, their propeller plane crash lands in cannibal territory deep in the jungle. With Kevin's expertise on tribes, and 'Nam veteran John's survival knowledge, the small group trek through the wilds avoiding the deadly snakes and piranhas and crocodiles before falling foul of an unscrupulous slave driver. *Cannibal Ferox 2* offers up some solid B-movie fun, and is even better than the original in many ways. Thankfully, there's no animal abuse this time, but there's no cannibalism either. Like Me Me Lai in Deodato's *The Last Cannibal World* (1977), the women in this film are made to run around topless for much of the running time. In the original *Ferox*, the tribe is portrayed as retaliating to the Westerner's nastiness, whereas this time they're depicted as evil from the start, kidnapping and murdering members of the group without any provocation. We get some great jungle locations, great use of Kevin's 'boomstick' which confuses the tribe as they've never seen anything like it before, but, like I said, Cannibalism is disappointingly off the menu here.

Captain's Pride, Volume 33 (2009?)

Dir: -Not credited-

A short six-minute clip which shows a woman in a cage being tormented by a man in a black ski mask. The cage is covered in animal skulls. The woman is carried out of the cage and chained up to a workbench. The man wears a Motorhead t-shirt. At this point we can make out other trussed up victims in the room. The woman has her ear cut off and her throat slashed. Mr. Motorhead then leaves the room and another enters wearing a Santo wrestling mask. He rapes her while she bleeds to death. Mr. Motorhead reappears and inflicts more damage on her throat wound with a home-made torture device. The end. This little clip was released anonymously onto the web in the late 00s and has been passed around on the underground horror circuit. It was shot on scratchy old 8mm film, and there's no audio except for the sound of the whirring projector. Nothing is known about the film's makers or what their intentions were. Presumably, they wanted to release this with as little information as possible in order to create an online 'buzz' about its supposed authenticity, but this is unmistakably fake.

Captifs (2010)

(aka *Caged*)

Dir: Yann Gozlan /France

Captifs is a routine, bloodless and rather predictable yarn about a woman who is kidnapped by a gang of Serbian organ traffickers. After the success of *Hostel* (2006) and *A Serbian Film* (2009), we have yet another film that centres on the paranoia of Europe's so-called 'Wild East.' Much of the film's drama takes place within the dull, grey cells where the 'captifs' are held, and in typical French-language tradition, the maniacs aren't just deviant killers, they're also driven by the greed for profit. Just like the sado-tourist club in *Hostel*, these organ traffickers have got their racket down to a well-oiled machine.

This underworld organisation seems far too professional, and this pushes credibility to breaking point. The film is set up as a trendy 'torture porn' horror, but then the gruesome details of the plot are avoided in favour of the heroine busting free and single-handedly wiping out all the bad guys. I mean, what is the point of putting women in peril anymore? We know that no challenge is too great for them. Women can do anything in horror movies nowadays; bust out of cells, kill an army of hardened maniacs, and outrun a pack of dogs while always finding something handy to stab people with, and even saving a little girl's life while they're at it. There are strong women and then there are ridiculously OTT movies. This falls into the latter category. It's an insultingly predictable film, I just wanted the smug bitch to fucking die.

Carver (2008)
Dir: Franklin Guerrero Jr. /USA
Another film supposedly based on true snuff events but is entirely fictional is *Carver* (2008), about a group of annoying campers who enter a barn and discover a collection of snuff reels featuring women and couples getting slaughtered in the woods. They soon realise that the murderers are the same men who run the local bar. And sure enough, the youngsters are hunted down. The most irritating dick weasel of the group is chained up in the rest room, has the contents of the toilet poured onto him and has his right testicle crushed in a nutcracker of all things. The blonde chick has a long nail hammered into her head. Another victim is beaten to death with a sledgehammer, and is not such a good-looking chap once his face has been pounded into pulp. *Carver* isn't a particularly good film, nor does it bring anything new to the genre, just a routine run-around where most of the annoying characters get to live longer than they should because the filmmakers assume we've grown to like them. Wrong assumption. Also, none of the killings are captured on the maniac's camera, which is another bum move. And, at just short of a hundred minutes, the film is way over-long and you'll be glad when it's over.

The Cars That Ate Paris (1974)
(aka *The Cars That Ate People*)

PHENOMENA

Dir: Peter Weir /Australia
Overblown and typically overrated since the director moved on to bigger things. Peter Weir marked his directorial debut with this black comedy which went on to inspire *Mad Max 2: The Road Warrior* (1981) and a homage in Quentin Tarantino's *Death Proof* (2007). Taking inspiration from rebel pics like *The Wild One* (1953) and westerns, such as *High Noon* (1952), here we have spiked car wrecks driven by fun-seeking youths through the streets of Paris, Australia, causing smash-ups. Turns out that the collisions are actually planned ahead and are engineered by the vulturous populace for economic and medical reasons. The looters profit by selling the salvage, and the town doctor performs immoral medical experiments on the victims. The film culminates in a bloodbath between the youths and the townsfolk.

Cassandra (1986)
Dir: Colin Eggleston /Australia
Tessa Humphries plays Cassandra, a girl plagued by recurring dreams of a shotgun suicide of someone she knew. She suspects the dreams are actually repressed childhood memories of some atrocity she witnessed, but she just can't remember exactly what it was. Her parents aren't very helpful, and they suspiciously do all they can to convince her that her experiences are nothing more than random nightmares. However, when a killer shows up bloodily dispatching a few locals, Cassandra is convinced that she shares psychic links with the maniac. This tense, atmospheric oddity is part mystery, part supernatural chiller, and part slasher movie that boasts superb roving, Raimi-esque camera work and an outstanding, creepy-as-hell synth score. The film owes a debt to other psychic link killer movies, such as *Eyes of Laura Mars* (1978), *Mind Over Murder* (1979), and the bloody awful *Blood Song* (1982). *Cassandra* would sit nicely on a double-bill with another Aussie psycho movie, *Out of the Body* (1989). Tessa Humphries is actually Dame Edna's daughter! Luckily for her, there's no family resemblance!

Cease to Exist (2008)
Dir: Ryan Okenberg /USA

This documentary takes a closer look at the link between the Manson Family and The Beach Boys' Dennis Wilson. According to this film, Manson exploited the fact that Dennis couldn't keep his cock in his trousers, and lured him into recording demos with the cult by offering him girls, soft drugs, and the opportunity to hang out at Spahn Ranch. Dennis is said to have spent $100,000 on the Family in one year alone. He even paid for their medical bills, which he called "the largest gonorrhea bill in medical history." The nastiness started when The Beach Boys recorded one of Manson's songs, 'Cease to Exist.' The band re-wrote the lyrics and changed the song's title to 'Never Learn Not to Love,' credited to Dennis. Charlie was infuriated, not only for the alterations, but for being cut out of the royalties, too. Dennis felt threatened and fled town just as Helter Skelter was taking off. He was later quoted as saying, "I know why Charles Manson did what he did. And some day I'll tell the world. I'll write a book and explain why he did it. Over the years though, people have always wanted to know what happened, what my relationship with Charlie was. We were just friends."

The Child (1976)
(aka *Children of the Night*)
Dir: Robert Voskanian /USA
A dreamy little film in which a child minder, Alicianne (Laurel Barnett) is hired to look after a little girl, Rosalie (Rosalie Cole) at a secluded house in the woods. She arrives at the eerie, fog-bound setting and soon learns that the girl's mother had died under mysterious circumstances. Her father is a bit loopy, and seems to be losing his mind altogether. And if things aren't weird enough, Rosalie is in contact with sinister zombie-like ghouls that dwell in a nearby graveyard. As Alicianne tries to make friends with Rosalie, her friendliness is met with mockery and the summoning of her 'friends' from the cemetery via telekinesis, whom she leads on a killing spree of those she believes have killed her mother...

After years of watching horror movies, I have learned through experience that certain films have to be watched while in a certain frame of mind, otherwise the magic can be lost. And for me, *The Child* is one of those movies. Like, say, *Eraserhead* (1976) or *Axe* (1974), I knew within the first five minutes that this is a film best suited to late night viewing. The mind is much more willing to latch onto strange movies, and be taken on a peculiar journey while in a sleepy haze. And *The Child* doesn't disappoint. From the opening shots, viewers are immediately plunged into a world that seems to exist in another slightly warped dimension. The music score (by Rob Wallace and Michael Quatro) alternates between eerie electric organ and wailing synthesizer effects; the camera is consistently posited at odd angles; the performances are stilted and defiantly drab; the 'plot' takes strange little detours that – interesting though they are – seldom lead anywhere, and the whole production walks a tightrope between amateur and avant-garde. Even the scratches and speckles on the print transfer somehow add to its vintage charms. Many horror fans have dismissed this film over the years, but if you sit back and relax, this weird and wonderful little gem might just work its peculiar magic on you.

Child's Play 2 (1990)
Dir: John Lafia /USA
Chucky tracks down little Andy and murders his foster parents. But before the evil doll can take over the child's body in a voodoo ritual, Andy and his foster sister put up a final battle in the Good Guy doll factory. Cue a lethal stitching machine, a vat of melted plastic, and a machine that inserts plastic eyeballs into dolls heads – all used as nasty weapons. A cartoony sequel which is perhaps more enjoyable than the original film. Also look out for the references to *Pinocchio*, the tale of another doll that wanted to be a real boy.

Children of the Corn (1984)
Dir: Fritz Kiersch /USA
Many Stephen King stories have been murdered on screen in cheapjack, 'couldn't-give-a-shit' cash-ins on his good name, and *Children of the Corn* was perhaps the earliest example of this shoddy treatment of his work. The story is set in an isolated town called Gatlin where the

children have turned to a strange religion, murdered all of the adults, and worship 'He who walks behind the rows.' A young couple driving through town witness a murder and come up against the mad children when they try to report it. King's original message about the damage religion can have on inexperienced minds is almost completely lost in the fake storms, rubber monsters and over-acting,. But the film was a cult success on home video, spawning no fewer than six sequels.

Choses secretes (2002)
(*Secret Things*)
Dir: Jean-Claude Brisseau /France
A pair of hot young women from the poor side of Paris take up office jobs for a bank near the Champs-Elysees. They intend to climb the professional ladder by using sex to ensnare the hearts of their easily-exploitable male colleagues. However, they don't bank on meeting someone like Christophe, an immaculate Patrick Bateman-type psychopath... Voted in the top ten films of the year by *Les Cahiers du cinema*, *Choses secretes* is a lurid tale of sex, tragedy and Machiavellian office politics, all dressed up in Visconti-esque eroticism and pretensions. The impressive performances of Sabrina Seyvecou and Coralie Revel as the manipulative women, Sandrine and Nathalie, rescue the film from what could easily have been an insufferable farce. But their sizzling screen chemistry makes their eventful journey a worthwhile watch. Fans of *Salo* (1975) and *Eyes Wide Shut* (1999) should enjoy.

Chromeskull: Laid To Rest 2 (2011)
Dir: Robert Hall /USA
Writer/director Robert Hall returns with a sequel to the enjoyable *Laid To Rest* (2009) with a dismal offering which picks up right where the first film left off. This offers more of the same as Chromeskull is repaired and resurrected by a sinister group of deviants, and finds a new group of dweebs to massacre. This time the plot is even lighter, the killings are twice as gruesome, and we even get a bit of back story on Chromeskull, who miraculously survived the head-crushing in part one.

But I suppose the most disturbing element in the film for me is the way in which technology is fetishized; all of the characters seem to document their entire lives – and deaths – on video, like sad tourists of life.

The City of the Dead (1960)
(aka *Horror Hotel*)
Dir: John Moxey /UK
A moody, atmospheric gem which shares similarities with Mario Bava's *Black Sunday*, which was made around the same time. The film opens on the scene of a suspected witch being burned at the stake during the Salem witch-hunts of 1692. She curses the townspeople and laughs as the flames rise around her. It then cuts forward to modern-day Massachussets where Christopher Lee plays a history professor who encourages his favourite student, Nan (Venetia Stevenson), to visit the strange misty town of Whitewood, the place where many a witch burning took place. Her trip will not only help her in her studies, but will also feed her own personal fascination with witchcraft. Things get creepy as soon as she enters the town, as her mysterious 'tour guide' disappears into the night. She takes a room in spooky hotel and begins to uncover some horrific home truths... But that turns out to be only half the story. With its dry ice and perpetual darkness, *City of the Dead* is one of the great horror movies of the early 60s, despite its low-budget. The 'town-full-of-hooded-Satanists' sub-genre flourished in the 70s, but this understated classic got there first.

Code Unknown (2000)
Dir: Michael Haneke /France /Germany /Romania
A mosiac drama in the mode of *Short Cuts* and *Magnolia* with stories of the modern world, including the homeless in Paris, Kosovo families and children at an inner-city school for the deaf. Haneke's film is much more cold and austere in its approach than the titles mentioned above, and is in keeping with the director's previous works which examine themes of contemporary dislocation. In the grand scheme of things, this is perhaps Haneke's most optimistic film to date, as Jessica Winter of

Village Voice pointed out: "[*Code Unknown* is] not a gaze into the void, but a fierce attempt to scramble out of it."

The Cohasset Snuff Film (2012)
Dir: Edward Payson /USA
Another 'based on a true story' offering is *The Cohasset Snuff Film,* which is presented as a series of internet clips in which school student Colin Mason murdered several class mates and posted the videos on the internet. The clips were available on the web for days before the police got wind of it. Colin Mason is a fictitious character but this film does share some disturbing similarities with the true case of that fame-hungry ice-pick loon whose name I won't even mention. Suffice it to say, if there was ever an *X Factor* for psychos, Simon Cowell would spooge himself inside out for him.

Color Me Blood Red (1965)
Dir: Herschell Gordon Lewis /USA
A troubled production, this tells the tale of Adam Sorg (Don Joseph), a frustrated artist who resorts to using human blood in his paintings. And before long, he ends up on a killing spree, wiping out his girlfriend and local residents for the sake of his art. Inspired by Roger Corman's *A Bucket of Blood* (1959) and going on to inspire Abel Ferrara's *The Driller Killer* (1979), *Color Me Blood Red* sees a definite drop in quality since the previous *Two Thousand Maniacs!* (1964). It's a claustrophobic take on encroaching madness that lacks the style and energy of his earlier films. Lewis and his producer, David F. Friedman, parted ways, and the movie was finished in post-production without their involvement, and that could perhaps explain the subdued mood and visual inconsistencies. Friedman continued in film production for years, with softcore credits like *The Erotic Adventures of Zorro* (1972), horror items such as *She Freak* (1967), and the notorious *Ilsa, She Wolf of The SS* (1975). Lewis continued making movies but didn't return to the gore genre until 1967 when he unleashed *The Gruesome Twosome*.

The Counselor (2013)
Dir: Ridley Scott /USA

Westray (Brad Pitt) – Have you ever seen a snuff film?

Counselor (Michael Fassbender) – No. You?

Westray – Would you?

Counselor – I would not.

Westray - ...'Cos, if the consumer of the product is essential to its production, one cannot watch without being an accessory to a murder.

Counselor – You know somebody who's seen one?

Westray – Yes I do. He said the girl was looking to the camera, crying when her head was lopped off.

Counselor – Jesus.

Westray – Think about that the next time you do a line.

Counselor – I don't do drugs.

Westray – Well, I'm glad to hear that 'cos what follows, I hope, would be beyond the power of your imagination... They let a figure in wearing only a hood with eye holes. Two. They address themselves to the headless and quivering corpse, of which you must remember, was selected because of her youth and beauty... And all of this is PAID for. So, what do you think that cost? Ballpark?

Counselor – Jesus.

Westray – Hmmm...

PHENOMENA

Counselor – God.

Westray – The point, Counselor, is that you may think there are things that these people are simply incapable of. There are not.

In a nutshell: Against the advice of friends and acquaintances, a counselor gets himself mixed up in a 'one-off' drug deal with a ruthless Mexican cartel. The plan is to get stinking rich and live happily ever after with his fiance. However, due to circumstances beyond his control, things go very wrong, and the cartel set out to destroy him by destroying the woman he loves...

You wouldn't expect a mainstream movie with a superstar director and star-studded cast to have its rightful place in this book, but *The Counselor* (2013) is one of the most horrifying and fascinating mainstream films to be released in a long while. The script, written by Cormac McCarthy, is dark, disturbing, poetic and downright Shakespearean in its plot mechanics. The film also explores areas of the soul which are rarely touched upon in mainstream cinema nowadays; Nietzschean concepts such as amorality, nihilism, existentialism, perspectivism. It was brought to the screen by director Ridley Scott, whose brother Tony (director of *The Hunger* and *True Romance*) had committed suicide in 2012 by jumping off the Vincent Thomas Bridge in L.A.. Back in the early 80s, Ridley Scott had initially turned down the opportunity of directing *Blade Runner* due to the sudden death of his other brother, Frank, but was later drawn to the script as a way of dealing with his loss and of facing the darkness and pessimism that had descended upon his psyche. And though he only learned of Tony's death while in the middle of shooting *The Counselor*, it's perhaps safe to assume that he had embraced a similar mindset to complete the picture.

The world depicted in *The Counselor* is one in which love is seen as a weakness, the innocent are fair game, manipulative, predatory divas always get their own way, and each of us live in our own self-determining universes. Philosophising cartel kings authorise barbaric snuff murders while loved ones plead with them to change their minds. Faith is an obsolete concept rotting on old billboards. And the ruthless will to power is seen as the philosopher's stone. Just think about that the next time you do a line.

The Counselor has all the hallmarks of a future cult classic; many critics didn't understand the film and tore it to shreds, the movie-star cast – which, alongside Pitt and Fassbender, also includes Cameron Diaz, Penelope Cruz and Javier Bardem – were ridiculed for appearing in the film, first time script writer McCarthy was accused of being indulgent and pretentious, and there were calls for Ridley Scott to retire. Even film critic Mark Kermode, who usually gets it right nine times out of ten, was so very very wrong in his casual dismissal of the film. All of which ensured that box-office receipts were thin on the ground. But mark my words, in ten or twenty years time, *The Counselor* will be basking in cult classic status, not in a camp, 'movie-stars-in-a-car-crash' sort of way, but as a legitimate, deeply penetrating film that was misunderstood for years.

Cradle of Fear (2001)
Dir: Alex Chandon /UK
Eli Roth claimed that the inspiration for *Hostel* came from a news story about a snuff website based in Thailand where paying punters could dictate murders in any specific way they wanted. This idea had already been explored in a segment of the British anthology horror, *Cradle of Fear* (2001). One of the stories centres on office worker, Richard, who chances upon a website called the 'Sick Room'. The site allows its customers to participate in brutal murders – by hammer, or beatings, or strangulation, etc – with anonymity, all from the safety of your own home, or office. Richard soon develops an obsession with the site, spending all of his money and getting into serious debt to feed his sadistic fantasies. First his girlfriend leaves him, then the bailiffs show up, and soon enough his home is repossessed altogether, but still he obsessively clicks away in the Sick Room. One day the website disappears, so he investigates and eventually tracks down the site's location... The other tales include a young woman (the beautiful Emily Boothe) having a one-night-stand with a goth guy (Dani Filth) whom she picks up at a club, only to suffer horrendous hallucinations the

following morning; an amputee willing to resort to murder to be able to walk again; and a couple of burglars who get more than they bargained for when they break into the wrong house. The stories have a wraparound segment featuring a notorious serial killer who makes a break for freedom. *Cradle of Fear* was released direct to DVD to many negative reviews. In fact, I personally don't know anyone apart from myself who enjoyed it. I've never understood why people are so quick to dismiss it. Yes, it's low-budget and shot on video, but the stories are quite engaging and the production values are pretty good for a film of its ilk. I've seen hundreds of shot-on-video horror movies over the years and *Cradle of Fear* is far superior to 90% of them. Yes, I know Dani Filth is a prick, but as far as EC Comics inspired movies go, *Cradle of Fear* is better than *Creepshow* (1982). I'm sorry if that's a controversial opinion. Fuck *you*.

The Card Player (2004) and *Untraceable* (2008) also use internet snuff as a starting point. *The Card Player* is about a serial killer who kidnaps women in Rome and challenges detectives to games of online poker. If the investigators loose, they can look forward to seeing the women being murdered live on web-cam. *Untraceable* has a similar mean-spirited killer who runs an untraceable website in which victims are murdered on a live stream. And, being aware of the public's desire to view forbidden material, he rigs the site so that the more people are logged on, the quicker the victims die. While having interesting premises, both of these films are ultimately let down by bland characters, join-the-dots plot-lines and a 'play-it-safe', '*Thesis* syndrome' of toning down the more disturbing elements in order to make them palatable for mainstream audiences. *The Card Player* is particularly disappointing considering director Dario Argento was once one of the kingpins of horror. It's an embarrassment, 'ooh, look, grandpa has discovered the internet!'

Crawlspace (1972)
Dir: John Newland /USA
A retired couple are set on edge when a strange young man is found sleeping in the cellar. After the old man padlocks the doors, the

bedraggled youngster flees into the night. The following evening he returns and tries the doors again. The couple hear him while in bed, and hug each other for comfort. In the morning they take food down to him, but the kid, Richard, doesn't seem interested in conversation. The old couple don't know where he came from or what his intentions are, and are reluctant to call the police for fears of antagonising him. So they try their best to ignore him. However, there is a bad smell coming up from the cellar... Eventually Richard begins to ingratiate himself into the household by helping out with the chores; chopping logs for the fire, shovelling snow, making morning coffee. The couple welcome him into their home, but Richard's violent streak ensures a lynch mob arrives on the doorstep to take him out... *Crawlspace* is more of a tragic story than out and out horror, which is a shame because the subtle rise in tension is expertly handled, but the horrific ending expected by the audience fizzles out in the final moments.

Creepozoids (1987)
Dir: David DeCoteau /USA
The creepozoids are a swarm of horribly mutated beasties who spread their contagion through a band of hardened survivors after a nuclear holocaust has ravaged the planet. It's the kind of micro-budget dreck that tries to depict the apocalypse by focusing on a few claustrophobic rooms on a movie set. A major let down.

Critters (1986)
Dir: Stephen Herek /USA
A group of Krites – sort of furry tumbleweeds with razor-sharp teeth – escape from a prison farm on an asteroid, steal a spaceship, and head for planet Earth while being pursued by shape-shifting bounty hunters. Meanwhile, on a Kansas farm, a family comes under attack from the carnivorous critters, and it's up to a resourceful ginger kid to save the day by fending them off with firecrackers. *Critters* is an endearing attempt to recapture the sense of fun in 50s space invasion movies, such as *Invaders From Mars* (1953) and *It Came From Outer Space* (1953), and for the most part it is successful in its aims. The creatures – their

design clearly influenced by Gremlins – are nasty little things, sort of like intergalactic piranhas covered in arse hairs that not only roll around biting chunks out of people, but are also capable of shooting sharp spines as projectiles out of their backs. We get the typical small-town setting, incompetent authority figures (including M. Emmett Walsh as a sceptical Sheriff), and a deliberately tongue-in-cheek script co-written by Don Opper (who went on to co-star in *Critters 3* and *Critters 4: In Space*, alongside newcomers Leonardo DiCaprio and Angela Bassett).

Cruel World (2005)
Dir: Kelsey T. Howard /USA
A comedy horror about a lunatic (Ed Furlong) who murders a reality TV show host after losing, and then sets up his own Big Brother-type show in which the losing contestants are " sent home," or executed. A woman is buried alive, another character is decapitated, and another impaled on a sword. It's a fun little slasher flick with a 'live on air' snuff gimmick.

Cruising (1980)
Dir: WilliamFriedkin /USA
Al Pacino plays an undercover cop in pursuit of a vicious serial killer who is targeting members of the gay community in New York. And, of course, as with any obsessed cop, the more embroiled in the case he becomes, the more his private life falls apart. *Cruising* – based on true events that took place in New York between 1962 and 1979 – was always going to be a controversial film. During filming, gay protesters turned up on set chanting slogans and throwing bags of urine at the crew members. And when the film was finally released – after United Artists literally destroyed around 40-minutes of footage – the protests only got bigger, with cops from the NYPD joining the pickets, outraged at the way their force was depicted in the film.

Cruising isn't the disaster many film critics would have you believe, nor is it anything special. Take away the gay angle and seedy setting, and you have a typical incognito cop movie, like a sub-par *Serpico* (1973) or *The French Connection* (1971). The film also has much in common with William Lustig's *Relentless* (1989), in that the killer in that film shares a similar psychosis to the one in Friedkin's pic. Pacino's investigation into the slashings is depicted as being like a literal descent into hell. The gay clubs he visits are dark, subterranean pits. Disturbingly, the man awaiting trial for the real-life murders, Paul Bateson, had previously appeared in a small part in Friedkin's earlier film, *The Exorcist* (1973). Friedkin even visited him in prison and used their conversation to help flesh out his film script.

Interestingly, during the making of *Dog Day Afternoon* (1975), Pacino famously refused to kiss his co-star on the lips as he felt it would have been a bit gay. However, just a few years later, during the making of *Cruising*, he seemed happy enough to get down and dirty with leather bars, mascara and anal fisting. Anal fisting! Blimey, talk about becoming comfortable with one's sexuality.

Curse of the Blue Lights (1988)
Dir: John Kenry Johnson /USA
A farmer finds a mutilated kitty on his land. His scarecrow then comes to life, foaming at the mouth with yellow bile, and kills him with a shovel. Teens bicker in a car. A trio of overweight ghouls plot in the shadows. Teens track a pair of mysterious blue lights in the woods. They find a frozen creature in the ground called the 'Maldoon Man.' The creature disappears and the cop doesn't believe their story. The teens enter a graveyard mausoleum and discover that a human corpse is being dissolved with acid by the overweight ghouls seen earlier. They're trying to resurrect the Maldoon creature. The kids are spotted and chased out of the graveyard. Things then become even *weirder* when a coin taken from the creature's chest begins to affect the environment, causing objects to levitate. Meanwhile, back in the mausoleum chamber, one of the captured teens is transformed into a snake. The kids take the coin to a witch. She crumbles to her knees at the sight of it. She tells them that the coin is very dangerous as it contains an evil from a dark netherworld. The kids are then picked off, one by one, by the ghouls and their spectral minions while the witch concocts a magic potion in her cauldron which the remaining kids use to battle against a

horde of zombies, the Maldoon Man and the fat ghouls.

Heavily inspired by *Children Shouldn't Play With Dead Things* (1972) and EC comics, *Curse of the Blue Lights* is a low-budget horror weirdy which – despite its obvious flaws – is a fun little movie to watch while you're stoned. It has enough green-headed ghouls, macabre reanimated corpses and mystical weirdness to keep viewers occupied for 95 minutes. Things fall apart a little in the third act as the narrative sort of tumbles out of control, but it remains far more engaging than the usual 80s video trash. And as for the significance of the mysterious blue lights? Who the fuck knows.

Curse of the Fly (1965)
Dir: Don Sharp /UK

The second sequel to *The Fly* (1958) after *Return of the Fly* (1959) switches locations from America to the UK where Henri continues his meddling with the unknown, despite almost coming to a sticky end in his father's teleportation chamber in his youth. He is also aided by his two sons, and together they have mastered the science of transatlantic teleportation, zapping back and forth between England and Canada. However, after a series of experimental failures, Henri's sons have an attack of the jitters and decide to stop. And things take a turn for the worse when one of the sons marries a woman who holds a few secrets concerning the 'curse' of the fly... Focusing more on the sci-fi elements this time, and playing down the horror, *Curse of the Fly* confines its monsters to the shadows. Hammer director Don Sharp and scriptwriter Harry Spalding do a good job of trying to restore the 'scientific' approach of the first film, but it's far too talky, and the budget restraints meant that the story couldn't be explored to the full.

Dagon (2001)
Dir: Stuart Gordon /Spain /USA

Director Stuart Gordon, producer Brian Yuzna and writer Denis Poali teamed up for the third time to tackle another HP Lovecraft project after the hits *Re-Animator* (1985) and *From Beyond* (1986), for the less successful *Dagon*. After a violent thunder storm ravages the coast of

Spain, blood spilled on a sailing yacht leaks into the sea, attracting a sea-dwelling tentacled monster. Two teenage love birds escape the boat (one of whom wears a 'Miskatonic' t-shirt), and head for the church for help. However, the place turns out to be a demonic fortress whose worshippers (the whole town) offers up human sacrifices for the beast. To make matters worse, the townsfolk transform into shambling ghouls after dark and target the youngsters. *Dagon* is a fast-paced, no-nonsense monster movie which offers up slimy scaly creatures, a small-town paranoia angle, and a moribund sense of humour at the expense of cheap holiday destinations. And though the film owes more to Lovecraft's *The Shadow Over Innsmouth* than *Dagon*, the impressive head-skinning sequence more than makes up for it.

Dario Argento: An Eye For Horror (2000)
Dir: Leon Furguson /UK

A documentary produced for Channel 4 in 2000 and narrated by Mark Kermode. This film traces Argento's life, from his isolated childhood where he found solace in the works of Edgar Allan Poe, to the filming of his – then – latest film, *Sleepless* (2000). People often complain that horror documentaries don't go deep enough into the subject, but how can it be otherwise? You can only pack so much information into an hour. If you want more detailed information on Argento, there have been many books written about him and his work – go read 'em. For those who understand the limitations of the documentary format, however, and aren't going to get all pissy about there not being enough 'details,' *An Eye For Horror* can be recommended as an interesting overview of Argento and his films. Writers Maitland McDonagh and Alan Jones gush lovingly about his work while George Romero, John Carpenter and Tom Savini swap anecdotes (Savini's story about the prop of Harvey Keitel's severed head is particularly memorable). Actors Michael Brandon, Piper Laurie and Jessica Harper relate their own personal stories of working with Argento, while the auteur's family members – daughters Asia and Fiore, ex-wife Daria Nicolodi and brother Claudio – add their own feelings about the man (and this includes Asia on the difficulties of shooting topless scenes with her dad). All of which builds to an interesting portrait of the artist who readily admits to disliking actors and the physical process of making films.

Darkroom (1981-1982)
Dir -Various- /USA

"You're in a house, maybe your own. Maybe one you've never seen before. You feel it, something evil... You run, but there's no escape, nowhere to turn... You feel something beckoning you, drawing you to the darkness, to the terror that awaits you in the darkroom." *Darkroom* was a short-lived horror anthology series that aired on America's ABC network in the early 80s, and disappeared pretty fast. A silver-haired James Coburn introduces the lacklustre short tales, most of which weren't worth the paper they were written on, let alone going to the trouble of assembling a cast and crew to film and broadcast them to a nation.

'Closed Circuit' stars Robert Webber as an employee of a TV studio who returns to work after suffering a minor stroke to discover that his identity has been stolen by a computer programme. *'Stay Tuned, We'll Be Right Back'* shows a man becoming obsessed with a transistor radio when he discovers he can pick up morse code and radio broadcasts from the 1940s. And even though it's forty years later, he convinces himself that he can end the war by intercepting German U-boat communications. In *'The Bogeyman Will Get You,'* a girl suspects an old family friend of being a vampire, but he turns out to be a werewolf instead. In *'Uncle George,'* a man convinces a homeless guy to live with him and his wife to take the place of his recently deceased uncle. In *'Needlepoint,'* a black pimp visits a witchdoctor who is also the grandmother of a recently killed hooker. He pleads with her to end the curse that was placed upon him, but to no avail. In *'Siege of 31 August,'* a young boy's toy soldiers come to life and attack the family farmhouse. *'A Quiet Funeral'* sees a murderer get the surprise of his life when he visits the open casket of his victim. *'Make Up'* stars Billie Crystal as a young man who acquires a make-up kit from the widow of a dead film actor whom no one has ever heard of. *'The Partnership'*

stars David Carradine as a hitch hiker who befriends a talkative loner in a diner, and together they visit a deserted fairground called 'Happy Land,' with deadly consequences. In '*Daisies*,' an adulterous lab technician is shot dead by his wife. In '*Catnip*' (penned by *Psycho*'s Robert Bloch), a young biker thug is terrorised by a witch's black cat. '*Lost In Translation*' sees a man hired by an archaeologist to translate an ancient Egyptian scroll which happens to be stolen, and cursed. In '*Guillotine*,' a French criminal desperately tries to avoid his execution by exploiting a loophole in the law. An untitled story stars Samantha Eggar as an influential theatre critic who comes face to face with an actor she had slagged off in the press. In '*Who's There?*' a man tries to talk a friend out of shooting dead his cheating wife. And finally, '*The Rarest of Wines*' sees two rich siblings squabbling over the details of their late mother's will.

With sixteen stories spread over six hour-long episodes, *Darkroom* never reaches above mediocre levels. *Daisies*, in particular, is especially bad; a dull, three-minute scene of a woman entering a science lab and shooting her husband dead. The acting and direction is flat and feels rushed, like we're watching loose rehearsals rather than the finished product. Amazingly, some episodes were considered too shocking for TV at the time, and were cobbled together for the anthology feature, *Nightmares* (1983).

Dark Shade Creek (2002)
Dir: David Mankey /USA
Dark Shade Creek is an unspeakably bland and generic 'slasher.' Unlucky campers run across 'Cyrus,' a homicidal degenerate bum whose brain has been frazzled with LSD. There are so many of these camping slasher movies nowadays, and they're all the same. These films don't have a single interesting idea among them. They have tacky credits sequences created in the hope that they will add a degree of professionalism, but no one is fooled. They have drony 'scores' created on cheap keyboards and programming equipment, failing to emulate the music of multiplex fodder. Of the cast members, there is always one who takes the film seriously, and he/she will play the role with much

dedication, but little talent, while the more camera-shy members of the cast – usually the director's friends and family – stand around looking like they feel like dicks.

In addition, these 'films' are always shot on bleary video, and yet the filmmakers desperately try to make them look more film-like by shooting with filters and adding 'scratch' effects in post-production. Again, no one is fooled, but they persist anyway. There are also the attempts to make the protagonists engaging by giving them inane dialogue, and mistaking boring childhood stories for character development; the tiresome commitment to obeying the 'rules of surviving a horror movie' laid down in *Scream* (1996), as if that film is somehow the gospel of slasher movies. It fucking well isn't, and if you think it is, then please, feel free to spend the rest of the night punching yourself in your stupid face. There are also characters who wear t-shirts with 'ironic' or 'cute' slogans ('Thundercock' in *Dark Shade Creek*, 'Insanitarium' in *V/H/S*, 'Cocksucker' in *Lake Noir*, etc); the over-use of slang terms, such as 'Dude,' 'Bro' and 'Butt-hurt;' out of place metal soundtracks crop up all the time. Oh, and imbeciles in baseball caps are another mainstay, too.

If you're a fan of low-budget slasher movies, the above paragraph will be an all-too-familiar and depressing read. Sometimes it feels unfair to criticise these movies; it's like scolding children for going 'out of the lines' in their colouring-in books. You feel like a bastard, but it has to be done. So, sort your movies out, you cultural sodomites, or I'll knife your parents.

Darkness Falls (2003)
Dir: Jonathan Liebesman /USA /Australia
By the early 00s, it was good to see the irony-constipated horror movies finally in their death throes, but during this time, what it was replaced with was an equally sad horror wasteland barren of any ideas or atmosphere, and the only laughs were of the unintentional variety. *Darkness Falls* represents the epitome of its era, with a hackneyed ghost story plot and a couple of unknowns (Chaney Kley and Emma Caulfield) being chased around by the 'tooth fairy,' an implausible

puppet-on-a-string monster that can only manifest itself in the dark. This film utterly fails on even the basic levels of horror – shock, suspense, creepiness – and while other movies of its type would resort to bombarding their audience with grue and gore as a way of compensating for their shortcomings, *Darkness Falls* fails there, too.

Day of the Dead II: Contagium (2005)
Dir: Ana Clavell & James Dudelson /USA

A Pennsylvania hospital is at the centre of a zombie outbreak. As you would expect, the army wants to 'blow the piss out of them,' whereas the doctors and other staff feel that the floppies should be quarantined until a cure is found. Interestingly, the cause of the epidemic strays away from George Romero's original (this supposed 'sequel' has nothing to do with Romero), and instead borrows a leaf from *Return of the Living Dead* (1985) and its sequels by putting the zombie uprising down to chemical and biological weapons spillage. Another change from the norm is that the stinkers possess telepathic capabilities during the early stages of the virus, due to an altering of the human DNA. But overall, this is an incredibly dull, slug-paced film in which the zombies don't cause any trouble until after the hour mark.

The Day of the Triffids (1962)
Dir: Steve Sekely [and Freddie Francis uncredited] /UK

Meteorites stream across the night skies, delivering dangerous killer plants to earth with fatal stingers. The glare of the meteorite shower has blinded those who witnessed the spectacle. Meanwhile, Bill Mason (Howard Keel) is recovering in hospital after an eye operation, and ironically, he's only one of very few people left who can actually see what's going on. As the chaos spreads across London, Bill rescues a young schoolgirl, and together they flee to France and Spain hoping to escape the alien threat, only to learn that the disaster is global... This adaptation of John Wyndham's classic novel starts with a great opener, but ultimately disappoints as the story progresses. The pointless trips to Paris and the Spanish countryside serve only to dish up scenarios that could have easily taken place back in London. There are also visual inconsistencies concerning the Triffids (in some scenes they look like giant alien orchids with creepy tendrils, and in others they sort of resemble spiky, hopping Christmas trees). Director Steve Sekely's original cut of the film was deemed so bad that Freddie Francis was brought in to shoot a new sub-plot in which a couple of characters are trapped in a lighthouse having to fend off the pesky plants. And this made way for the silly ending in which they use plain old seawater to destroy the pests (as was later ridiculed in Tim Burton's *Mars Attacks!* (1996), though M. Night Shyamalan later recycled the idea again in *Signs* (2002)). The film became much talked about thanks to its regular screenings on late-night television, and has influenced various filmmakers over the years (including the 'main-character-awakens-in-hospital' opener in Danny Boyle's *28 Days Later* (2001) and the scenario of Fernando Meirelles' *Blindness* (2008)), but it was the power of Wyndham's original plot that seems to have resonated the most, rather than its lacklustre screen adaptation.

The Day of the Triffids (2009)
Dir: -Director not credited- /UK
After the BBC's impressive five-part mini-series in 1981 (which is still the definitive screen adaptation of Wyndham's novel), the Beeb had another crack at the whip in 2009, delivering a two-part TV special set in the modern-day that starts off well before being bogged down in the usual BBC quagmire of sentimental, mediocre nonsense. Episode one begins at Triffoil, an energy corporation that has been farming thousands of Triffid plants in warehouses across the UK so that they can be drained of their oil-like substance that is used as fuel. Bill Mason (this time played by Dougray Scott) is a biochemist who works at the London plant, and he has to deal with a situation in which a 'Triffid rights' activist (an underused Ewen Bremmer) intrudes on the premises attempting to free the killer plants. Mason suffers eye damage from the lights while trying to protect a colleague by giving her his protective glasses, and as a result, finds himself in hospital temporarily blinded. Thus starts the familiar scenario of the light show in the sky that blinds most of mankind while Dr. Mason recovers in a hospital

ward. After leaving, he witnesses the chaos and hysteria in the streets as the public roam around trying to make sense of their helpless situation. He rescues a blonde news reporter, Jo (Joely Richardson) from the clutches of a panicked policeman, and together they eventually make it to the 'gherkin' tower in central London that has been fashioned into a fortified sighted community run by the establishment and protected by the military. This community is overthrown shortly thereafter by socialists, and every sighted person is handcuffed to a blind man and transported to a nearby pub. And after the characters are attacked by the Triffids in a food storage warehouse, the power struggle continue when another group takes control with a brutal efficiency. Mason and his American buddy, Coker (Jason Priestley) manage to escape, and they end up at a church which serves as a makeshift refuge for the blind, while Jo stays behind and is sweet-talked by Torrence (Eddie Izzard), a mysterious drifter whose allegiances are not made clear until the end... Despite the decent set-up, this version of *Triffids* goes tits-up at around the two-hour mark (which still leaves a further 60-minutes of torturous tedium to sit through). Things simmer down into the usual BBC territory where the writers slap the viewers across the chops with just about every cliché they can get their hands on, ensuring that the product can never rise above its formulaic, crowdsource-approved, tangled-in-red-tape, BBC origins. And modern-day news reporters are actually decent people with souls, apparently.

Dead Creatures (2001)
Dir: Andrew Parkinson /UK

A very rare attempt to make a zombie movie from the zombie's perspectives. Lucio Fulci had previously broached the concept in the finale of *The Beyond* (1981) where his two protagonists found themselves trapped in a 'sea of darkness', an eternal empty space where their eyes were blanked out – a superb image of existential despair. Clive Barker also addressed the theme in his short story, 'Scape-goats' (from *Books of Blood Volume 3*), another vision of eternal emptiness as the female protagonist became an underwater zombie, condemned to drift in her own "sea of darkness" forever. With *Dead Creatures* we explore the concept once again, but disappointingly, in very little detail, and with nothing new to bring to the plate, so to speak. Instead, what we get is a 'neorealist'/Ken Loach approach to the subject-matter which may find favour with critics but is sure to bore the rest of us to death. The story follows women who 'live' with some kind of zombie/cannibal infection as they wallow in 'dead time', a post-mortem existence where they're condemned to sit around watching soaps on TV and drift around from flat to flat, all the while casually feasting on human corpses. There's an obvious subtextual strain here concerning the underclass and AIDS, elements which were later updated in the French *Les revenants* (2004).

The Dead Don't Die (1975)
Dir: Curtis Harrington /USA

Perhaps the least inspired of Curtis Harrington's films is *The Dead Don't Die*, in which George Hamilton suspects that his brother – who was recently executed by electric chair – has been reanimated via voodoo sorcery. And when he digs up his grave he finds an empty box and a small zombie army out to get him. This is painfully boring, and difficult to believe that it was directed by the same man who made *Ruby* (1977) and *The Killing Kind* (1973).

Dead Girls (1990)
Dir: Dennis Devine /USA

The lead singer of an all-girl goth band is haunted by the suicide of her sister while a skull-faced maniac goes on a killing spree. This is bottom of the barrel slasher nonsense, shot on bleary video, and stuffed with pointless red herrings, needless exposition, zero suspense, lacklustre kills, wooden acting - all the usual.

The Deadly Bees (1966)
Dir: Freddie Francis /UK

Pop star Suzanna Leigh is exhausted after a gruelling schedule and takes time out to visit an exclusive island resort. However, rather than having a relaxing time of peace and quiet, she finds herself in the middle of chaos after a number of people die as a result of bee stings. It soon becomes apparent that somebody is training the swarm of nuisances to kill. Perhaps the local bee keepers, Frank Findlay and Guy Doleman, are to blame? This is middling, tedious fare by Francis, who – though he became a legendary cinematographer – had never concealed his lack of warmth towards the horror genre. Look out for future Rolling Stones bassist, Ronnie Wood, as a teenage douche bag.

The Deadly Dream (1971)
Dir: Alf Kjellin /USA
Neuroscientist Lloyd Bridges is haunted by a series of persecution nightmares in which those who die also die in real life. The dreams may have something to do with his breakthrough project which involves genetic experimentations on the brain. Or, he could just be losing his mind... The scariest thing about this film is the horrendous fashions on display; there's Janet Leigh's grotesquely coloured outfits and her head-dipped-in-a-bucket-of-jizz hairdo, and Bridges running around in a pair of old man pantaloons. The dream/reality confusion and treacherous wife plot could have been inspired by Philip K. Dick's *Do Androids Dream of Electric Sheep?* which was later filmed as *Total Recall* (1990).

Deadly Game (1991)
Dir: Thomas J. Wright /USA
A vengeful millionaire by the name of Cyrus invites a disparate group of characters to his private island – a Japanese yakuza, a businessman, a Vietnam veteran, etc – and lets them loose on his land while hunting them down with armed henchmen and a pack of bloodhounds. The victims try to work out why they are being targeted this way, and gradually piece together the things they have in common. Turns out that each character committed a deadly act against Cyrus in their pasts; Jack stole a car and crashed it, killing his reluctant passengers; Peterson committed atrocities in Vietnam, and left a fellow soldier burning to death; and Dr. Harrand (*Fright Night*'s Roddy McDowell) failed to restore Cyrus' burnt face. *Deadly Game* is a little seen but excellent TV

movie. Fans of *Dr. Phibes* and *Battle Royale* should lap it up.

Deadly Lessons (1983)
Dir: William Wiard /USA
Donna Read settles into the Starkwater Hall boarding school only to find that there's a killer on the loose. This is a by-the-numbers ABC TV movie of the week, which has a small role for Bill Paxton as a backward farmhand. Don't expect any bloody violence here, just routine, mediocre fare. Dario Argento's superior *Phenomena* (1983) is similar to this, and was made around the same time.

The Deadly Spawn (1982)
Dir: Douglas McKeown /USA
A sleepy American town is awoken by the arrival of a meteorite carrying a spawn of toothy alien creatures that feast on human prey. A young monster movie fan discovers the creatures in the family basement. And, with the help of his older brother and friends, he sets to work eliminating the pests... *The Deadly Spawn* is a pean to the monster movie, and is a must-see for fans of *Critters* (1986) and *Phantasm* (1979). For such a low-budget film, this boasts a superb score and sound design, along with a great imagination, likeable characters, gruesome special effects, and a genuine love for monster movies of old. Most of the budget was wisely spent on the creation of John Dods' space alienss; the FX guy did a marvellous job of constructing the critters, which look like giant reddish mouths with row upon row of uneven teeth dripping with alien slime. In their infant stages, the baby spawn look like oversized tadpoles, or the blood parasites in Cronenberg's *Shivers* (1974), slithering around in the waterlogged basement. The result is a 50s-style invasion movie by way of HR Giger.

Deathwatch (2002)
Dir: Michael J. Bassett /UK /Germany
Spooky World War 1 drama set on the Western front where British soldiers come across a supernatural evil after capturing a German trench. *Saving Private Ryan* meets *Event Horizon* in this warped horror

flick, which – despite baring a mundane title – has much to commend it. With a solid cast and some inventive use of rats and barbed wire, *Deathwatch* is concerned with the evils of war, told in an allegorical style, in which both sides of the conflict are ultimately at the mercy of an incomprehensible power beyond their control.

Death at Love House (1976)
Dir: E.W. Schwakhamer /USA
Robert Wagner moves with his wife (Kate Jackson) into a Hollywood mansion to write a book. But the house is haunted by the spirit of a dead actress, Lorna Love, whose body is entombed in a glass shrine on the grounds. *Death at Love House* is a lacklustre TV movie which pre-dates – and also anticipates – certain themes that cropped up in Stephen King's *The Shining*, such as the ballroom scene in which Wagner dances with ghosts. Other similarities include Wagner slowly transforming into his father, the betrayal of his wife, his finding 'comfort' in the arms of a haggard old ghost, his writer's block and lack of progress on his book; and his slow psychological breakdown. Also, the film shares a gas poisoning scene with *Burnt Offerings* (1976), which was made around the same time.

Death Moon (1978)
Dir: Bruce Kessler /USA
A workaholic is forced by his boss to take a vacation, so he chooses Hawaii. And while he's there trying to relax and chatting up the women, the full moon transforms him into a werewolf. He spends the rest of his holiday intermittently perusing the island, and killing people with his furry face. The closest we get to a transformation sequence here is close-up shots of the protagonist's face straining as if he's taking a shit or on the verge of sexual climax, or both. And crucially, the man's lycanthropy wasn't triggered by a werewolf bite, but a curse; turns out his ancestors were missionaries who destroyed a sacred temple on the island in the late 19th Century. For die hard werewolf freaks only.

Death Occurred Last Night (1970)

(Orig title: *La morte risale a ieri sera*)

Dir: Duccio Tessari /Italy /W. Germany

A desperate father tries to track down his kidnapped daughter, in parallel to the official police investigation led by Inspector Lamberti (Frank Wolff). This is a slow and routine addition to the giallo formula, and has been neglected on home video over the years. The lack of all-out star power and set-pieces ensures its absence on DVD. Director Tessari's only other giallo effort was the superior *The Bloodstained Butterfly* (1971).

The Death Train (1978)

Dir: Igor Auzins /Australia

An investigator for an insurance firm enters a strange town called Clematis to ascertain the cause of death of a man who had died three months earlier. The townsfolk prove very unhelpful to outsiders, and so the investigator trudges on alone (with a little help from a horny, van driving chick), and uncovers a legend about a phantom train that has been passing through the town and flattening the locals. Like a *Scooby Doo* episode, we get the usual goofy humour and ghostly goings on that turn out to have an all-too-human explanation.

Decay (2012)

Dir: Luke Thompson & Michael Mazur /UK

Set at CERN's large Hedron Collider in Switzerland, we get a group of British students fighting off a zombie outbreak in the building when particles bring back the dead, or some shit. And if the acting and dialogue isn't bad enough for you, wait 'til you get a load of the zombies; a bunch of bleary-eyed, middle-class bell-wipes who look like they've been queuing all night for Coldplay tickets.

Demented (1980)

Dir: Arthur Jeffreys /USA

In the prologue, Sallee Elyse is gang-raped by country boys wearing tights on their heads. She has been badly affected by the experience, and is edgy and suffers from constant flashbacks. She begins to rebuild her life with the help of her cheating scumbag husband (Harry Reems). However, when intruders break into her house one night with the intention of raping her, she finally snaps altogether and gets even with the assailants by hacking at throats with a meat cleaver, and offing another's testicles with cheese wire. *Demented* is essentially an also-ran of the rape/revenge sub-genre, thanks to an awful performance by leading lady Elyse, and the pedestrian directorial style by one-time helmer, Arthur Jeffries. However, the film is worth a watch if only for the demented finale in which Elyse goes all twisted on us; she laughs whilst playing with the blood of her victims, and dresses in lingerie while humming a happy tune. Like *I Spit On Your Grave* (1978), *Demented* is basically a melodramatic version of Zarchi's film; the castrated character even gets to vent his sorry excuses for wanting to rape the woman ("We just wanted a bit of fun"). But after listening to Elyse's annoying tirades in this film, it's easier to admire the way Zarchi decided to keep Camille Keaton's character mostly silent during her revenge spree in *I Spit On Your Grave*.

Demonia (1990)
Dir: Lucio Fulci /Italy
Archaeologists unleash hell when they dig at a monastery where evil nuns were crucified in 1486. *Demonia* is as graphic and gruesome as we have come to expect from director Lucio Fulci. There's baby burning, blood draining, tongue hammering, death by cats, and – perhaps most notoriously – the 'wishbone' scene in which a man is strung upside down by his ankles and is literally torn in half. The special effects are quite lousy, however, and the narrative is sluggishly paced.

Demon City – Shinjuku (1988)
(Orig title: *Makaitoshi Shinjuku*; aka *Monster City*)
Dir: Yoshiaki Kawajiri /Japan
The influence of HP Lovecraft was also felt in Japanese anime in which tentacled creatures from the portals of hell have long been the norm.

Wicked City (1987), *Demon City – Shinjuku* (1988), the *Urotsukidoji* series (1988-1996) and *Tokko* (2006), to name only a few. These movies and TV shows share a fondness for sexually-frustrated tentacled demons from hell. The Japanese also add their own perverse touch, which often includes the sight of pretty young females hoisted skyward by the monsters and raped in every orifice by the phallic-like prongs. In a change from the usual demon rape anime, *Demon City* includes a sequence in which a tentacled demoness attempts to have her wicked way with a man in a deserted bar room, only to be overpowered, beaten, and almost drowned with a bottle of whisky poured down her throat. Apparently, only women are permitted to be raped by tentacles in Japanese movies.

The Demon Murder Case (1983)
Dir: Billy Hale USA
TV movie based on a 'true story' that supposedly happened in Brookfield, Connecticut. The film borrows heavily from the previous year's *Amityville II: The Possession* (1982), and, like that film, this is basically just post-*Exorcist,* child possession shenanigans, with Satanic forces sending the boy's belongings violently hurling across his bedroom, as he convulses and makes growling noises while family members struggle to pin him down to the bed. At least this film doesn't waste any time in getting down to the good stuff: The child changes, and the demonologist is called in within the first twenty minutes. After that, things lead to an unintentionally amusing showdown in a church. This movie is goofy as hell with its levitations, a sceptical priest who refuses to believe that the child is possessed, yet has no trouble believing in a magic being in the sky. Add to this some horse shit dialogue, lame, *Omen*-inspired 'accidents,' an evil madness that seems to hop from one person to another, and you've got a real 80s shitter. At one point, a lady reporter asks a priest what's going on, to which he deadpans, "What's going on? A divine comedy." No shit, Father! But I suppose the silliest aspect of the film is that top-billed actors, Kevin Bacon and Liane Langland, play the teenage love birds and do nothing but sit around the house looking stoned.

Devil Dog: The Hound of Hell (1978)

Dir: Curtis Harrington /USA

A Satanic cult purchases a cute puppy, conducts some kind of black magic ceremony on it, and then unleashes it back into society. Meanwhile, a family grieving the death of their own pet, procures the evil puppy, christen it 'Lucky,' and then all *Omen*-like hell breaks loose in the household. Created as a TV movie to cash-in on the theatrical hit, *Zoltan, Dracula's Dog* (1978), *Devil Dog: The Hound of Hell* boasts a star-studded, overqualified cast which includes Richard Crenna, Yvette Mimieux and Martin Beswick. The hound sets the housemaid on fire, tries to shred the father's hand in the blades of a lawnmower, kills a neighbour dog, a few locals, and causes demonic behaviour in the kids. The parents are so enthralled with love for their pet that they don't make the obvious connections between the deadly goings on and the evil mutt until it's too late. The film has proven so popular over the years that it was released as a double-disc special edition on DVD, which is largely unheard of for a 70s TV movie.

The Devil Rides Out (1968)

Dir: Terence Fisher /UK

One of the high points of British horror in the 60s, Christopher Lee gets to momentarily drop his Dracula cape and take on the hero role in this Richard Matherson-adapted tale based on Dennis Wheatley's novel about a naïve young man, Patrick Mower, who dabbles with evil. It was brought to the screen by director Terence Fisher, a man who had a knack for creating unmatchable scenes of delirious Satanic rites. Wheatley was the Stephen King of his day, and sold paperbacks by the shed load. He wrote before, during and after the war, but hit paydirt in the 50s and 60s with the arrival of the mass paperback market. His books can be on the lengthy side, but he was one of the first modern novelists to explore the themes of Arthur Machen and Arthur Collier. And he took his subject seriously enough to include a preface warning his readers not to mess around with the black arts. The film reaches a climactic point of full-on allegorical melodrama with the night of the pentacle during which the forces of evil are met head-on by Lee. *The*

Devil Rides Out is also notable for introducing aspects of mythology that the cinema had completely ignored up to that point.

Devil's Pond (2003)
Dir: Joel Viertel /USA
A newly-wed couple spend their honeymoon in a lake island cabin in the middle of nowhere. And things get interesting when hubby turns out to be a complete whack-a-loon. Oh, you lucky lady! She misses her family and has a spoilt brat temper tantrum when he refuses to pack up and head off home with her. Her failure to live up to his idea of the easy-going, nature-loving wifey brings out his nasty side, with revelations that he had been stalking her for a long time before they met, and had murdered her previous boyfriend and even his own father. If you ask me, they deserve each other. *Devil's Pond* is different from the usual interloper movies in that the audience never gets to see how the husband interacts with her family and friends, save for a brief scene of their wedding ceremony at the beginning. And though there are only two main characters on screen for most of the running time, things never get boring. Actors Tara Reid and Kip Pardue should be commended for carrying the weight of this film on their shoulders and succeeding admirably. You can imagine Lars Von Trier watching this and gaining the inspiration for *Antichrist* (2009).

Diabel (1972)
(*The Devil*)
Dir: Andrzej Zulawski /Poland
Set during the Prussian occupation of Poland in the 1790s, a black-cloaked stranger sets a prisoner free. The prisoner, Jakub (Leszek Teleszynski), eventually gets back home across the snowy wilderness only to find that his family has fallen apart. He then finds himself embarking on a vicious killing spree. Still one of the most criminally overlooked filmmakers in cinema history, Andrzej Zulawski is only familiar to the most adventurous of film fans. *Diabel* was his second feature after the controversial World War II epic, *The Third Part of the Night* (1971), and here he confirms his early promise with an

allegorical tale about the monstrousness of the – then – current communist rule. Zulawski's quirks for which he is most well known for are all in evidence here: shrieking, hysterical women, rapid hand-held camera work, interesting use of music, political provocation and strong bloody violence. Unsurprisingly, the communist authorities didn't look too kindly on the film, and promptly banned it for many years. The DVD looks a bit rough in places, especially around reel changes, but it's a minor miracle that this film still exists at all.

Dog Soldiers (2002)
Dir: Neil Marshall /UK
Southern Comfort with werewolves and humour and live ammo. A British army battalion on a training exercise deep in the woods come up against a vicious pack of lycanthropes. When *Dog Soldiers* was first released, the British movie media – namely *Total Film* and *Empire* magazines – were so desperate for a home-grown hit that they basically lived in writer/director Neil Marshall's arsehole for five months, heaping lavish praise on the film as if it was some sort of cinematic masterpiece. It wasn't. At best, it's a fun little monster movie which delivers on the chills and laughs in pretty much equal measure. For a low-budget horror movie, the special effects are pretty good, but the characters are mostly bland and annoying. One of them is a Geordie who says the word 'bone' every five minutes and complains that he's missing the England v Germany footie match, and he's super annoying for those reasons alone. I'm on the werewolves' side.

Dolly Dearest (1991)
Dir: Maria Lease /USA
An American family moves down to Mexico to open a doll factory on the cheap. However, the factory is located next to an ancient Mayan tomb, and the young daughter of the family, Jessica (Candy Hutson), comes into possession of 'Dolly,' a doll inhabited by the spirit of an evil force that attempts to create a Devil Child. *Dolly Dearest* is a well-made, haunting little movie that is still very much worth watching today. But the problem is that the film is guilty of the very same faults

the film itself is railing against; the film stands as a critique on the American trend of heading south of the border and using their wealth to get rich quick by exploiting the cheap materials, low tax rates and cheap labour. And, as the film itself was made in Mexico where the filmmakers enjoyed the very same cheap labour, the overall message – though legit – can be taken with a pinch of salt.

Don't Turn Out the Light (1987)
(aka *Night of Retribution*; *Skull: A Night of Terror*; *One Eyed Killer*)
Dir: Robert Bergman /Canada
It's bad soap opera time as a wife-cheating traumatised cop tries to protect his family from dangerous killers who have busted out of a prison truck. This is a guilty pleasure, an action-packed, Z-grade piece of nonsense, but hey, we can't watch *Straw Dogs* (1971) or *Assault On Precinct 13* (1976) every night, can we? The big, bollock-headed Robbie Rox steals the show as the eye-patch wearing maniac called 'Skull,' who is just as adept at chewing off his intended rape victim's blouse as he is at chewing the scenery. Unintentionally hilarious but endless fun, especially when the cop dresses in pieces of makeshift armour and climbs on his house like some kind of drug-crazed superhero wannabe. The shit movie *par excellence*.

Do's Final Exit (1997)
-Director not credited- /USA
Recorded in March 1997, just days before the infamous mass suicide of Heaven's Gate members, this 89-minute tape sees cult leader Marshall Applewhite (now known as 'Do') delivering his final speech. He denies that his group are committing suicide because suicide is an escape from life, whereas what they're doing is entering a new kingdom. He predicts the media's condemnation of their actions and also encourages viewers to follow them. According to him, this world is barbaric, and Heaven's Gate offers a better world, a higher plane of existence. You're hearing it from the horses mouth. He sits on a white plastic lawn chair in front of a large television screen which is relaying the footage being recorded, so we see a 'mirroring' effect of his head reflected larger and larger into

infinity, which I think is a nice visual metaphor for the man's stupendous ego. When he speaks, he reminds me of Uri Geller in the way he uses hand gestures and his softly spoken voice and his big, starey eyes – which rarely blink – to mesmerise the viewers and inflict a bit of spoon-bending on their minds.

He then spins the camera around and films the excited members of the cult who show off their Star Trek-like uniforms and basically do as they're told. They look to be servile, timid mouse-types; shy, easily controlled, happy for the acceptance. Do controls everything here, including when they should laugh. Their smiles rise and fall depending on whether Do is making a serious statement or not. It soon becomes clear that the smallest details of their lives are controlled in the form of 'classes.' And some of the cult members look so young it's truly tragic. Do never tries to qualify his outlandish claims with any kind of logic or evidence; we're expected to take his word for it.

Down (2001)
(aka *The Shaft*)
Dir: Dick Maas /USA /Holland
A remake of Dick Maas' own enjoyable Dutch flick, *The Lift* (1983), which revisits the concept of an evil elevator that is controlled by a military bio-chip. Resilient reporter (Naomi Watts in *Ring* mode) and a lift technician (James Marshall) uncover the malicious conspiracy, but the real fun here comes from the scenes in which the crafty machine plunges a pregnant woman down twenty storeys, lures a vicious blind man and his guide dog down the shaft, decapitates security guards and plays games with a little girl.

Downfall (2004)
(Orig title: *Der Untergang*)
Dir: Oliver Herschbiegel /Germany /Austria /Italy
Hitler's secretary, Traudl Junge, recalls the last grim days in the Berlin bunker before the Fuhrer killed himself and the Red Army advanced on the city. This film charts the chaos and hysteria of those final days with a detached quality. Bruno Ganz's performance is one of the finest

portrayals of Hitler in film history. *Downfall* caused much controversy at the time in the German press where many misread the film's calm, neutral and non-judgemental approach as siding with the Third Reich. If you don't openly condemn the Nazis in an obvious propaganda-ish way, then you must agree with what they stood for, apparently. Quentin Tarantino later cast Ganz to reprise his Hitler role in *Inglorious Basterds*.

Down In It (1989)
Dir: Eric Zimmerman /USA

On the music video front, *Down In It* was a promo by Nine Inch Nails that was mired in 'snuff movie' controversy. The video depicts frontman Trent Reznor ascending the stairs of a deserted building, followed by a couple of band members. And when he reaches the top, he either falls or jumps to his death. The directors used helium balloons to lift the camera into the air for the overhead shots, and the balloons were secured to the ground with rope. Somehow the balloons got loose, and the camera – which contained raw, unedited footage of the shoot – drifted over 200 miles from Chicago to Michigan where it landed in a farmer's field. The person who found the camera looked at the tape and, thinking it was real death footage, alerted the police. The FBI launched an investigation under the assumption that the tape contained footage of a genuine suicide. They even declared it to be a 'snuff film.' And even when Trent Reznor was identified as the man on the tape, and that he was still very much among the living, the band's manager had to convince the authorities that none of the band members were involved in Satanism or any kind of illegal activity.

Dracula 2000 (2000)
(aka *Dracula 2001*)
Dir: Patrick Lussier /USA

Produced by Wes Craven, this film sees Van Helsing (Christopher Plummer) deliberately injecting himself with Dracula's blood so that he can immortally keep track of the bloodsucker indefinitely. Complications arise due to Van Helsing's daughter Mary carrying the same blood, and this allows her a connection to Dracula. Much of the action takes place in the French Quarter of New Orleans during Mardi Gras, which allows the recently risen vampire the opportunity to pick off the revellers who have invaded the area. The filmmakers have revised the back-story of the Count, and traced his history back beyond that of Vlad the Impaler of the 1400s, as was established in Bram Stoker's original novel. Other changes to the myth include Dracula (Gerard Butler) informing Mary that he was Judas Iscariot, the biblical betrayer of Jesus – an act he now seems to regret. This revisionism ironically makes the 'blasphemous' content of Stoker's original more acceptable to the Christian crowd. But what's the point of that? Presumably, the film was made so that we could all sit back and say "Ooh, Wes, what an intelligent, creative genius you are! You've reinvented an entire genre once again! How do you do it?!" Ugh, I'm not buying it. *Dracula 2000* was followed by two sequels, *Dracula II: The Ascension* (2003) and *Dracula III: Legacy* (2005).

I have an idea for a reality TV show, and I should try to pitching it to Hollywood. It's called *Wes Craven's Brown Eye*, and features the celebrated director of *A Nightmare On Elm Street* and *Scream* running naked through city streets. The idea is, he has to press his bum against as many clear glass surfaces as possible – which includes climbing on car bonnets and spreading his buttocks across windshields; slowly defecating against coffee shop windows, bus shelters, motorcyclist"s helmets, and smearing the poo with his bottom – until the police show up and arrest him. Viewers are then encouraged to donate bail money via a hotline, so that we can set him free and watch him do it all over again.

Dracula II: The Ascension (2003)
Dir: Patrick Lussier /USA /Romania
This direct-to-DVD sequel to *Dracula 2000* sees Craig Sheffer reviving the Judas Dracula (Stephen Billington, in replacement for Gerard Butler), and spends a large chunk of the running time avoiding the simple escape that conveniently sets up the third instalment in the series. This passable nonsense looks better than most bargain bin DVD

releases but has nothing going for it beyond the blatant Virgin product placements.

Dracula III: Legacy (2005)
Dir: Patrick Lussier /USA /Romania
In this third and final entry in the series, it's the turn of Rutger Hauer to take on the Dracula role and head for war-torn Transylvania where he orders his henchmen to kidnap Romanian peasants for his blood thirst. However, he is soon under attack from a couple of vampire hunters who have teamed up with a TV news journalist. This time the filmmakers turn away from the hip young bloodsuckers of the earlier films and instead try to stay more in line with its revisionist gothic roots. But oddly, it doesn't work. And what we're left with is a stale commitment to get on your nerves like a lingering vampire fart.

Dracula, Pages From a Virgin's Diary (2002)
Dir: Guy Maddin/Canada
With a knowing irony, director Guy Maddin uses such long-extinct silent cinema techniques as tinting, masks and irises in this ballet based on Bram Stoker's classic novel. With its Victorian setting and the resurrection of the 'undead,' this film isn't simply a tinkering with Murneau's *Nosferatu*, but a dark and original re-telling of the old story. I'm not a fan of ballet. In fact, I'd rather eat razor blades than sit through *Swan Lake*, but Zhang Wei-Qiang's imposing performance as the Count is equally seductive as it is menacing. And Paul Suderman's camera work is fantastic. This arty approach may alienate 90% of horror fans, but, judged as a stand-alone effort, this unique film has style and wit in abundance.

Dr Phibes Rises Again (1972)
Dir: Robert Fuest /USA
An entertaining sequel to *The Abominable Dr Phibes*. This time the immortal doctor returns with his assistant from the dead in search of an Egyptian elixir of life, and winds up clashing with a Satanic Egyptologist. Despite the Monthly Film Bulletin claiming it to be

superior to the original film, I have to disagree; it has a zippy pace but is quite uneven in places. If anything, Phibes is much more ruthless and less charming this time around.

Duel (1971)
Dir: Steven Spielberg /USA
Produced as a TV movie in America but released theatrically in Europe, *Duel* pits an ordinary family man (Dennis Weaver) against a menacing truck whose driver relentlessly persecutes him across the wide-open desert roads of America. It was Spielberg's debut feature, made when he was just 23 years old. He shot it in 16 days and discarded most of writer Richard Matheson's dialogue between the drivers, preferring a much more sinister, non-verbal approach. The result is a wonderfully crafted nail-biter, a horror classic whose director went on to become the most famous movie-maker on the planet.

Eaten Alive! (1980)
(Orig title: *Mangiati vivi!*)
Dir: Umberto Lenzi /Italy
Umberto Lenzi's finest film sees New Yorker, Janet Agren, head out to New Guinea to find her sister whom, it is feared, has gotten herself mixed up in a dangerous pain-worshipping cult out in the jungle. The cult leader, Jonas (Ivan Rassimov), is a bloodthirsty maniac who subjects his followers to rape, beheadings and castration. While Janet tries to rescue her sister, Jonas keeps control over his flock by threatening to banish all wrong-doers out of the community and into the jungle surrounding them which is teeming with savage cannibals. When things slip out of his control, he encourages a Jim Jones-type mass suicide, and those who refuse to die are stabbed to death. *Eaten Alive!* is an underrated curio, which – despite the oodles of stock footage of tribesmen hanging on meat hooks, fire walkers, and the usual animal footage – is far more riveting and enjoyable than it had any right to be. The direction is well handled, and the sense of foreboding and being isolated with lunatics is evident throughout. Footage is also taken from *Mountain of the Cannibal God* (1978) and Lenzi's own *The Man From*

Deep River (1975). Also, Me Me Lai runs around with her tits out again in footage taken from Deodato's *The Last Cannibal World* (1977).

Effects (1980)
Dir: Dusty Nelson /USA
The long unreleased *Effects* is a calmer, more contemplative version of *The Last House On Dead End Street*. A filmmaker shows his cast and crew a realistic film of a woman being tortured and killed by a fat guy in a mask. When the viewers express their anger at being subjected to the footage, the director assures them that it's all fake. However, the camera man is not entirely convinced, and, after snooping around on set, he discovers that there is another film being made behind the scenes, something truly sinister which endangers everyone on set. *Effects* is a nicely subdued take on the snuff myth, avoiding all-out blood and guts in favour of a slow, horrific build-up and psychological tension. It has a slow start but patient viewers are rewarded with a great final third when the shit hits the fan. Fans of George Romero will spot a few familiar faces from his films, such as the director played by John Harrison who went on to compose the music for *Day of the Dead* (he also composed the score for this film, too, which sounds similar to Joe Delia's score for *Ms.45*, made around the same time). Also look out for Joe "Choke on 'em!!!" Pilato as the camera man who went on to play Captain Rhodes in *Day of the Dead*. Tom Savini also appears as Mick, a hard partying coke-head who turns very nasty. *Effects* was never released in any format and basically sat gathering dust on a shelf for 25 years before being released on DVD by Synapse in 2005.

8mm (1999)
Dir: Joel Schumaker /USA
A snuff film showing the killing of a teenage girl is discovered by a widow while sorting through her dead husband's belongings. She hires Nicolas Cage to investigate. A dull, unrealistic 'thriller' indebted to *Hardcore* (1979) and set in the seedy world of snuff.

Elephant (2003)
Dir: Gus Van Sant /USA

Elephant is about two disaffected high school students who decide to massacre their fellow students and teachers at their school in Portland, Oregon. This is a slow, posturing movie based on the Columbine killings. Director Gus Van Sant succeeds at probing those feelings of alienation felt by the outcasts, where slights and taunts result in tragic consequences. But the problem is that Van Sant has never had an original idea in his head. Strange then that in 2003, *Elephant* won the Palme D'Or at Cannes and Van Sant won Best Director. I'm still not convinced by him as a filmmaker. His pointless remake of *Psycho* in colour (or "anti-remake," as he called it), and *The Last Days*, which is supposedly based on the last days of Kurt Cobain, but comes off as a teenage angst fantasy. To me his films are all rather pointless and juvenile.

Embryo (1976)
Dir: Ralph Nelson /USA

Dr. Paul Holliston (Rock Hudson) attempts to grow foetuses outside the womb after successfully experimenting with a pregnant dog he hit with his car. But alas, he soon discovers that human genetics are very different to that of our four-legged friends, and the results turn out to be, ur, mildly unpleasant... With its big budget and all-star cast, *Embryo* rivals *Exorcist II: The Heretic* (1977) in the 'what the fuck were they thinking?' sweepstakes. From its ludicrous script, hammy acting and the downright unbelievable interactions between the characters, *Embryo* is less a 'mad scientist' movie than a 'mad filmmaker' movie, and has become a schlock-horror classic among train wreck rubberneckers everywhere.

Eternal Evil (1985)
Dr: George Mihalka /Canada /USA

A director of TV commercials experiences astral projection and commits murder. Constructed like a Stephen King-based TV movie, and owing more than a little to Ray Danton's *Psychic Killer* (1975),

Eternal Evil is a dull, run-of-the-mill 'thriller' offering nothing out of the usual. Floppy-haired protagonist, Winston Rekert, is not a particularly engaging character, and it's difficult to give shit what's happening much of the time.

Evil Dead (2013)
Dir: Fede Alvarez /USA

The Evil Dead minus the charm and humour. Some of the visuals look *Antichrist*-y, and the fact that the youngsters have brought a girl out to the woods as a form of 'therapy' also relates it Von Trier's film. And while there are plenty of *Evil Dead* elements here - the possession theme, the silly necklace, the fruit cellar, the evil book of the dead, the cabin in the woods, the possessed hand, the 'force' in the woods, the incantations, the demons, the girl violated by a tree, etc - it just doesn't feel like an *Evil Dead* movie of old; it completely lacks the weird, tongue-in-cheek vibe of the originals, and has more in common with latter-day turds like *Drag Me To Hell*. The nearest we get to a gag is when the demons shout foul-mouthed insults at the teens. If it has anything to commend it, it would be the fact that there's lots and lots of nasty, brutal violence in this film, and that should be enough for some. Also, there is a loud air raid siren on the soundtrack which has nothing to do with the plot or the environment the characters are in, and seems to have been added as a way of instilling a tense, 'alarmed' reaction in the audience as it's a sound designed to send people running for safety (or at least it was in the 1940s). It's a good idea but it doesn't really work in this film. The air raid siren is supposed to inflict a primal sense of danger in those who hear it, but here it just serves as an alarm clock to keep the bored viewers awake.

Evilenko (2004)
Dir: David Grieco /Italy

If *Citizen X* (1985) concentrated on the hunt for Andrei Chikatilo and the set-backs caused by the Soviet bureaucratic system, *Evilenko* instead focuses on the man himself, the serial killer who took dozens of victims. This film portrays him from his days as a lecherous, impotent school teacher sacked for attempting to molest a young girl. The indignation of it all seems to fire him up, and he begins raping, slaughtering and eating children. Malcolm McDowell is brilliant as the quietly deranged psychopath, and the film includes lots of uncomfortable details of the murders and molestations which are sure to upset a lot of viewers. The bureaucratic hurdles, such as the killer's connections to the KGB, sees him getting off the hook more than once. Annoyingly, Chikatilo is also portrayed as having some kind of hypnotic power that overwhelms his victims, meaning he can have his way with them without a struggle. A silly and unnecessary move. In fact, so much of the real life details on the man and the case have been altered that the filmmakers felt compelled to change the killer's name to Evilenko, a silly boogeyman name. In one ridiculous scene – which is worth the price of the DVD alone – the killer, while in police custody, strips off and attempts to sexually molest the chief officer assigned to the case. Absolutely riveting for all the wrong reasons. See it to believe it.

Evil Things (2009)
Dir: Dominic Perez /USA
A group of friends on the road are terrorized by a van driver who also films them while they sleep. Derivative of movies like *Duel* and *Jeepers Creepers*, it also has a hand-held, *Blair Witch*-type documentary feel, but is ultimately let down by some piss-poor improvised dialogue and bad acting. For those willing to stick around, however, the action really picks up in the last half hour or so, and the end credits sequence, which shows the killer's footage, is especially creepy, if slightly underwhelming due to it being tacked on to the end of a sub-par movie.

The Evolution of Snuff (1978)
(aka *Confessions of a Blue Movie Star*)
Dir: Andrzej Kostenko & Karl Martine /W. Germany
Filmmakers sometimes promote their movies with claims of a factual basis. Michael and Roberta Findlay's *Snuff* (1975) was the first snuff-

based horror film to adopt such marketing tactics, but it wasn't the last. Just a few years later and along came *The Evolution of Snuff* (aka *Confessions of a Blue Movie Star*), an amusing mockumentary about the making of a porn movie which came to an end when the lead performer committed suicide. The film includes a talking head sequence with Roman Polanski and the discovery of a snuff film which is passed off as genuine and is shown at the end (it's actually footage of David Hess as Krug killing one of the girls in a deleted scene from *The Last House On The Left)*.

eXistenZ (1999)
Dir: David Cronenberg /USA
In the near future, a video game designer survives an assassination attempt while demonstrating her latest game creation. Cronenberg returns to *Videodrome*-like territory with *eXistenZ*, this time by exploring Virtual Reality and the eventual difficulties of separating games from real-life as technologies become increasingly sophisticated and realistic. The result is a bizarre, convoluted mystery where the idea is to work out what is fiction and what is real. *eXistenZ* is similar in concept to *Total Recall* (1990), a project David Cronenberg was originally set to direct. How different the film would have been if Cronenberg made it can only be guessed at, but *eXistenZ* confirms he has much to say on the themes of fantasy, reality, technology and the melding of the three.

Exorcist III (1990)
Dir: William Peter Blatty /USA
This much underrated third instalment in the *Exorcist* saga was directed by Blatty himself and based on his own novel, *Legion*. It's just a shame the studio hacked it up to meet their 'crowdsourced' demands. Horror fans are still awaiting the release of a director's cut. Set 15 years after the original, *Exorcist 3* sees a new evil stalking the rainswept streets of Georgetown with a series of brutal murders. George C. Scott plays Detective Kinderman who discovers that all clues lead to the Gemini Killer (Brad Dourif) and Regan's original exorcism... Warner Bros.

insisted that there should be an exorcism in the film, so Blatty's slick serial killer movie went through re-shoots and had an inferior ending forced upon it to keep the film in line with *Exorcist* tradition. In the original film, the Devil possessed the young and innocent Regan, whereas in this third entry in the series, evil turns its attentions onto society's outcasts – the hopeless, the abandoned, the senile, and the criminally insane. It's a world of cynicism, of society going to pot, of aged men clinging to the past because they have no future, and the present is too bleak to contemplate.

Das Experiment (2001)
Dir: Oliver Hirschbiegel /Germany
In a scientific experiment, volunteers are assigned the roles of guards and prisoners. But those who are the guards begin to brutalize the others. Having taken its inspiration from an experiment which was conducted at Stanford University in the early 70s, which showed how power ultimately corrupts, this disappointing film wastes much of its fascinating premise and is merely content to dish out some action-style violence and visuals. The American remake in 2010 was even worse, substituting unedifying shallowness for deeper scrutiny.

Eyes of Fire (1983)
Dir: Avery Crounse /USA
Set near the American frontier in 1750, a preacher is persecuted from his town for polygamy and witchcraft, so he escapes with his children to a remote forest deep in French colonial territory. After surviving out in the wilderness for months, they find themselves at battle with an evil spirit that dwells among the trees. *Eyes of Fire* is a beautiful, absorbing period fantasy that has been unfairly overlooked for years. It isn't a particularly scary movie, but it balances wonderful flights of fancy with grim period details, producing magic and menace at every turn. Highly recommended.

The Farm House (2008)
Dir: George Bessudo /USA

A young couple in debt to the mob leave their home in San Diego and set off in their car to start a new life in Washington. However, the man falls asleep at the wheel after driving all night, and he crashes the vehicle in the quiet wilderness. Stranded, they head to a nearby farm house for help. But the sinister couple who live there prove to be far more dangerous than anything they had left behind them... What starts off as an interesting set-up soon descends into the norm, as *The Farm House* is basically a watered down version of *Frontiers* without the political subtext. The cheese grater scene was the torture highlight, and there's a supernatural spin at the end right out of leftfield, but there's really nothing here for a jaded old horror fart like me to warm to. Director George Bessudo shows his inexperience by relying on overhead helicopter shots to establish each new scene, and the warring couples scream and fight their way through every tired cliché of the genre.

Fatal Games (1984)
Dir: Michael Elliot /USA
The ultimate 'chick with a dick' slasher movie, in which a transexual killer does the rounds of a sports college, skewering the students with a javelin. See also *Sleepaway Camp* (1983) and *Terror Firmer* (2000).

Fear (1990)
Dir: Rockne S O'Bannon /USA
A best-selling author and psychic helps police to track down 'The Shadowman,' a serial killer who is also psychic and can read the author's mind. Typical thriller nonsense that was done much better in *Hideaway* (1995).

Feardotcom (2002)
Dir: William Malone /UK /Germany
An unremarkable effort which borrows heavily from *Ringu*, but transfers the horror from a spooky videotape to a spooky website in which those who log in die 48 hours later. Those investigating the strange deaths decide to enter the site to find clues. Turns out that

PHENOMENA

Feardotcom is a snuff site where victims are murdered on camera, and the viewers later succumb to their worst fears. The rest of us, however, are left to die of sheer boredom. Other snuff-based website movies include *My Little Eye* (2002), *Cradle of Fear* (2000), *Halloween: Resurrection* (2002), *The Card Player* (2004), *Untraceable* (2008) and *Snuff-Movie* (2005).

Fear of the Dark (2003)
Dir: K.C. Bascombe /Canada
A modestly effective PG-13 chiller, *Fear of the Dark* tells the tale of a boy who suffers from acute noctophobia. While his parents are out partying one night, the kid has to spend the evening at home with his affectionately bothersome older brother. And when the house is plunged into darkness after a power cut, both brothers begin to see things in the shadows, as formless fears are manifested in the shape of movie-world boogey men. The dialogue and banter between the boys is well written and performed, and the film is confident enough in its simple premise to allow it to unfold without any annoying 'false alarm' jump-scares in the build-up. Good stuff.

Postscript: Return of the Repressed
Picture the scene: You're in the bathroom. The window is open and the birds are singing. It's a glorious day. You're sitting on the toilet, squeezing your bowels, and – after a long strain and a glimmer of orgasmic fulfilment flashing across your face as your eyes roll to the back of your head for a moment – your stool hits the water with a 'splash.' After wiping, flushing and washing your hands, you leave the bathroom ready to face the day.

Miraculously, as soon as you hit the flush button, your turd vanishes into another dimension. But of course, it doesn't really. It's still there, probably being washed down the pipe that runs down the side of your house. It's a strange phenomenon how we completely forget about the excrement once it has been flushed away; it's as if it no longer exists in this world. If we compare the process of flushing the toilet with the process of repressed memories, we can see how the toilet works as an effective metaphor for the way the mind works. We rarely pay any thought to the bad stuff once it has been disposed of, even though if we consider it rationally we know that Mr. Turd is currently passing through a dark and dingy water slide to the underground sewage system. But we rarely think about that. For most of us, once the turd has been flushed away it no longer exists. Even the *idea* of the bad stuff is not allowed to exist in day-to-day reality, hence the old adage that mankind only became truly human once we figured out how to banish our manure.

So, there you are walking down the street, your mind completely free of the bad stuff. However, just yards away, under the ground, perhaps Mr. Turd is there following you, passing through the sewage system's waste pipes with all the other neighbourhood crap and scurrying rats. Just think about that the next time you poop one out down the bowl. Imagine a horror movie set in a town where every home is suddenly under threat from the bad stuff, where the refuse from every household makes a significant return. Late one night, while the residents are sleeping, all the piss and shit and tampons and tissues from the neighbourhood returns in the form of huge 10-foot tall, oily brown 'manure monsters' that break through the toilet bowls of every home, leaving enormous shitty paw prints on the walls and smothering the families to death with their huge shitty hands, choking them on their own repressed and horrifying primordial dirt. It would be the ultimate 'return of the repressed' horror movie; the Freudian nightmare in the stink. How about it Hollywood, is it worth a pitch?

Of course, it wouldn't be the first time the movies had tackled the return of the bad stuff in metaphorical ways. In fact, a large part of the horror genre has relied on it for many of its classic (and not so classic) offerings. Take Samantha Eggar in *The Brood* (1979), for example. In this classic Cronenberg shocker, her repressed anxieties are spawned through the pores of her skin in the form of pint-sized mutants (or little shits) who venture out and murder the objects of their 'mother's' rage. In *Signs* (2002), a family's guilt over the death of the mother returns in the form of extraterrestrial excrement, a gaggle of otherworldly beings who lay siege to their isolated farmhouse. And funnily enough, the aliens retreat at the first sign of H20, so dealing with the invasion finally boils down to the simple act of 'flushing' them away. And what's Dracula if not a representation of the repressed sexual impulses of mankind?

Slavoj Zizek once compared the home of Norman Bates with his psychological layers. The three levels of the *Psycho* house reproduce the three levels of subjectivity: The ground floor represents his ego, the place where Norman behaves like a somewhat normal person; upstairs represents his super-ego, or the maternal super-ego, because the dead mother is basically a figure of super-ego. The bedroom is the place where the mother's dominance reigns supreme, the place where she barks out her orders. And the fruit cellar represents the id, the reservoir of illicit drives, the place where Norman's dead rotting mother sits in a chair, carefully concealed in the place where the bad stuff dwells.

These layers of subjectivity can also help us to interpret films like *Phantom of the Opera* and *Fight Club*. In the many different versions of *Phantom*, including Gaston Leroux's original, the Paris Opera House can be seen as representing the three levels of Christine's subjectivity: the auditorium, with its heightened stage and demanding audience, represents the super-ego; backstage represents the realm of the ego, the place of her normal, everyday being; and the subterranean caverns beneath represents the id, the dark doldrums, the disgusting, chaotic realm of the deformed 'phantom' (Erik), who serves as an engine for her own illicit desires.

According to Freud himself, the super-ego and the id are intrinsically connected. When Norman Bates carries his mother's rotting skeleton from the bedroom down into the fruit cellar, we see how his mind is transposing the domineering super-ego to the id. The mother (in Norman's deranged mind) demands that he put her down, and she chastises him as to why he is doing this to her. And then almost immediately she begins to be more obscene about it, suggesting that his carrying her down to the fruit cellar is his way of having his illicit way with her ("You think I'm fruity, huh?"). "Super-ego is not an ethical agency," says Zizek. "Super-ego is an obscene agency bombarding us with impossible orders, laughing at us when – of course – we cannot ever fulfil its demands. The more we obey it the more it makes us guilty. There is always some aspect of an obscene madman in the agency of the super-ego."

In *Fight Club*, the narrator (Edward Norton) has an imaginary friend in Tyler Durden (Brad Pitt). Durden plays out the narrator's own super-ego: "I look like you wanna look, I fuck like you want to fuck," etc. Durden gives the narrator a series of impossible tasks to carry out, like fighting with himself in a car park, and demanding that he blow up his condo and turn his back on his job as an insurance investigator (and because this is a movie we're talking about, the narrator has little trouble actually carrying out these orders until the end when Tyler sets out to destroy the world's economic infrastructure). The narrator becomes on-off friends with Marla (Helena Bonham Carter), and though it's never made clear in the film, she could also be entirely imaginary. Marla, for the most part, serves as a mirror to Ed Norton's character, in the way she shows up at support groups for cancer patients, and thus exposing the darkness within himself. Her presence at the various groups reminds him of just how fucked up his illicit desires have become. Of course, Marla represents his id, his skeleton in the closet, or fruit cellar. And he tries to push her away and keep her in a repressed state. The super-ego and the id become connected when Tyler and Marla engage in a casual sexual relationship. And the obscenity becomes clear when Marla says "I haven't been fucked like that since grade school" (the original line in the script was, "I want to have your abortion," but was dropped for being too controversial). If Marla really was an imaginary friend, it would have been fitting if she'd have uttered the words "I am Jack's slimy bowel movement."

The horror genre is full of movies which deal with the return of the repressed. We get more abusive mother madness in *Don't Go In the House* (1979) and *Maniac* (1980); repressed sexuality in any number of vampire films, from *The Velvet Vampire* (1971) to *True Blood* (2008-2011); more repressed sexuality in *The Haunting* (1963), *Singapore Sling* (1990), *Island of Death* (1975), *Tenebrae* (1982), and *The Corruption of Chris Miller* (1973); personal guilt in *Audition* (2000) and *Antichrist* (2009); collective guilt in *Candyman* (1992) and *The Mist* (2007); even a nation's guilt in *Auschwitz* (2011). Also, anxieties of every conceivable kind, such as alienation in *Society* (1989), *Invasion of the Body Snatchers* (1978), *The Stepford Wives* (1975), and *Disturbing Behaviour* (1999); return of repressed criminal deeds in *Les Diaboliques* (1955), *Ruby* (1977), and *Frenzy* (1972); more destructive imaginary 'friends' in *The Other* (1972), *Dolly Dearest* (1988) and *The Ugly* (1996). Since the dawn of cinema, the horror genre has attempted to make viewers face up to the things we'd rather forget about. And they do it not just to mess with our heads, but to allow us to take our anxieties and explore them in a safe and controlled form.

52 Pick-Up (1986)
Dir: John Frankenheimer /USA

An exceptional thriller based on the novel by Elmore Leonard. When successful business man Harry's (Roy Schneider's) infidelity is caught on camera, he is blackmailed into paying $105,000 to a shady trio of thugs. When he refuses to pay up, however, the gang resorts to murdering his mistress on camera by shooting her in the chest and framing him for her murder. In order to save his skin and his wife's political ambitions, Harry refuses to inform the police and instead sets out to play the thugs at their own game, using his intelligence to drive the blackmailers apart. But the gang's leader, Allan (John Glover), proves himself to be much more dangerous and cunning than he lets on... *52 Pick-Up* was one of the last films made by Cannon before the company went bankrupt, and was given very little in the way of an ad campaign, disappearing from theatres pretty fast before becoming a cult classic on home video. It's a hard boiled 70s crime thriller lost in an ocean of 80s sleaze, and can't be recommended highly enough.

Firestarter 2: Rekindled (2002)
Dir: Robert Iscove /USA

If it wasn't such a sprawling three-hour TV movie, *Firestarter: Rekindled* might have been a whole lot of fun. A sequel spawned from a Stephen King novel, it features Marguerite Moreau taking on the Drew Barrymore role as now-grown-up pyrokinetic heroine. The long-slumming Malcolm McDowell plays John Rainbird, a scarred Man In

Black-type shady government agent who is in charge of destructive mutant kids who are hell-bent on taking over the world. Not even the late great Dennis Hopper as a failed drug guinea pig can save this one.

The First Power (1990)
Dir:Robert Resnikoff /USA

The First Power borrows the plot of Wes Craven's *Shocker* (1989), and adds a whole lotta "mumbo jumbo occult bullshit" to the mix, as detective Lou Diamond Phillips attempts to stop a serial killer who continues his killing spree even after his execution. Cheesy and rife with police procedural cliches.

Flatliners (1990)
Dir: Joel Schumacher /USA

Flatliners was perhaps the first anti-yuppie movie, coming after a decade of 'Reganomics' and 'greed is good' mentality. Here, viewers are confronted with horror as metaphysical dread. Embossed with director Joel Schumacher's usual flashy surface style, *Flatliners* is about a group of arrogant med students who embark on a series of dangerous experiments. They each undergo a Near Death Experience, and under those conditions, while their bodies have ceased to function, they experience horrifying, DMT-like trips in which their wrong doings from days of yore come back to haunt them. At heart, *Flatliners* is an old-fashioned morality tale that can be interpreted by Christians as a fable on the afterlife, and by athiests as a purely psychological horror.

Flight of the Living Dead (2007)
(aka *Plane of the Dead*)
Dir: Scott Thomas /USA

On a passenger plane heading for Paris, a re-animated medical patient escapes from the cargo hold and spreads her infection, turning the passengers into flesh-eating zombies. It's up to a sky marshal and a wise-cracking con man – who is being extradited to France – to slay the ghouls and save the day. However, for reasons of national security, fighter planes are scrambled to blow the jet out of the sky... *Flight of the Living Dead* is a low-budget zombie flick that was made to cash-in on the success of *Snakes On a Plane* (2006), with the added bonus of lots of blood, guts and brains splattered across the place. The flight passengers are routine zombie fodder – the bickering black couple, the bickering teens, flight staff, and of course, the scientists whose meddling with nature has unleashed their worst nightmares, EC comics style. This is a competent little film that basically does what it says on the tin. The kills aren't particularly memorable - apart from a shredded zombie that is sucked into the engine, and a nun having her legs ripped off – but, for a standard sized plane, there seems to be an unlimited supply of ghouls to kill. Also, be warned: If you have epilepsy, the amount of flashing 'thunder' lighting effects in this film will cause you to wriggle off the couch like Michael J. Fox at a foam party.

The Forest (1981)
Dir: Don Jones /USA
Two California couples take a camping trip to the Sequoia National Park. A pair of ghostly children warn them not to stick around. And when the campers fail to heed the warning, a cannibal madman begins offing the couples with a hunting knife... *The Forest* is an eerie slasher movie from the early 80s which has as much in common with supernatural shockers like *The House By the Cemetery* (1982) as it does with the usual backwoods slashers of the time, like *Don't Go In the Woods* (1980) and *Friday the 13th Part 2* (1981). Although the film was made on a low budget and is let down by some awful songs with dreadful lyrics, *The Forest* is worth a watch for its 'out there' supernatural angle, and for the interesting back-story: Here we learn that the killer had fled to the woods with his children after killing his cheating wife. He survived by killing and eating backpackers. The kids couldn't take it any longer and committed suicide. Since then, the maniac has survived alone in the woods with his insanity going unchecked, while the ghosts of his children try to warn travellers to stay away. Writer/director Don Jones re-mortgaged his house to finance the project, only to be burned by crooked distributors on both its short theatrical run and on home video. Not only did he make no money for

his efforts, but he lost his house too.

Forced Entry (2002)
Dir: LizzyBorden /USA
Not to be confused with Shaun Costello's 1973 film, this *Forced Entry* is loosely based on the crimes of California serial killer Richard Ramirez, and is presented as a repulsive, XXX pseudo-snuff video. In a particularly ugly scene, Ramirez and his two accomplices record themselves raping a pregnant woman before shooting her and her dog. In a later scene, another woman is forced into the killer's van and is filmed being beaten, raped and stabbed. This is a shot-on-video micro-production all the way; the filmmakers aren't breaking any new ground here. They 're not breaking any new holes, either. The victims in this film are obviously no strangers to the world of adult entertainment production – they have that modern porn 'look' with their pouting lips and shaved pussy-lips, and have clearly been double-penetrated dozens of times before (talk about gazing into the gaping abyss). The film caused controversy while still in production; a film crew making a documentary about the porn industry walked off the set in disgust during one of the rougher scenes, and subsequent reviews have been generally scathing, accusing Extreme Associates and their productions of being "disgusting," "abhorrent" and "evil." I know the cast were all pretending, but you do get the feeling that there is a genuine mean-spiritedness behind this video.

1408 (2007)
Dir: Mikael Hafstrom /USA
Paranormal investigator, John Cusack, takes a hotel room at the Dolphin in New York that is reputed to be haunted. His room – 1408 – has been the location of dozens of deaths over the years, to the point where hotel staff have closed it off as 'out of bounds' to the public. However, Cusack meets the manager (Samuel L. Jackson) and threatens to dig up some journalistic dirt on the hotel unless he is allowed to use the room. *1408* – based on Stephen King's short story from his *Everything's Eventual* collection – starts off well, but it just isn't scary

in the slightest. You'll realise you've seen it all before within the first 20 minutes, as the ghosts dig up his psychological dirt and smears it in his face like a bad mushroom trip, in the same way as *The Haunting* (1963), *Event Horizon* (1997), *Deathwatch* (2002), *Session 9* (2001) and *Malefique* (2002).

Frankenstein Unbound (1990)
Dir: Roger Corman /USA
John Hurt inadvertently goes back in time from 2031 to the late 19th Century, where he encounters Dr. Frankenstein and Mary Shelley, and attempts to destroy Frankenstein's monster with the use of his own deadly weapon, a 'particle beam weapon' he had developed for the US Military. Visually, this is one of Corman's finest films, but the plot feels stretched and confusing at times.

Frayed (2007)
Dir: Norbert Caoili /USA
Standard slasher movie with an escaped mental patient, kids camping in the woods and a twist ending. Though overlong at 110 minutes, this film relies on atmosphere and tension rather than bloody slayings, and for once, it's all the better for it. Plus, it has another rarity: a genuinely creepy killer clown.

Freakshow (1989)
Dir: Constantino Magnatta /Canada
A mass shooting outside a cinema compels a TV news reporter to investigate. She chances upon the 'Freakshow,' a strange museum whose proprietor tells her a quartet of macabre tales. The first one sees a heroin addict resort to murder and poodle chasing to get his fix. In the second story, a pizza delivery guy stops by at 1313 Bram Stoker Blvd, a large crooked mansion which houses a coven of vampires. Next up, a catatonic girl finds herself in an autopsy room after as it was presumed she had died of a drug overdose. And finally, we get zombies tearing up a golf course in search of the dirt that was stolen from their graves (!). It's strongly hinted throughout the film that the museum's proprietor

has the power to hypnotise people into committing heinous acts, such as the cinema shooting at the start. And the film ends with the TV reporter now under his demonic influence. It then cuts to a cinema audience that – presumably – is about to step outside to be massacred by her, which would bring the narrative full circle, as is popular in the anthology horror tradition, dating back to the classic *Dead of Night* (1945).

Freakshow is a fairly ambitious little movie but it never steps beyond trashy fun. None of the stories are anything new to horror fans, and the execution of the tales concentrated more on fancy lighting and a tongue-in-cheek attitude rather than a serious attempt to unnerve its viewers. However, the film is worth a watch today if only for the murder sequence which has striking similarities to the murder scene of the fat, obnoxious TV guy in *Henry – Portrait of a Serial Killer* (1986) with the stabbed hand and the television set plonked on his head ("plug it in"). Except here it's a microwave that is crashed onto the victim's head and is used to cook his brains.

The Freeway Maniac (1989)
Dir: Paul Winters /USA
80s video trashola about a psychotic killer, who - institutionalised since embarking on a childhood killing spree - escapes from the nuthouse, leaving a trail of bodies behind as he heads off to a remote movie set in the middle of the California desert. He also has his sights set on a dumb blonde. Like Michael Myers before him, this maniac has superhuman – or plain old retard – strength, and is impervious to bullets. Once the films hits third gear, it's so ridiculous and over-the-top, you'll realise you're watching a spoof on crappy slasher movies disguised as a crappy slasher movie... Or, at least that's what *I* got from it. If that's right, then it's a bloody good disguise.

Friday The 13th (2009)
Dir: Marcus Nispel /USA
After a couple of extended prologues which recap the ending of the original *Friday* to promulgate the urban legend of Jason Voorhees, a

new bunch of irritating youngsters stop by the camp to be slaughtered. The house on Crystal Lake looks similar to the house in Mario Bava's *A Bay of Blood* (1971), the film which served as a prototype for the original *Friday The 13th*. This remake stands as an unremarkable rehash of moments from *Friday* sequels, and was later released on Blu-Ray in an 'Extended Killer Cut,' which supposedly heaps on the bloody carnage. But the difference isn't all that noticeable. In the age of political correctness, and the suspicion of the supposed links between misogyny and slasher movies, you can expect all the white male characters in the film to be graphically butchered, but the female killings are all quick and bloodless or take place off-screen.

The Gate II: Trespassers (1990)
Dir: Tibor Takacs /USA /Canada
In this sequel, Louis Tripp returns as the young demonologist, Terry, who wishes to re-experience 'the greatest night of my life' by summoning more demon minions. This time, however, the ritual goes wrong when local thugs show up and shoot the tiny demon with a pistol. If the original film was an enjoyable horror aimed at kids, this sequel is a major disappointment; the script is terrible, there are no ideas, no budget, and – worst of all – there's only one demon, and this pathetic creature spends the entire 90-minutes running time being kicked around and abused. Hardly the most fearsome villain in the movies.

Ghost (1990)
Dir: Jerry Zucker /USA
Wall Street yuppie, Patrick Swayze is murdered by a money-laundering colleague, and his spirit stays behind to enlist the help of spiritual advisor, Whoopie Goldberg, to communicate with his surviving girlfriend, Demi Moore. Though it's remembered nowadays as a slushy, sentimental romance, *Ghost,* for all its lame humour and slushiness, has an 'end-of-an-era' feel to it, in that the yuppie dream was coming to an end, and there was lots of soul-searching going on. Like *Flatliners* (1990) – which was made around the same time – *Ghost* presents

viewers with a good old Christian universe in which good deeds are rewarded and evil is punished in the afterlife. Horror fans will especially appreciate the scenes in which dark, Grim Reaper-like spirits drag evil souls to hell after rising out of the ground.

Ghost Rider (2007)
Dir: Mark Steven Johnson /USA
Pale Rider and *Sleepy Hollow* gets the Marvel Comics treatment with *Ghost Rider*, which starts out with an interesting stunt biker back-story before descending into the usual superhero nonsense with an over-reliance on dunce-dazzling CGI effects. A bloated Nicholas Cage takes on the hero role which is no different than the roles of Batman or Iron Man or The Crow, except that Ghost Rider thwarts the bad guys while on a stunt bike with a burning skull for a face. A sequel followed, *Ghost Rider: Spirit of Vengeance* (2011), but I couldn't bring myself to watch it.

Ghosthouse (1988)
(Orig title: *La Casa 3*)
Dir: Humphrey Humbert [Umberto Lenzi] /Italy
A young man receives a strange radio signal, so he and his girl visit the abandoned mansion in the wilderness where it came from. And once there, they soon find themselves terrorised by exploding jars, a rocking camper van, a ghost dog, a makeshift guillotine, and a ghost girl holding a sinister doll. *Ghosthouse* was released in its native Italy as an unofficial sequel to *The Evil Dead*, but let's face it, Umberto Lenzi is no Sam Raimi, and dumpy lead actor Greg Scott is no Bruce Campbell. Even regular fans of Eurohorror tend to dislike the late 80s Italian productions, but personally, I've always had a soft spot for goofy curios like Fulci's *House of Clocks* (1989), Deodato's *Bodycount* (1987), Lamberto Bava's *Demons* (1987) and especially *Demons 2* (1988). *Ghosthouse* is in the same vein as those mentioned, with the bad acting, bad direction, nonsensical dialogue and all-round cheapness somehow adding to its demented charm. My only gripe is that I wish the filmmakers had included Deadite-like creatures, in keeping with the

Evil Dead series, but perhaps they were wary of being sued, so they stuck to the pee-brained ghosts instead. Two more sequels followed, *La casa 4* and *La casa 5*, which were equally cheesy and mildly entertaining.

Ghosts... of the Civil Dead (1988)
Dir: John Hillcoat /Australia

A new prisoner soon learns of the brutal system in an Australian jail by being victimized and having the word 'CUNT' tattooed on his forehead, and who witnesses much more victimisation and injustice behind bars. Filmed in an almost documentary-like style, *Ghosts... of The Civil Dead* is a gritty and downbeat movie that nonetheless offers up some fantastic performances from David Field (who looks a bit like UK MMA fighter, Ross Pearson) and Nick Cave, whose turn as the psychotic maximum-security prisoner, Maynard, is as insane as they come.

Ghostwatch (1992)
Dir: Lesley Manning /UK

Ghostwatch was originally aired on Halloween night, 1992, on the BBC as a supposedly real documentary filmed live from 'the most haunted house in Britain.' It was in fact entirely fake, but the viewing public weren't told that. The show was supposed to be a bit of fun, a harmless little spook show for families to enjoy on Halloween. However, just like Orson Welles' *War of the Worlds* radio broadcast from 1938 in which thousands of Americans ran screaming from their homes after believing they were listening to news coverage of a genuine Marsian invasion, *Ghostwatch* traumatised a nation's youth in a similar way. I was eleven years old when it aired. I was scared shitless. It affected me for days. Watching it again for the first time, 22 years later, feels weird. I'm surprised by how much of it I remember; usually, my mind will dress memories up to make them seem more satisfying, especially when it comes to movies. I remember watching Hitchcock's *The Birds* for the first time since I was a kid. I hadn't seen it for years, and I was shocked by how many of my memories of the film were completely made up or viewed in my hazy mind from completely different angles. But there was none of that when it came to revisiting *Ghostwatch*; it seems etched on my psyche like an abuse memory. Looking back on it all these years later, it's remarkable how TV has changed; the presenters were much more strait-laced and well-spoken back then, unlike nowadays with gaping arseholes like Ant and Dec, and that loud-mouthed, horse-headed cunt, Justin Lee Collins, clogging up the airwaves. I was expecting *Ghostwatch* to be cheesy, but the 'live on air' gimmick is done quite convincingly, with all the real life untidiness, fluffed lines, awkwardness and technical faults all adding to the illusion of authenticity.

Gods and Monsters (1998)
Dir: Bill Condon /USA
An elegiac meditation on the final days of legendary horror director James Whale (*Frankenstein, The Invisible Man, The Old Dark House, The Bride of Frankenstein*), who was found dead in his Hollywood swimming pool in 1957 under mysterious circumstances. The ailing director looks back on his life while attempting to seduce one of his gardeners. The material is sometimes quite thin, but the film offers up Oscar nominated performances from Ian Mckellen and Lynn Redgrave. It has its moments, but after watching I couldn't help feeling that Whale's memory had been shat on by the filmmakers. His character is portrayed as though he had a sick desperation about him in the way he would pester the young men around him. It left me feeling annoyed that such liberties were taken with this fiction. I even found myself agreeing with Alexander Walker of the London Evening Standard who commented, "I dare say some people will find it all touchingly affectionate, but to me it's posthumous libelling of James Whale, without a shred of evidence for most of its fictions. It proves that death is not the last thing one has to fear."

Goke: Body Snatcher From Hell (1968)
(Orig title: *Kyuketsuki Gokemidoro*)
Dir: Hajime Sato /Japan

In the early 00s, DVD and video companies were falling over themselves to uncover and release the most bizarre and twisted treasures they could find. And DVD addicts were spoilt for choice with the sheer amount of cult material on the shelves. And when Quentin Tarantino paid homage to *Goke: Body Snatcher From Hell* in a key sequence *Kill Bill Vol.1* (look for the red skies), it was only a matter of time before a company came along and released the film in an anamorphic, digitally-remastered transfer. *Goke* is an obscure sci-fi/horror/disaster movie from Japan that somehow manages to cram a jetliner diverted by a bomb threat, a fleeing political assassin out to prolong the Vietnam War, a close encounter with a UFO, and a crash in the wilderness into the first ten minutes pre-credits sequence. After that, things become even more bizarre as blue jello creatures ooze in and out of vertical slots in character's heads, which turns them into vampiric aliens who lament on mankind's destructive ways. Long live DVD!

The Gore Gore Girls (1972)
Dir: Herschell Gordon Lewis /USA

The Gore Gore Girls is upbeat fun from start to finish, with its catchy rock 'n' roll grindhouse numbers, amusing script and the bickering lead players who are on the hunt for a serial killer, and who gradually warm to each other as things progress. It's also a film packed with outrageous gore and splatter, including the sight of a woman having her face hacked up with a meat cleaver, in close-up, until there's nothing left but a mound of red pulp; another girl is beaten on her derriere with a meat tenderiser, to which the killer adds salt and pepper to the pulverised mess; another victim has her nipples snipped off with scissors, resulting in streams of white milk and chocolate milk; one girl takes a whack to the back of the head while blowing bubble gum, and the bubble fills with blood; one victim has her head shoved into a deep fryer, and another has her face scolded with a hot iron. Yet despite all the gratuitous nastiness on display, it's so over-the-top that it can't be taken seriously. Lewis went on to make his fortune in advertising and stayed away from filmmaking for decades until he returned for the ill-advised *Blood Feast 2: All You Can Eat* (2001).

Grave Halloween (2013)
Dir: Steven R. Monroe /Canada
TV movie made for the Syfy channel in which a group of North American students head out to 'suicide forest' in Japan. Their intention is to make a documentary about Maiko's mother who had killed herself. However, no sooner do they arrive at the forest when they are menaced by yurei, the restless, angry souls of those who took their own lives and have been prevented from a peaceful afterlife. Despite its vague title, *Grave Halloween* is a modest, engaging little movie that borrows just as much from *The Blair Witch Project* as it does from Japanese folklore. The black-haired yurei spirits first appeared in kabuki theatre before being immortalised in the Japanese horror classic *Kwaidan* (1964).

The Gravedancers (2006)
Dir: Mike Mendez /USA
Three mourners visit the grave of their friend after dark. One of them reads aloud from what he thinks is a poem left by another mourner, but it's actually some kind of incantation. And, after the friends dance and party in the graveyard (like the punks in *Return of the Living Dead* (1985)), they unwittingly unleash malignant entities; the evil spirits of dead psychos that are hell-bent on sending the friends to their graves... *The Gravedancers* is a pleasant surprise; an independent horror film with an original premise, likeable characters and decent storyline. It isn't perfect – there are one or two slow moments, and the evil spirits lack a certain panache – but this little gem can stand shoulder to shoulder with any independent horror movie of the 00s.

Graveyard Shift (1990)
Dir: Ralph S. Singleton /USA
Night cleaners come up against carnivorous bats in the basement of a mill. Not only is this a decent little horror flick, but the subtextual strains of Stephen King's source novel – concerning the exploitation of American workers – is in full force, too.

The Great American Snuff Film (2003)
Dir: Sean Tretta /USA

Narrative-based movies got in on the 'snuff myth' with 'based on a true story' claims tacked onto sub-par horror movies. *The Great American Snuff Film* introduces a pair of sickos, Bill and Roy (Mike Marsh and Ryan Hutman). Bill keeps a journal and Roy is a retarded redneck type. They kidnap two women with the aim of making a snuff movie. Bill narrates the film with a smug self-righteouness; he has a serious mission in mind for the slaughter. His voice sounds like he has glandular fever, or he has spent five years in a cock-sucking factory or something. His plans for a "grand" and "elaborate" snuff project is ruined when Roy winds up killing one of the girls before the camera rolls. So Bill shoots his friend in the head and downscales his ambitious project to focus on the remaining girl... We're led to believe that this is a true crime story based on William Allen Grone, a sociopath who made snuff films and kept a journal detailing his ideas and plans. But it's actually entirely fictional. The film gained notoriety on the web for the end sequence which supposedly shows the 'actual' snuff film made by Grone and now belonging to Montgomery County Police Dep. in Maryland. Alas, it's fake. There was no William Allen Grone, thank goodness.

Gremlins (1984)
Dir: Joe Dante /USA

A cute but mysterious pet of Oriental origin causes trouble in an American suburb when the 'Mogwai's' owner disobeys a few basic rules and helps to spawn a host of evil, slimy creatures. The film shifts tone from a cute, Spielbergian family movie to a full-on monster fest as the gremlin pests get nasty, and the film oozes an adult-themed social satire. Warner Bros balked at Chris Columbus' original screenplay which included a scene of gremlins feasting on a pet dog, and a sequence in which the slimy creatures invade a McDonalds restaurant and devour the diners while leaving the ghastly Big Macs untouched. Fortunately, scenes of a strangled Santa Claus and a gremlin cooked in a microwave made it to the screen.

Gremlins 2: The New Batch (1990)
Dir: Joe Dante /USA

Director Joe Dante returned for the sequel which is even more impressive than the original. This time the filmmakers target everything that is wrong with modern culture while the gremlins cause chaos in a technologically-advanced, fully-automated office building in New York City. It's Donald Trump who cops for much of the sly humour in a thinly-disguised character called 'Daniel Clamp,' a fat cat billionaire. Also, much of the humour is derived from the business jargon of the times; office workers are encouraged to find their 'synergy' and 'take it to the next level;' career aspirations are referred to as 'situational long term outlook perspectives.' Even the building's light bulbs are referred to as part of an 'illumination system.' For all the fun of *Gremlins 2*, the real point is Dante's lamenting on the fact that American culture had sunk to the point where everything is a product or a machination designed to squeeze out every last drop of profit – Yes, even in the form of sequelized monster movies, a self-deprecating jibe not lost on the film's makers.

Grim Prairie Tales (1990)
Dir: Wayne Coe /USA

A decent, western-themed anthology horror, the highlight of which is the tale *'Grassy Hills of the Great Divide,'* a creepy and well executed story about a man who encounters a pregnant woman, only to be devoured whole by her vagina. Talk about man eater! The woman then roams around again in her 'pregnant' state awaiting the arrival of her next victim.

The Gruesome Twosome (1967)
Dir: Herschell Gordon Lewis /USA

This looks to be a gory spoof on *The Adams Family*. The story follows the criminal escapades of a wig store owner, Mrs. Pringle (Elizabeth Davis) and her retarded son, Rodney (Chris Martell) who lure college girls into the shop so that Rodney can scalp them in graphic detail with an electric carving knife. Heavy on jokes and silliness this time around,

The Gruesome Twosome is the one which includes the legendary opening scene of two styrofoam heads having a conversation before one of them is stabbed. Lewis claimed he shot that sequence simply to bring the production up to the required feature length. Another troubled production, the cast and crew were thrown out of one particular shooting location after the 'electrician' accidentally set fire to the place.

The Guardian (1990)
Dir: William Friedkin /USA

A tree-worshipping druid princess called Camilla lands the job of guardian for a baby boy, but she turns out to be an evil interloper, and a powerful woodland tree aids her in offing her enemies in brutal fashion. The couple who hired the strange woman as nanny don't realise the danger they're in until it's too late. *The Guardian* is your typical interloper horror tale, albeit with a supernatural twist. Director William Friedkin has come under attack from many a critic for basically wasting his talents on what is essentially a hokey old tale, but the film does have its intriguing moments; the 'love' scene between the tree and the druidess is very weird, as in some shots it looks like the tree is 'fingering' her. Also, there is an excellent sequence in which an admirer of Camilla follows her into the woods, sees what's she's up to, runs off home, and is then attacked in his home by the wolves. Friedkin once remarked, 'I'd rather work with tree stumps than actors.' Here he got the best of both worlds.

Gummo (1997)
Dir: Harmony Korine /USA

A group of youngsters search for ways of passing the time in a run-down town in Ohio that has been devastated by a tornado. Bernardo Bertolucci called it one of the most important films of the 90s, but casual viewers will no doubt find it all too much to take. It's a deliberately disturbing account of fractured lives and seems to serve as some kind of grotesque freak show. Sight and Sound magazine called it "a high watermark of 90s White Trash Chic." Amazingly, Linda Manz (who played Cebe in *Out of The Blue*) here plays the title character's mother who enjoys feeding her son chocolate bars while he takes a bath. It's a rare performance by one of cult cinema's most enduring icons (she also appeared in a small role in David Fincher's underrated *The Game* in the same year).

Gurozuka (2005)
Dir: Yoichi Nishiyama /Japan
A group of school girls who intend on making a horror movie based on true events in which a movie club was closed down after the disappearance of one of its members and the mental breakdown another. The movie is to be shot at a secluded lodge, but plans are put on hold when the girls watch an old video which depicts one of the actresses being butchered to death with a meat cleaver by someone wearing a Noh mask. The next day their supplies are stolen and pretty soon the girls realise they're stranded with evil in their midst. Recommended to J-Horror completists only, *Gurozuka* is painfully boring and takes an age for anything of significance to happen. Of course, the cursed video tape was tackled much better in *Ringu*. But, to this film's credit, the snuff video, while not particularly graphic, has a very creepy 8th generation blurry VHS feel to it, with the masks and ritualised murder.

Hack! (2007)
Dir: Matt Flynn /USA
A group of students on a trip to an island become the victims of a pair of deranged killers who enjoy recording their crimes for their later amusement. The film basically serves as a fanboy homage, with literally dozens of references to horror movies and horror fiction, past and present, and this is at the expense of everything, from the story line and dialogue to everything else. References to *Psycho*, *The Birds*, *Hellraiser*, *The Texas Chain Saw Massacre*, *Friday The 13th*- even *Orca, The Killer Whale*. Notice character names relating to horror heroes, such as the teacher (Mr. Argento), the murderous eccentric (Mary Shelley), Victor (King, as in Stephen), the boat captain (Bates) and the Sheriff (Stoker). This kind of thing was archaic in the 90s in

films like *The Dead Hate the Living!* (1999), but here it's simply overkill.

La Haine (1995)
(*Hate*)
Dir: Mathieu Kassovitz /France
La Haine presents a day in the life of three unemployed youths - a black man, a Jew and an Arab - as they get themselves involved in a riot on their housing estate against the hostilities of the local police. This is a furious and passionate movie which takes the side of the downtrodden masses, filmed in a hand-held documentary style before it was 'cool' to do so. The film caused so much controversy in France that the Prime Minister, Alain Juppe, insisted that his entire cabinet watch it. Writer/director Kassovitz won the Best Director prize at Cannes, and the film also won Europe's Felix as the Best Young Film.

Halloween: Resurrection (2002)
Dir: Rick Rosenthal /USA
The eighth entry in the *Halloween* series serves as a mindless *My Little Eye* clone in which a group of wannabes volunteer to spend Halloween night in Michael Myers' old derelict house in Haddonfield, Illinois. The event is broadcast live on the web, and it's no surprise when Michael shows up with a huge Ginsu knife. This time it's Busta Rhymes who takes on the LL Cool J role of rapper-turned-shit-actor who presumably had it in his contract to destroy Mr Myers and save the day. And instead of telling him to go away, the producers indulged him, and together they made an absolute stinker. Oh, and everyone involved in the film seemed to have ignored the fact that Myers was decapitated at the end of the previous sequel, *Halloween H20* (1998).

Happiness (1998)
Dir: Todd Solondz /USA
Three sisters in New Jersey struggle to deal with dysfunctional relationships of different kinds. Cynical and pessimistic to the extreme, this is an excrutiatingly funny tapestry of unfulfilled lives which

confirmed the promise of Solondz's earlier *Welcome To The Dollhouse*. The film's most disturbing and superbly subversive thread centres on the angst of a suburban paedophile; the scene where he attempts to dose a young boy with a sedative in his food so that he can sexually abuse the boy is Hitchcockian in the most subversive and perverse sense of the word, in that he somehow manipulates the conventions of the movie thriller and sets up a 'will he/won't he' scenario in which the audience is gripped on the 'excitement' of seeing weather the paedophile can have his wicked way with the kid or not. It's a masterclass in viewer manipulation and a way of thumbing its nose at the audience. Solondz utilises tricks that filmmakers often use in thrillers, and uses them to create an appalling sequence that plays against the viewer's own morality, and demonstrates how mainstream cinematic techniques are often used simply as a way of controlling the viewers like puppets and dictating how they should feel. *Happiness* is also relentless in its insistence that sex ultimately destroys us. A masterpiece.

Hardcore Poisoned Eyes (2000)
Dir: Sal Ciavarello /USA
A group of idiot youngsters head out to a cabin in the snowy wilderness in upstate New York and are terrorized by a robed Satanist. This film relies heavily on actresses hysterically conveying their speeches about the history of Devil worship to show that the filmmakers did their research on the subject. With a bigger budget and some technical know-how behind the camera, this film could have been interesting. But as it stands, the inexperienced cast and crew, and the lacklustre script renders it borderline amateur.

Hardware (1990)
Dir: Richard Stanley /UK /USA
Richard Stanley's debut feature is heavily inspired by *The Terminator* (1984), as a military killing machine plunges itself into the electricity grid and targets a group of friends for extermination. Described by one critic as 'a fascist cyberpunk nightmare,' the cyborg here – named M.A.R.K. 13 – even goes as far as rampaging with a phallic drill, just

like Tamora Taguchi in *Tetsuo the Iron Man* (1988). The film had to be drastically cut in America to avoid the X rating, while the British censors left it intact for release on VHS.

The Haunting In Connecticut (2009)
Dir: Peter Cornwell /USA /Canada

Candyman's Virginia Madsen plays Sara, a housewife whose teenage son, Matt (Kyle Gallner), is undergoing chemotherapy. Sara and Matt move in to a new house with the rest of the Campbell family, a place they can't really afford – just like the Lutz family in *The Amityville Horror* (1979) – and almost immediately Matt begins to see some strange things. Later, the family discover that their new home was once a funeral parlour, and Matt's behaviour becomes increasingly erratic. Is it the medicine that is causing the trouble, or is it something truly sinister within the house? *The Haunting In Connecticut* is a pleasant surprise after such disappointing Hollywood ghost/possession movies that were released in the same decade (*The Amityville Horror* remake, *The Exorcism of Emily Rose*, etc). There is an interesting back-story to the house that the characters learn about through old photographs, newspaper clippings, and even a box of human eyelids. The story unfolds in a believable way, and it rarely feels like you're treading on old territory. Even the ending is allowed to unfold in a sensible and subtle manner, instead of the usual shouty-screamy-flashing-lights-effects-and-mumbo-jumbo bollocks. The film was inspired by 'true' claims of paranormal activity at the Snedeker family home in Southington, Connecticut in the 1980s, as investigated by Ed and Lorraine Warren. The claims were published in a book, *In a Dark Place: The Story of a True Haunting* (1992), whose co-author, Ray Garton, has since admitted that he and Ed Warren had fabricated many of the events and details to spice up the book in order to shift more copies.

The Haunting of Helen Walker (1995)
Dir: Tom McLoughlin /USA

Henry James' novel, *The Turn of the Screw*, is remade yet again for this above-average TV movie, which, despite the now predictable trappings of the tale, offers up a great performance by Valerie Bertinelli as the Governess, one or two creepy moments, fine period details and a great location for the spooky old mansion. See also *The Innocents* (1961), *Dark Shadows* (1966-71) and *The Others* (2001).

The Haunting of Morella (1990)
Dir: Jim Wynorski /USA

A tits and lightning anti-epic produced by Roger Corman and directed by Jim Wynorski. This film is supposedly based on Poe's story, *Morella*, but the end result has more in common with soft core cable TV than any 19th Century gothic literature. An executed witch who had sworn revenge before her death returns to possess her daughter, Lenore. For all its shortcomings, the film does at least deserve credit as a warm tribute to Hammer, with numerous references to everything from *Countess Dracula* (1970), *The Vampire Lovers* (1970) and *Lust for a Vampire* (1972). And lots of bare tits.

The Haunting of Seacliff Inn (1994)
Dir: Walter Klenhard /USA

An industrious couple purchase a beautiful cliff-side house from the daughter of a deceased old lady. They renovate the place with the intention of transforming it into a guest house. However, the resident entity soon puts a stop to that idea and creates havoc in the house through mishaps, infidelity and jealousy, all engineered as a way of driving the couple apart... *Seacliff Inn* is a soft, daytime TV movie for bored housewives who idolise bland, emotionless yuppies in the latest catalogue wear. With not a single memorable scene to choose form, this bore-fest vanishes from the mind before the credits have even finished. And, am I the only person who thinks that investing in such a wonderful home and then turning it into a B&B is a crazy idea? Having strangers scurrying around your beautiful abode like gormless, farting rodents, and even allowing them to stay overnight is ghastly to me. Fuck that noise.

Haunts of the Very Rich (1972)

Dir: Paul Wendkos /USA

This TV movie - based on a story by T.K. Brown – sees wealthy passengers on a luxury airliner travelling to a mysterious destination called Portals of Eden. They arrive at the tropical paradise and are greeted by Seacrist (Moses Gunn), a white-suited black man who serves as their tour guide. The passengers argue about where they are; some reckon Central America, others the Caribbean. They stay in a grand, opulent hotel, where they're free to pamper themselves and enjoy their luxurious surroundings. However, the characters soon begin to question the reality of their environment while the lecherous millionaire, David Woodruf (Lloyd Bridges) tries to sleaze his dick into every female he meets, even when he knows they're married. A thunderstorm cuts off the electricity, which means no phones, no TV, and no air conditioning. Food supplies are also running low. And their tropical paradise slowly darkens into a hellish nightmare as they realise they could all be dead.

Haute Tension (2002)

(*High Tension*; aka *Switchblade Romance*)

Dir: Alexandre Aja /France

A brutal slasher/chase movie which helped to kick-start the 'new French extremity' movement of recent years. Philippe Nahon plays the maniac who barges his way into a random country house and proceeds to slaughter the occupants for no apparent reason. Daughter Alex is kidnapped and kept alive, so her friend pursues the killer's van in the hope that she can rescue her. Much of this film is breath-taking, heart-stopping stuff, but the ridiculous twist at the end – one of the most unconvincing of all time – does a lot to ruin its sheer aggressive power. The final third of this film will leave you scratching your head while you try to piece together the events that led to that point, only to realise that you have been duped, as it just doesn't make any logical – or psychological – sense. Interestingly, this film owes much to Dean Koontz's novel, *Intensity*. In fact, most of the film plays as a direct adaptation of the first half of the book. Even the original French title,

Haute Tension, is a literal translation of the word 'intensity.' Furthermore, Koontz's name is never mentioned in the credits. What a bunch of koont holes.

Headhunter (1988)
Dir: Peter Scheffer /USA /South Africa
In this routine police procedural monster movie, a detective whose wife has become a "muff diver" investigates a series of brutal voodoo beheadings among the Nigerian community of Miami. The detective (Wayne Crawford) and his colleague Katherine (Kay Lenz) put their own heads on the line in their attempts to track down the culprit, which turns out to be an overgrown, hideous-sun-demon-with-a-hangover lookalike.

Heart of Midnight (1988)
Dir: Matthew Chapman /USA
A disturbed young woman, Carol (Jennifer Jason Leigh), inherits an old nightclub from her uncle. And rather than sell the place, she decides to continue with the refurbishments and keep the place running, in keeping with her uncle's wishes. However, the workmen are an obtuse bunch who refuse to listen to her suggestions on the designs of the bar layout, and they constantly pretend to listen to her while carrying on with the original plans. One night, the workers attempt to rape her, but she makes a run for it and triggers the fire alarm, causing the men to flee. And with her history of mental instability, the experience – combined with the feelings of isolation of living alone in the sinister old building – leaves her feeling very fragile... Similar to Roman Polanski's *Repulsion* (1965) and Stanley Kubrick's *The Shining* (1980), *Heart of Midnight* presents us with a character in a crumbling mental state. She dislikes sex, and she dislikes the fact that men are constantly intruding on her personal space. The film also has some seemingly supernatural elements; a bicycle tosses itself down the stairs, the bathroom mirror cabinet opens by itself. And there are menacing, shadowy figures dashing around the building. Like Carole in *Repulsion*, this Carol also experiences terrifying visions of things breaking through

the bathroom door – in this case, a giant eyeball – and strange, psycho-sexual visions, such as the phallic prong which juts out from her bed sheets and closes in between her legs. But unlike *Repulsion*, this time we get a brief back-story on Carol, with revelations that she may have been molested by her uncle as a child.

Heavenly Creatures (1994)
Dir: Peter Jackson /New Zealand
Two New Zealand schoolgirls form an intense, close relationship based on their shared fantasy world, and eventually end up killing one of their mothers to prevent their separation. Based on the true story of Pauline Parker and Juliet Hulme (which also inspired the French movie, *Don't Deliver Us From Evil*), *Heavenly Creatures* is a bizarre, hallucinatory film which erupts into a horrific act of violence. It's a film which bridges the gap between Peter Jackson's early gore trilogy and his more mainstream work in Hollywood. The real-life Juliet Hulme now lives in Scotland and writes mystery novels set in Victorian times under the pseudonym Anne Perry.

He Knows You're Alone (1980)
Dir: Armand Mastrioianni /USA
A notorious serial killer whom detectives have failed to catch over the years, returns and continues his killing spree while setting his sights on a young woman who is soon to be married. This is a routine slasher movie which starts out quite promising. The opening scene set in the cinema with the film-within-a-film gimmick proved so effective an idea that the producers secured funding to make the film based entirely on the pitch of that opening scene. Spanish filmmaker, Bigas Luna, was so impressed he stole the idea and managed to wring an entire tension-packed 90-minutes from the same idea for the excellent *Anguish* (1986). As for *He Knows You're Alone*, the bright start is soon muddied with a lacklustre and charmless middle and end.

Hell Roller (1992)
Dir: G. J. Levinson /USA

A bitter, wheelchair-bound teen goes on a voyeuristic killing spree ("God help the next 'normal' who fucks with me!"). Funny in places, and also aware of its own shortcomings, which means that the performers are permitted to ham it up without ruining what is already sub-standard, amateur fare in the first place. You could team it up with *Feto Morto* (2003) for a double-bill of lame, disabled revenge movies.

The Hidden (1987)
Dir: Jack Sholder /USA
This film opens with a superb sequence in which a stockbroker with a distant look in his eyes robs a bank, helps himself to a Ferrari and drives recklessly through police blockades while listening to blaring rock music. It's a sequence I must have replayed two dozen times when I rented the tape as a kid. Finally, the police force the car into a blazing crash that sends the injured driver to hospital. Later on, a mysterious FBI agent, Lloyd Gallagher (Kyle Maclachlan), arrives at police HQ to enlist the help of a veteran detective (Michael Nouri) in tracking down the fugitive. Meanwhile, the bank robber dies, and a slimy slug-like alien creature crawls out of his mouth and into the body of another patient in a nearby bed. And pretty soon the mayhem begins anew... *The Hidden* is a genre hybrid, mixing sci-fi, horror and cop thriller into an exciting and often darkly amusing blend. Filmed on a bigger budget than usual, and offering up decent performances all around, especially from Nouri and Maclachlan, the latter's character feels like a dry-run for Agent Cooper in David Lynch's *Twin Peaks: Fire Walk With Me* (1992). A childhood classic!

The Hidden II (1993)
Dir: Seth Pinsker /USA
Starting with a 15-minute recap of the ending of the first film, *The Hidden II* begins proper with the death of the alien creature. But Lloyd sticks around to deal with the problem of the alien eggs which are hatching and threatening to plunge the city into chaos all over again, only this time even dogs are used as hosts for parasitical alien invaders... This is a middle-of-the-road sequel offering nothing of

interest and a lame ending. It completely lacks the excitement and charm of the first film.

Hideaway (1995)
Dir: Brett Leonard /USA
After ritualistically killing his mother and sister, a teen commits suicide in a self-sacrifice to Satan. His condemned soul then travels, DMT-like, through fractal tunnels to become a Hell dweller. Later, Jeff Goldblum has a near-death experience after his family are involved in a road accident in which he gets a glimpse of the afterlife and briefly gets to meet his dead daughter. Upon recovery, he is never quite the same: He has visions of himself slashing throats, and his wife finds him sleeping outside beside the pool. He soon learns that the girls in his visions are being murdered in real life, so he vows to prevent any further murders from happening. Turns out that the Satan kid who committed suicide in the prologue has been brought back to life to do Satan's bidding. And when the killer, Vassago (brilliantly played by Jeremy Sisto), puts Goldblum's wife and surviving daughter in danger, the race is on to save the day. *Hideaway* is a bad Dean Koontz adaptation, but as a stand-alone film, this really isn't the disaster that many have dismissed it as. It has a routine, predictable finale, but is easy, engaging viewing from start to finish (and it also contains a nice little surprise after the end credits).

Hiruko The Goblin (1991)
(Orig title:*Yokai hanta: Hiruko*)
Dir: Shinya Tsukamoto /Japan
This film is much more conventional than Tsukamoto's other works (*Tetsuo, Tokyo Fist, Nightmare Detective*), even if it does feature demon spiders with humanoid faces on their backs spilling out of a gateway to hell under a Japanese high school. A student and a professor team up to investigate deaths and eventually go head to head with the Hiruko demon. This is a run-of-the-mill teenage horror flick, presumably made so that the director could head more towards the mainstream. That didn't happen. In the following year, Tsukamoto went back to what he

knows best for the delirious *Tetsuo II: Body Hammer* (1992).

His Name is Jason: 30 Years of Friday the 13th (2009)
Dir: Daniel Farrands /USA
Tom Savini presents a look back at the *Friday the 13th* series. The casts and crews of all the Jason-related movies swap the usual stories and anecdotes that anyone familiar with the series has heard a million times before. With talking head sequences and a plethora of clips, Vorhees is discussed as if he is some kind of deeply complex Shakespearean villain or something, rather than the retarded killing machine he is. Everyone does all they can to make the *Friday* films seem deeper and more culturally influential than they really are.

The Hitcher II: I've Been Waiting (2002)
Dir: Louis Morneau /USA
A long-delayed sequel to the cult classic, *The Hitcher*, which sees the return of C. Thomas Howell (though not for long) to be menaced by a new hitcher who is somehow the same as the one who wrecked his life back in the mid-80s. The story continues with Kari Wuhrer as a crop-dusting pilot who is framed for increasingly elaborate crimes by the demented Jake Busey, who looks to be channelling not only Rutger Hauer of the original film, but also his father Gary as a sinister psycho who even resorts to cutting off his own finger in order to get the heroine into more trouble. It's formulaic stuff all the way, but the cast are very good and director Louis Morneau works wonders with the widescreen landscapes, making this an above-average direct-to-DVD offering.

The Hook of Woodland Heights (1988)
Dir: Michael Savino & Mark Veau /USA
A 40-minute amateur video in which an escaped lunatic goes on a murder spree using his metallic hook on his victims. Despite a variety of creative kills (including a clipboard frisbee'd into a guy's head and another unfortunate getting genital'd by the hook), this has nothing on other 'killer hook' movies, such as *Scream Bloody Murder* (1972) and

Candyman (1992), but could pass as mild entertainment on a slow afternoon.

The Horseman (2008)
Dir: Steven Kastrissios /Australia
The grieving father of a murdered girl receives a video in the mail which shows her being abused before she died. He then sets out on a brutal revenge mission with the aid of a hefty toolbox that he carries around with him. This sometimes exhilarating revenge movie is let down by the usual problems which crop up in low-budget SOV efforts – sub-par performances, cliché bad guys, a routine mediocre 'score', etc – but if you're a fan of Uwe Boll's later works, like *Rampage* or *Postal*, those things can be overlooked in favour of the gripping story. The horseman meets a young woman on the road and they bond pretty quickly, and this is when the film hovers between redemption and cruel irony as he takes her on the warpath with him. See also *Dead Man's Shoes* (2004) and *The Beasts* (1980), films which share similar story lines.

House of Bones (2010)
Dir: Jeffrey Lando /USA
Made for the Syfy Channel, *House of Bones* is about a reality TV show called 'Sinister Sites' whose presenters also act as paranormal investigators. In the latest episode, the investigators chance upon the 'wicker house,' a deserted residence in which a young boy is said to have disappeared in the early 1950s. Within moments of arriving at the old house, we learn that the crew and presenters are a cynical bunch with no belief or interest in the paranormal, and are just there for the pay cheques. Someone has even gone to the trouble of decorating the back yard with old doll parts dangling from pieces of string. However, once the live broadcast begins, viewers can expect all the usual clichés of haunted house movies as sinister audio and visual recordings are picked up, along with an evil force that enjoys impaling coppers and ramming glass shards down women's throats. *House of Bones* isn't too bad for a Syfy TV movie (I was expecting a lot worse), but it fails to

rise above its hokey premise, despite having characters cacooned in the walls with blood and guts, and a derelict house right out of Dickens' *Great Expectations*. Actress Charisma Carpenter is very hot, and her presence turns the place into a house of boners. It's just a shame she has the 'charisma' of a frozen puddle.

House of the Dead (1978)
(aka *Alien Zone*)
Dir: Sharron Miller /USA
An anthology horror that has nothing to do with aliens, in case you were wondering. A mortician tells four tales about how the latest bodies have wound up in his establishment. The first story is about a highly-strung school teacher whose home is invaded by sinister masked children. The third story depicts a battle of wills between two of the world's finest detectives. And the fourth sees a journalist trapped in a basement of horrors after he falls down a lift shaft. But it's the second story which is the most unusual. It's about a serial killer who lures women back to his house so that he can strangle them to death in front of his video camera. Though the acting and dialogue is often clunky, this segment stands out from the other routine stories as it just doesn't sit right with the usual horror fair of the time. The other stories wouldn't have been out of place in an Amicus production, but the story here, however, explores much more down to earth horrors, and by default this gives it a disturbing edge. Too bad it was directed with little care as a throwaway piece. In its favour, *House of the Dead* stands as one of the earliest narrative films to explore the snuff legend just as home movie cameras were becoming much more readily available to the public. It's a difficult film to track down nowadays. Have fun trying to find it.

The House on Tombstone Hill (1988)
(aka *The Dead Come Home*; aka *Dead Dudes in the House*)
Dir: James Riffel /USA
Enjoyable nonsense from Tromaville in which a group of youngsters set about renovating a newly purchased house whose previous owner,

Annabelle, had murdered her husband there in the 1940s. One of the goons smashes a nearby headstone, and this act of vandalism seems to bring back Annabelle's ugly corpse as a frail – but very deadly – zombie, or ghost, or something. Who knows what she is supposed to be, but the characters are so irksome even the house itself takes an instant dislike to them, and shows its contempt by locking 'em in and leaving them to their fates... Memorable death scenes include one of the 'dudes' losing his hands, and another cut in half by a window pane, complete with twitching severed legs (perhaps in tribute to *Superstition* (1982) which includes a death scene that is very similar). Also look out for the homages to classics like *An American Werewolf in London* (dead friends coming back to life to crack a few jokes) and *The Shining* ("What about MY responsibilities?!!").

The House That Dripped Blood (1970)
Dir: Peter Duffell /UK

Amicus anthology based on the stories of Robert Bloch and set in a spooky old house. Writer John Bennett is tormented by 'the stranger,' a horror character of his own invention. Peter Cushing is the next tenant, and he finds horrors in the local wax museum. And private tutor, Nyree Dawn Porter, gets herself mixed up in witchcraft when she is hired to home teach Christopher Lee's troubled young daughter. And finally, the last occupant is film star Paul Henderson (Jon Pertwee), who purchases an authentic vampire cape for his performance in his latest picture, 'Curse of the Bloodsuckers,' a role he really gets his teeth into.

Humains (2009)
(*Humans*)
Dir: Jacques-Oliver Molon & Pierre-Oliver Thevenin /France

Phillipe Nahon returned with another 'there's-something-scary-in-the-woods' tale where he plays a professor up against rampaging neanderthals. A very disappointing film, it was directed by a couple of special effects technicians, Jacques-Oliver Molon and Pierre-Oliver Thevenin, who had previously worked on the special FX for *Inside* (2009), but their writing and directing skills are atrocious. Other French dog turds to avoid include *I Am the Ripper* (2009), *Broceliande* (2002), *Promenons-nous dans les bois* (2000, aka *Deep In the Woods*), *Eden Log* (2007), *Fear(s) of the Dark* (2007), *Hellphone* (2007), *In the Shadow* (2010) and *Last Screening* (2011).

The Hunger (1983)
Dir: Tony Scott /USA

A stylish, dream-like vampire movie in which Catherine Deneuve plays Miriam, a bisexual bloodsucker. Throughout the course of thousands of years, the immortal Miriam repeatedly falls in love with her consorts and promises to give them eternal life. However, unlike her, they eventually die of old age after a few centuries. She keeps her lost loves in coffins in the cellar of her New York apartment. Her latest soulmate, John (David Bowie), is rapidly reaching the end of his tenure on earth, and he urgently seeks the help of Sarah (Susan Sarandon), a doctor who is researching how blood diseases relate to the ageing process. After John's disintegration, Miriam falls in love with Sarah. And when Sarah learns of Miriam's vampiric ways, she resorts to drastic measures to put an end to the vampire queen... *The Hunger* was Tony Scott's first mainstream movie, and is based on the novel by alien abductee, Whitley Strieber. It's a moody, visually-dazzling, pop promo of a film, where the billowing curtains, swirling dry ice and neo-noir shadows rarely get in the way of what is essentially a solid story told in the style of a modern-day gothic fairytale. Abel Ferrara borrowed the look of Scott's film for his crypto-vampire tale, *King of New York* (1990).

Hypnosis (1999)
(Orig title: *Saimin*)
Dir: Masayuki Ochiai /Japan

A *Ringu*-like J-Horror with gimmicky but effective death sequences. After a series of bizarre suicides linked by the victims uttering the words "green monkey" before they expire, a cop assigned to the case works out that it has something to do with a strange girl who was hypnotised on a light entertainment TV show. With lots of mystery and suspense, and a glut of gruesome imaginings, including a man 'washing' his face with fire from a stove, this is an unusual film even by Japan's standards. The only downside is that things become a bit convoluted and confusing in the final quarter.

I Am Curious - Yellow (1967)
(Orig title: *Jag ar nyfiken-gul*)
Dir: Vilgot Sjorman /Sweden

A drama student playing the role of a sociologist questions the public on their opinions to such matters as education, class and military service while also discovering her own sexuality. An important, ground-breaking 60s documentary largely influenced by the French new wave and launching a full-scale attack on bourgeois attitudes of the time. Though rather tame by today's standards, the uninhibited sex scenes caused much controversy at the time of its release and led to it becoming banned following a trial, but the verdict was later overturned by the Court of Appeals. Much of the footage was recycled in the less interesting sequel, *I Am Curious - Blue* (1968).

I Know Who Killed Me (2007)
Dir: Chris Sivertson /USA

The raspy-voiced rat, Lindsay Lohan, stars in this disappointing 'torture porn' mess. The film stars Lohan as Aubrey, a high school girl who is kidnapped and tortured in a killer's lair. She has her right hand and foot amputated, and is later found alive in the woods. She awakens in hospital convinced that she is not Aubrey but the daughter of a crack addict called Dakota. And Dakota happens to be a fictional character whom Aubrey created before her abduction, for a writing project. Has she suffered some kind of brain damage or deep psychological trauma that has caused her to completely disassociate her identity, or is there something else going on?

I must admit, I found this to be an interesting premise – How does the mind react to such an extremely stressful situation of being strapped down onto a table and being completely helpless while your limbs are slowly frozen off by a maniac? But – surprise, surprise – the filmmakers make a total pig's ear of things. The potential for a daring and challenging psychological thriller is squandered by having the storyline dumbed down to the point where even a supermarket trolley collector could feel intellectually superior. We also get 'passionate' sex scenes; we know they're passionate because they tear each other's clothes off and hump like dogs having asthma attacks. Oh look, their clothes are all ruined – Gasp! - they must be really *really* passionate! The end result is like a lobotomised Lynch trying to remake '*Fire Walk With Me*'.

I Saw What You Did (1988)
Dir: Fred Walton /USA

A TV movie remake of the 1965 film, itself based on the novel by Ursula Curtis. A prank phone call goes wrong for a couple of teenage girls when a maniac suspects them of listening in to a murder he has recently committed. Directed by Fred Walton, the man behind the other telephone-based horror, *When a Stranger Calls* (1979), this is actually superior to the original, despite its TV feel and sometimes unconvincing plot turns.

I Was a Zombie for the F.B.I. (1982)
Dir: Marius Penczner /USA

Retro-inflected nonsense in the style of a 50s B-movie. A crashed UFO gives off radiation which causes the dead to walk. 'Zombie' criminals are sent by the F.B.I. to infiltrate and destroy the alien invaders, or some shit. Just like the 30th Anniversary Edition of *Night of the Living Dead*, this film was later re-released on DVD with 'improved' special effects, extra scenes and a dreadful new soundtrack which obliterates the 50s illusion and ruins what was already a pretty terrible movie in the first place. Crucially, these are not rotting, flesh-eating ghouls, but mute, catatonic in-patients.

Iguana With the Tongue of Fire (1971)
(Orig title: *L'Iguana Dalla Linga Di Fuoco*)
Dir: Willy Pareto [Riccardo Freda] /Italy

In Dublin, a woman retiring to bed has acid doused in her face and her throat slashed by a black-gloved killer. The next morning her body is discovered in the boot of a car whose chauffeur stands out as an immediate red herring. The wife of the Swiss Ambassador to Ireland calls the police, and Inspector Lawrence gets started on the case. Lawrence soon begins to piece together a political conspiracy that involves greed, lust, jealousy, hidden doorways and a shadowy maniac who destroys his victim's faces in an attempt to conceal their identities. However, just as the detective moves in on the suspect, more mutilated bodies show up as the killer taunts and plays games with his pursuer. *Iguana With the Tongue of Fire* is a below average giallo offering from Italian horror trailblazer, Riccardo Freda (*I Vampiri*, *Tragic Ceremony*). It isn't a bad film, but it isn't particularly great either. It's a very workman-like approach to a standard murder mystery. With no characters to root for, or any kind of memorable set-piece, the film disappears from memory pretty quickly. The Italian gialli of the time often had exotic-sounding titles like *The Bloodstained Butterfly*, *The Bird With the Crystal Plumage* and *The Case of the Scorpion's Tail*. *Iguana With the Tongue of Fire* keeps up the tradition, but the exotic illusion of the title is soon shattered when the film reveals itself to be set in dreary old Ireland with a detective who talks too much. They could have named the film 'Paddy With the Gob of Shite' instead.

Incubus (1982)
Dir: John Hough /Canada
A doctor (John Cassevetes) and local Sheriff are puzzled by a series of rape-murders in a small New England town while a young man has severe nightmares about black-cloaked figures conducting evil Satanic rituals. The vicious killings continue, and the perpetrator looks to be inhuman, some kind of incredibly strong beast that fires such a high volume of spunk that the coroners believe the girls to have been gang-raped. *Incubus* is an ever so tasteful approach to the monster rapist horror sub-genre, but is worth a look if only for the monster itself; a kind of bald-headed toothy ogre who could probably father a whole squad of Wayne Rooneys with one load. Now *that's* scary.

Infested (2002)
Dir:Josh Olson /USA

A group of thirtysomethings gather at a friend's funeral and whine about their relationships, resentments and selling out. They attempt to remedy their discontent by wallowing in 80s nostalgia. However, things take a turn for the worse when mutant flying bugs show up and infect people, turning them into shambling zombie-like creatures who besiege a house, *a la Night of the Living Dead* (1968). The script is nicely written in places and obviously played for laughs (the dancing zombies is a highlight), but the CGI bugs are piss-poor. A worthwhile rental but don't expect much.

Intimacy (2000)
Dir: Patrice Chereau /France /UK

A bleak and sexually explicit drama about a barman who has anonymous sex every Wednesday with a married woman. But perhaps inevitably he begins to desire to know more about his mysterious lover and risks putting their meetings to en end. Featuring raw performances from the two leads (Mark Rylance and Kerry Fox) and seedy environments, *Intimacy* has very little to offer its viewers beyond the cold loveless affair. The plot is quite similar to Bertolucci's *Last Tango In Paris*, but here the sex scenes are all real and unsimulated and surprisingly passed uncut by the BBFC.

I Spit On Your Grave (2010)
Dir : Steven R. Monroe /USA

A 21st Century updated (read 'politically correct') version of Meir Zarchi's notorious rape/revenge shocker. This time, the victim, Jennifer (Sarah Butler), is only raped once but has to endure extended scenes of psychological torture, too, in order to keep the product trendy in the age of 'torture porn'. One of the tormentors blows a harmonica just like Flavia Bucci in *Night Train Murders*. After her ordeal, Jennifer walks in a trance-like state into the river, just like one of the victims in *The Last House On The Left (*1972). She then returns with sodden dark hair draped across her face in vengeful mode looking like she has just stepped out of a 00s J-horror, and sets about her ruthless retribution. The film includes some deviously fiendish traps which involves horrendous suffering, with one guy having his eyeballs eaten by crows while he is still alive, and another getting shot-gunned in the arse. Hey, she's a novelist after all, so her imaginative revenge traps aren't as far-fetched as you'd think. If anything, *I Spit On Your Grave* shows that America's 'eye for an eye' mentality is still very much in full force today.

It Came From Beneath the Sea (1955)
Dir: Robert Gordon /USA
In the deep depths of the Pacific Ocean, atomic bomb tests awakens a giant angry octopus which rampages through San Francisco. Can the citizens outrun this dangerous rubbery monster? Enjoyable sci-fi nonsense which is perhaps one of the first disaster movies ever made (though *King Kong* pre-dates it by more than 20 years), with special effects straight out of a cereal packet and ludicrous wooden acting. Submarine captain Kenneth Lobey and Faith Domergue try their hardest to act scared of the Ray Harryhausen creation.

Jack Frost (1997)
Dir: Michael Cooney /USA
A serial killer escapes from a prison van only to be doused in liquid nitrogen following a crash with a truck loaded with the stuff. He is then transformed into a wise-cracking killer snowman and targets the arresting Sheriff's family. This is a lame-brained attempt at comedy horror which misses the target more often than not. After killing a man with an axe, the snowman quips "God, I only axed you for a smoke. Ha ha ha ha!" Other highlights include death by Christmas tree and the snowman raping a girl in a bathtub ("Looks like Christmas came a little early!").

Jack Frost 2: Revenge of the Mutant Killer Snowman (2000)
Dir: Michael Cooney /USA
Set a year after the first film, the Sheriff takes his family on a vacation

to Hawaii. But the tropical heat doesn't stop Jack from bringing his own brand of sub-zero terror to the island for much of the same slaughter and giggles. Nothing much to commend it, except to say it's marginally more amusing than the original.

Jacob's Ladder (1990)
Dir: Adrian Lyne /USA
Tim Robbins stars as a wounded Vietnam soldier who returns home to New York and experiences terrifying hallucinations. And just as he is about to uncover some evil government conspiracy about US marines being chemically 'altered' with psychedelics, he learns that he is actually dying and watching his possible future pass before his eyes... Loved and hated in pretty much equal measure by film fans, *Jacob's Ladder* is nonetheless a stylish cult classic that depicts hell as urban blight in a perpetually gloomy 1970s. The story owes an obvious debt to Ambrose Bierce's short, *An Occurance at Owl Creek Bridge* (1890), and also to Herk Harvey's horror classic, *Carnival of Souls* (1962), but director Adrian Lyne offers up a fascinating, personal and psychological vision of death. In tune with the Buddhist beliefs, the film is ultimately about the difficulties of accepting death, and the process of coming to peace with it. Independent filmmaker, Gaspar Noe, delved even deeper into the subject with his *Enter the Void* (2009).

Jesus Camp (2007)
Dir: Heidi E. Ewing & Rachel Grady /USA
In a North Dakota Christian summer camp, children are taught to accept evangelical religion, creationism, and encouraged to participate in anti-abortion rallies while demonizing mainstream culture. This is a sobering documentary about the brainwashing of children. There are moments where you'll be tempted to laugh out loud at the ridiculous propaganda on view, but more often than not you'll be dismayed at how young and innocent minds are twisted and bent out of shape, and saddened by the children's eager acceptance of it all. It's a disturbing glimpse into the world of the American religious right where Harry Potter is considered a "warlock of Satan" (they may have a point there),

and is ultimately a breeding ground for fundamentalism and bigotry.

Jingles the Clown (2009)

Dir: Tommy Brunswick /USA

A serial killer clown who hosts a children's television show abducts a family and records himself murdering a little girl's parents and sister while forcing her to watch. The police show up and shoot the killer, and, presuming he is dead, they dump his body in the trunk of the police car. The next day, however, Jingles escapes leaving dead cops behind... Many years later, producers of the TV series, 'Haunted Maniacs' attempt to film an episode at Jingles' old house. And sure enough, the killer clown shows up for more bloodshed.

Joshua (2007)

Dir: George Ratliff /USA

Mainstream cinema has often explored the sickness of serial killers in movies that posit normal, everyday characters against sicko psychopaths who are hell-bent on wrecking lives. These psychos - also known as interlopers - are often portrayed as friendly at first (some are even the victim's relatives), but eventually show their true colours once the coast is clear. These interlopers are often chameleon-like and usually very intelligent and experts in manipulating others to get them on side to the point where the victim(s) is alienated to the brink of madness. A common thread that runs through these types of films is a cautionary one about being careful of whom you trust, and also a primal fear that a person close to you could be a deranged sociopath. The victims are usually nice, middle-class characters, whereas the psychos often – but not always – come from a lower social strata. The template for this was *Play Misty For Me* (1971), in which a radio DJ (Clint Eastwood) has a drunken one-night-stand with a fan only to later find that she's a raging 'bunny-boiler'-type with a strong homicidal streak. Sixteen years later, and *Fatal Attraction* (1987) upped the ante by exaggerating the homicidal mania and thus hightening the paranoia forever more.

The success of *Fatal Attraction* ensured a slew of similar films with a slight variation, and creating a new sub-genre in the process: We have a psycho stepdad in *The Stepfather* (1987) and *Stepfather 2* (1989), psycho husbands in *Sleeping With the Enemy* (1991) and *Devil's Pond* (2003), a psycho landlord in *Crawlspace* (1986), a psycho tenant in *Pacific Heights* (1990), a psycho teenager in *The Crush* (1993), psycho neighbours in *The Neighbor* (1993) and *Disturbia* (2007), psycho kids in *Mikey* (1992), *The Good Son* (1993) and *The Paperboy* (1994), psycho flatmates in *Deadbolt* (1992) and *Single White Female* (1992), a psycho cop in *Unlawful Entry* (1992), psycho teachers in *The Substitute* (1993) and *Scarred* (1994), the psycho ex in *Mother's Boys* (1994) and *The Ex* (1997), psycho work colleagues in *The Temp* (1993) and *Disclosure* (1994), a psycho saviour in *Misery* (1990), a psycho handyman in *Retribution Sight Unseen* (1993), a psycho celebrity stalker in *Crazy Love For You* (1992), psycho foster parents in *The Glass House* (2001), another psycho fling in *Malicious* (1995), and a psycho orphan in *The Orphan* (2009). That's a lot of psychos.

Perhaps the creepiest entry in this sub-genre is *Joshua* (2007), which centres on a psycho son whose behaviour becomes increasingly destructive after the birth of his baby sister. And while his mother is slumped out in post-natal depression, and his father is a busy stockbroker in the city, nine-year-old Joshua sabotages his gift as a piano prodigy, dissects his pet hamster, drives his mother insane, poisons the family's four-legged friend, and kills his grandmother. Basically, he's determined to destroy everyone around him in order to be able to spend quality time with his uncle, the only person in his life who ever showed a genuine interest in the piano.

Joshua keeps up the tradition of these movies by relating to them on numerous levels. Just like many other interlopers in this field, he is intelligent, highly manipulative, remorseless, cunning, and he never falters in his determination. The viewer is also drawn into the web because, despite his behaviour, Joshua is, after all, just a boy in need of love and encouragement. But these films often make a conservative stance in implying that these psychos are simply beyond the pale and that there's nothing anyone can do about it. Note too that many of the psychos in this realm only get nasty when the people around them fail to live up to expectations: Kathy Bates in *Misery* only torments writer Paul Sheldon when he acts in ways contrary to her idea of the idealised novelist, and Terry O' Quinn in *The Stepfather* only enters psycho mode when his adopted family behave in ways contrary to his impossible standards of a well-to-do, middle-class existence.

Julien Donkey-Boy (1999)
Dir: Harmony Korine /USA

A violent schizophrenic youth (Ewen Bremner) lives with his equally dysfunctional family in New Jersey. With subject-matter ranging from incest to death, and shot in a hand-held, haphazard, Dogme-style, it has its moments but will be a major turn-off for most casual viewers. Overall, the film lacks the ideas of *Gummo* (1997) and the chaotic spark of *Trash Humpers* (2009), but is worth a watch if only for Bremmer's great performance, which is sort of a more sustained version of his role as the hick mutant in *Judge Dredd* (1995)

Junk (2000)
(Orig title: *Junk: Shiryo-gari*)
Dir: Atsushi Muroga /Japan

Japanese horror doesn't come any more cheap or unambitious than *Junk*, a grubby homage to George Romero's zombie movies that owes more to the *Resident Evil* films with its gangsters and military men squaring off against the zombie hordes in ugly industrial settings. Has its fun moments but the posing with guns stuff is super fucking irritating.

The Keep (1983)
Dir: Michael Mann /USA

German troops in 1942 occupy a citadel in the mountains of Romania. A pair of soldiers attempt to steal silver from the tombs and unleash a vengeful, Golem-like entity that begins murdering the troops. When the SS arrives to investigate the deaths, they release a Jewish scholar from a concentration camp to help them deal with the crisis. However, the scholar and the Jew entity form an alliance to eliminate the Nazis... For the first 50-minutes of its running time, *The Keep* plays as a marvellous,visually-stunning, haunting masterpiece-in-the-making. But then things go seriously to pot in about five minutes flat, and the film never recovers. And what's left of the plot limps along in a frenzy of silly melodrama and even sillier special effects. The film is based on the vampire novel by F. Paul Wilson (who famously hated the movie so much, he later went on to write *Cuts*, a story about a writer who puts a voodoo curse on a film director who mangled his work), and also shares similarities with *Castle Keep* (1969) – also set during World War II in which American soldiers occupy a 10th Century castle and defend it with their lives... Or, perhaps they were dead the whole time? As for the entity itself, director Michael Mann – himself a Jew – has clearly drawn on the ancient Jewish legend of the Golem, a being made of clay and lacking a soul, which seeks vengeance against its creators. The films central message – whether Nazi or Jew – is a warning of how raw power ultimately corrupts. It's just a shame that the message is easily lost among the daft dialogue and billowing dry ice.

The Key (1984)
Dir: Tinto Brass /Italy
A tale set against the backdrop of Musolini's rise to power, *The Key* centres on an art professor who keeps a diary detailing his frustrations over his wife's prudery. She, in turn, begins her own diary detailing her affair with her daughter's boyfriend. Typical softcore nonsense from Tinto Brass, who is to arses what Russ Meyer is to big tits, except this particular film addresses such themes as transvestitism, necrophilia and urolagnia, and includes a scene where Franck Finlay dresses in bra and suspenders, and who suffers a heart attack while having sex. As the Virgin Film Yearbook put it best: "Where there's muck there's brass; and where there's cinematic muck, there's Tinto Brass."

Killer Tomatoes Eat France! (1991)
Dir: John De Bello /USA
Director John De Bello returned with the fourth - and hopefully the last – in the *Killer Tomatoes* series. Gangreen the nutty scientist tries to take

over the world yet again by placing a dupe on the throne in France (even though France hasn't had a king since the Revolution in 1798). This is absolute dog shit, what can I say? A cartoon series based on these films was aired in 1991 on Fox. De Bello has only made one film since, *Black Dawn* (1997), but after watching this silly series in a marathon, I have no desire whatsoever to see it. I hope De Bello gets the nastiest arse cancer for inflicting these movies on us, the kind of gravelly arse cancer that grows out of the back of his long-johns like an overripe, inflamed, throbbing tomato. And I hope his dog takes a nibble out of it every time he walks by.

Killer Tomatoes Strike Back (1990)
Dir: John De Bello /USA
This second sequel to *Attack of the Killer Tomatoes* (1978) sees a cop team up with a 'tomatologist' to save the world from the evil scientist, Gangreen, and his bid for world domination with yet another tomato attack. Truly dire, even the *Police Academy* series can look down on this turd. It was followed by yet another sequel, *Killer Tomatoes Eat France!* (1991).

The Killers Are Our Guests (1974)
(Orig title: *Gli assassini sono nostri ospiti*)
After a bungled diamond heist, armed robbers make their getaway and arrive at the home of a doctor and his wife. One of the crims has taken a bullet in the shoot-out and needs urgent medical attention. And though the doctor does what he can to save the injured robber, the robbers target the couple for rape and other forms of abuse... *The Killers* is a home invasion movie which pre-dates *House on the Edge of the Park* (1980). And though it never quite reaches the levels of degradation found in Deodato's film, this is still a fairly watchable addition to the Italian exploitation film.

King of the Ants (2003)
Dir: Stuart Gordon /USA
In one of the oddest team-ups of the early 00s, director Stuart Gordon

(*Re-Animator, From Beyond*) collaborated with British actor and writer Charlie Higson (*The Fast Show*) for this bizarre and strangely comic horror weirdy. Handyman Chris McKenna is hired by a sketchy businessman to murder his boss. And after Chris blunders his way through the killing, the businessman has a change of heart. He then punishes McKenna by ordering him to accept a daily whack to the head with a golf club. In the ongoing, day-to-day torture, McKenna's head is literally – and metaphorically – beaten out of shape. Unfortunately, after this intriguing build-up, the film looses its way and rushes its final third with many unconvincing plot turns.

Kingdom of the Spiders (1977)
Dir: John 'Bud' Cardos /USA
A blonde entomologist investigates a series of spider bites on animals at an Arizona ranch while William Shatner tries to get into her panties with lines like 'you're kinda pretty, for a girl.' And soon enough the furry arachnids turn their attentions onto human prey, killing off the characters with venomous bites and wrapping the bodies in cacoon-like webs. By the hour mark, the whole town is overrun with the silent killers that serve as a stand-in for the killer flocks of *The Birds*. It's a decent little creature feature which is basically a re-run of the classic Hitchcock film.

Kojitmal (1999)
(aka *Lies*)
Dir: Jang Sun Woo /South Korea
An 18-year-old schoolgirl gets involved in an obsessive sadomasochistic relationship with a middle-aged married man. The power dynamics shift from the apparently stronger to the seemingly weaker partner. The sexual scenes are often brutal and unflinching, but there are also absurd moments, like when the two main characters decide which poles to use to beat the other. The novel, '*Tell Me a Lie*', By Jang Jung II on which the film is based, was deemed pornographic and was banned in Korea after only a month of its publication. And Jang Jung II spent time in prison.

Labyrinth of Passion (1982)
(Orig title: *Laberinto de pasiones*)
Dir: Pedro Almodovar /Spain
Described by Sight and Sound magazine as "The quintessential Spanish cult movie," this film follows the sexual adventures of a nymphomaniac and the homosexual son of an emperor. The result is a weird blend of sex and psychology in the vein of an Andy Warhol movie which seems all-out to shock and amuse its audience. *Labyrinth of Passion* is a cult classic in its native Spain where it played at midnight every Saturday for 10 years at Madrid's legendary Alphaville cinema.

Laid To Rest (2009)
Dir: Robert Hall /USA
A young woman awakens in a coffin (or "dead box"), then climbs out to discover she's in a funeral home. To make matters worse, she is terrorized by a lunatic wearing a chrome mask and holding a video camera. She manages to escape and hitches a ride with a kindly truck driver. Back at his house, however, the evil Mr. Chromeskull shows up and slaughters the driver's wife with a hunting knife while wearing the camera on his shoulder. The truck driver and the girl escape, so Chromeskull resorts to killing everyone in the neighbourhood. *Laid To Rest* is one of those horror movies set in a small town in the middle of nowhere, where the phone lines are always down, the local Sheriff's Department has been wiped out, and the internet is still a curious novelty ("make that [computer] thing look for missing girls in Florida"). The 'plot' is light on the ground but the knowing humour and decent production values makes it easy viewing. The film's setting, in and around funeral home with coffins and a demonic hearse, evokes a *Phantasm*-like vibe. The villain's motivation is never explained: all we know about him is that he likes to record himself butchering people and sending the videos to the police. The snuff angle has absolutely no bearing on the story and could have been easily dropped from the plot without causing any major changes in the script. Indeed, the fact that Chromeskull wears the camera on his shoulder makes me wonder whether the snuff element was added to the project as a last minute

thing, to give the film a more depraved edge. It was followed by *Chromeskull: Laid To Rest 2* (2011).

The Last Horror Movie (2004)
Dir: Julian Roberts /UK

A British variation on *Man Bites Dog* (1992) which drops the satire in favour of lame lectures on the nature of evil. The film opens with a scene in a diner where a young woman is stalked and about to be killed in typical slasher movie style. But then the screen fuzzes over and a man appears talking directly to camera. He claims he has recorded over the rental tape (i.e. the film we were just watching). He then takes us on a tour of Hammersmith and claims to be a serial killer who enjoys recording his crimes on camera. The guy is a bit of a smart-arse, jeans and blazer-type tosser; he puts on this noble facade, but is actually just a low-grade Hannibal Lector wannabe. And he works as a wedding photographer. His camera man follows him around while he prepares dinner for his friends, dribbles on about his lame-arse philosophy and murders random people by beating them to death with hammers, stabbing them with knives, or burning them alive. He is also fond of suffocation and strangulation.

Not only does this film lack the dark humour of *Man Bites Dog*, but it's also unsuccessful in its attempts to be subversive. The maniac addresses the viewers about our complicitness with the murders, and our desires to watch violence and death on screen, but it doesn't work because we're not actually watching violence and death, we're watching bad actors playing out fictional scenarios. He claims he wants to teach people "lessons in humanity" and yet he is a self-proclaimed psychopath who doesn't care about anyone and regularly paraphrases Sade about his smallest desires being more important than anything else in the world. Us Brits suck at making movies.

Last Rites (1980)
(aka *Dracula's Last Rites*)
Dir: Dominic Paris /USA

After a road race leads to a fatal crash, one of the surviving girls has her throat bitten and is then staked through the heart by medical staff at the hospital. The son-in-law of a recently deceased woman becomes suspicious when the staff refuse to hand over the body. He eventually uncovers a vampire conspiracy which also involves the town coroner and local Sheriff. *Last Rites* is a heavy-handed critique of corporate health institutions, but is a decent little vampire flick which has much in common with Peter Weir's *The Cars That Ate Paris* (1974). The film also pre-dates such similarly themed movies as *A Return to Salem's Lot* (1987) and *Blood on the Highway* (2007).

Legend of the Demon Womb (1990)

(Orig title: *Urotsukidoji II*)
Dir: Hideki Takayama /Japan
More bizarre mayhem ensues in this sequel to *Legend of the Overfiend* which has only a loose connection to the original film. We get the usual demons and man-beasts with massive tentacle dicks, but also a battle to prevent the son of a crazy Nazi from gaining unlimited powers by murdering the child who is destined to be the overfiend, the ultimate god of gods. Those hoping for a delirious, outrageous anime won't be disappointed as we also get the usual extremely gruesome fantasies, graphic sex, fellatio, masturbation, lesbianism, and rape, decapitations, mad Nazis, multiple bloody murders and human sacrifice. Two more sequels followed, *Urotsukidoji III & IV*.

Live Feed (2006)

Dir: Ryan Nicholson /Canada
In the mid-00s the 'torture-porn' movement hit the mainstream with *Saw* (2004) and *Hostel* (2005). Suddenly, video racks were overrun with cheapjack imitations set in cold, dank warehouses with pretty young victims sliced and diced by an assortment of sadistic maniacs. *Live Feed* (2006) was the first of the *Hostel* clones to add a snuff element. And this time the setting was shifted from Eastern Europe to East Asia (though English-language street signs can be seen). But still, we have similar stupid characters and set-up. One of the Canadian tourists upsets a Triad boss at a bar, and they end up being held captive

in a seedy old porno theatre which serves as some kind of sex and slaughter house. The tourists then become the latest victims of the Triads whose boss enjoys watching people getting murdered by a brute wearing an apron and a gimp mask, via video relay. *Live Feed* was the debut feature of Ryan Nicholson – primarily a special effects artist – and was a major disappointment after his promising short, *Torched* (2004). He later redeemed himself somewhat with the gory-comic *Gutterballs* (2008).

Livid (2011)
(Orig title: *Livide*)
Dir: Alexandre Bustillo & Julien Maury /France
After *Inside*, directors Alexandre Bustillo and Julien Maury returned with their follow-up, *Livid*. Turning more towards the supernatural this time around, *Livid* is a vampiric tale about a trainee nurse who visits the home of an elderly woman, a former ballet teacher, and discovers that the house holds many treasures. She later brings along her friends and they force their way into the basement. And soon enough all hell breaks loose... It doesn't come close to the sheer visceral terror of *Inside*, but *Livid* does have its moments; the initial set-up is very well done, and also includes lots of creepy scenes with the use of stuffed animals and even the stuffed body of a young ballerina that serves as a life-sized musical box, complete with a slow turning figure and an accompanying tinkling tune. But ultimately, *Livid* is let down by a rather silly and over-the-top ending.

The Loch Ness Horror (1981)
Dir: Larry Buchanan /USA
Scummy scuba divers steal a Nessie egg in the hope that it will bring them riches, but what it brings instead is a very angry monster mother who savages the locals with her big rubber head. Featuring bad acting, bad dialogue and atrocious 'Scottish' accents (which amounts to American actors over-pronouncing their 'R's'), the most unforgivable sin in this film is that it wasn't filmed in Scotland but in sunny California. Sacrrrrrilege!!

Loch Ness Terror (2008)
(aka *Beyond Loch Ness*)
Dir: Paul Ziller /Canada

A shop assistant tags along with a rugged cryptozoologist to track down a plesiosaur that has been munching the locals. The prologue is set in 1972 where a group of researchers are attacked by a large, CGI Nessie that strolls out of the loch and chomps down on a couple of characters while whipping others 30-feet into the air with her tail. Thirty-odd years later, and the setting has shifted from Scotland to Lake Superior in Canada. And somehow – for reasons never explained – 'Nessie' and her young are terrorising a bunch of Canucks thousands of miles away from home... *Loch Ness Terror* is basically a modern-day re-working of films like *The Beast From 20,000 Fathoms* (1953) and *The Crater Lake Monster* (1977) with the added spectacle of blood, guts and CGI effects. The characters and the action are just your typical join-the-dots monster movie staples, but Brian Krause as the cryptic crypozoologist – who, it turns out, is the now grown-up kid that survived the massacre in the prologue – is interesting to watch because he looks to be doing a permanent Clint Eastwood impersonation.

Love Me Deadly (1973)
Dir: Jacques LaCerte /USA

Lindsey (Mary Wilcox), a troubled young woman with daddy issues, falls in with a coven of evil Satanists whose deranged activities include embalming live humans and gang-banging fresh cadavers. Lindsey desperately tries to repress her necrophiliac urges by dating a regular guy and even marrying an older man. However, one sniff of dead man's balls, and she's riding them like Frankie Dattori on a prized stallion. Things end tragically when her husband inevitably discovers her secret. *Love Me Deadly* feels very different to most American horror movies of the time. Much of the drama takes place in and around the Morningside Mortuary, with its morbid props of casks and coffins and mourners. And Lindsey's perversion is treated as an excuse to wring every last drop of soap opera-style tension from the narrative. The film clearly had a big influence on Lynne Stopkewich's *Kissed* (1996).

Malice@doll (2001)
Dir: Keitaro Montonaga /Japan

A bizarre CGI future fantasy from Japan. Long after the human race has become extinct, robotic sex droids get bored and transform into monstrous predators which attack the weaker robots. Malice, the kind heroic one, becomes a flesh human and helps the victims. With an aesthetic borrowing just as much from Terry Gilliam as HR Giger, this is a dull, overlong excuse to have girl-shaped things abused on screen.

Maniac Cop (1988)
Dir: William Lustig /USA

A killer dressed as a cop plagues New York. The killer has superhuman strength and is apparently 'undead.' He snaps necks with ease, and also slashes throats and tosses victims through car windows. His face is usually concealed in shadows, and, unlike the usual movie killers, people actually run to him for help. It's an odd movie for sure, which also mixes in action sequences with shoot-outs and car chases, and Bruce Campbell plays a patrolman who is framed for the killings and endures endless physical abuse.

Maniac Cop 2 (1990)
Dir: William Lustig /USA

Much of the same cast and crew returned for the sequel, though campbell gets offed at around the 20-minute mark. This time the killer 'cop' forges an alliance with Turkell (Leo Rossi), a deranged serial killer who preys on strippers. The stunts and action sequences are even more impressive here than those in the original, with one sequence showing cop Cordell attacking an urban police precinct. Cue lots of gleeful destruction as cops are launched through ceilings and blood spills everywhere.

Maniac Cop 3: Badge of Silence (1992)
Dir: William Lustig /USA

Badge of silence is perhaps the more satisfying entry in the *Maniac Cop* series. Cordell is resurrected by occult methods and resumes his vigilante assault to protect the reputation of a policewoman who ate a bullet during a robbery, and has been accused of killing an innocent hostage.

Maniacal (2003)
Dir: Joe Castro /USA
An artless, amateurish *Halloween* rip-off shot on a cheap camcorder. A bald lunatic attempts to murder his family, is locked up in an institution, and upon release dons a clown mask and attacks a slumber party. With an endless supply of ketchup and rubber heads to smash and stab, director – and special effects guy – Joe Castro slips beyond his usual shoddy standards with this cheap and unimaginative shitter. The DVD release by Hardgore was snipped of 10 seconds of sexualized violence by the BBFC.

Manson Family Movies (1984)
Dir: John Aes-Nihil /USA
Created to stimulate the rumours that Charles Manson and his gang actually filmed their murders on stolen television equipment, serial killer aficionado, John Aes-Nihil, created this cheap, deliberately grotty-looking faux-snuff footage of the cult murders which has been an underground video staple for years. Interestingly, the footage in this film was shot in the same locations where the events actually took place, and Manson himself even contributes to the soundtrack, along with Aes-Nihil's band, Beyond Joy and Evil, and the punk group, Sloppy Titty Freaks, whose song. 'Die Bitch,' is played over a particularly tasteless scene in which the pregnant Sharon Tate is repeatedly stabbed in the stomach.

Mark of the Devil (1969)
Dir: Michael Armstrong /West Germany
With a theme tune similar to Ritz Ortolani's for *Cannibal Holocaust*, *Mark of The Devil* presents the activites of an evil, bloodthirsty witchfinder whose devious work is usurped by an even more sadistic aristocrat who acts in the name of the Church. This is a nasty period

horror that was heavily influenced by Michael Reeves' *Witchfinder General* (released the previous year), but *Mark of The Devil* ups the ante by lingering on graphic scenes of brutal torture - hacked off limbs, burnings, brandings, beatings, rape, tongues "removed by the root," etc - It claims to be based on cases 'taken from historical documents', but the end result looks more like an exploitative cash-in on Reeves' film. *Mark of The Devil* was banned outright in the UK, and an unregulated VHS release quickly disappeared in the 80s. Sick bags were handed out to audiences when the film played in America.

Melancholie Der Engel (2009)
(*Angel's Melancholy*)
Dir: Marian Dora /Germany
After the shocking extremes of *Cannibal*, director Marian Dora returned with his toughest film yet, *Melancholie Der Engel*, and in the process stole the infamy of Jorg Buttgereit to crown himself the new dark prince of extreme German horror. But unfortunately, this film is a dull and pretentious bore fest. We basically have a bunch of repugnant characters sitting around talking absolute crap, pretending to be deep and cryptic to conceal the fact that they have nothing interesting to say. Amongst the crude and depraved activities on screen, viewers can look forward to such heart warming scenes as a woman watching a snuff movie in which a pregnant woman is severely beaten and her baby aborted. The foetus is then cut into pieces. The woman watching the tape begins to masturbate, and spreads blood across her vagina and stomach. Also, an old man (played by Ulli Lommel, director of *Tenderness of the Wolves*) is burned alive. As usual, Dora's cinematography has a very closed-in feel about it as though it was shot on 8mm on zoom mode (it was actually shot on 16mil). Shots are awkwardly framed with heads and faces partially obscured from view – it's a very up-close and personal style of filming. The shots also have a soft-focus, powdery texture to them that makes the film look decades old, like Jean Rollin's movies. Maybe I watched this in a bad translation (there is still no English-friendly DVD release, to my knowledge), but there's barely a single sentence in this film that makes any sense, and

I'm not exaggerating. I don't believe killing animals is acceptable in any type of entertainment or 'art,' but the fact that *Angels' Melancholy* is such an over-long, dull and pretentious piece of garbage somehow makes the animal sacrifices ten times more offensive. Amusingly, some of the cast members had to undergo psychological counselling at the end of filming. Perhaps they would have been better getting their heads examined *before* embarking on this turd.

Mimic (1997)
Dir: Guillermo Del Toro /USA
Mutant killer bugs, genetically engineered to rid New York of a deadly plague, evolve into creatures that can disguise themselves as human beings. This is an effective and atmospheric bug movie, with the bulk of the action taking place in the city's subway tunnels. The film manages to create a sense of unease without resorting to silly jump-scares or OTT gore sequences. To be honest, I'm still not convinced by Del Toro as a director; I think his films are generally overrated. For me, his early work, like *Mimic* – and especially *Cronos* – remain his finest achievements. It's those earlier films which show his sure hand and unique visual style before it was diluted in the Hollywood system.

Mimic 2 (2001)
Dir: Jean de Segonzac /USA
A direct-to-DVD quickie which sees the return of the genetically-engineered super-cockroaches that can take on human-shaped form. Here they descend upon a leftover character from part one – the emtomologist science teacher (Alik Koromzay) – and attempt to make her queen of the bug nest. But before they do, they see to it that any potential romantic love-interest is spectacularly disembowelled. Then they threaten to inseminate her. Koromzay is an engaging character, but the rest are very one-dimensional and stereotypical, such as the cop and the shady military men. *Mimic 2* had potential to be an effective little crowd-pleaser but squandered it all by having the characters run around trying to evade the piss-poor CGI bugs.

Mimic 3: Sentinel (2003)
Dir: J.T. Petty /USA
This final entry in the *Mimic* series strays into *Rear Window* territory with a plot involving an asthmatic, allergic photographer who is confined to his apartment and who spies on the neighbours in the opposite building. And sure enough, it isn't long before he witnesses those pesky bugs taking out a few locals. With its emphasis on voyeurism and paranoia, *Mimic 3* – another in a long line of direct-to-DVD-sequels – is far better than many expected. Taking its time with an interesting and unsettling build-up before unleashing the bugs, the film doesn't require any prior knowledge of the earlier entries, and can be enjoyed as a stand-alone episode. The third entry ends the series on its best form. It's perhaps the best of the series.

Minbo no Onna (1992)
(aka *Anti-Extortion Woman*)
Dir: Juzo Itami /Japan
Follow-up to *Violent Cop*. A female lawyer is brought in to deal with a yakuza gang who are attempting to blackmail the manager of a high-class hotel. This broad satire wastes no time in mocking Japanese gangsters and exposing their methods of extortion, intimidation and other nasty tricks. The film is well known for upsetting the yakuza; six days after its premiere, writer/director Juzo Itami was hospitalized after having his face and throat slashed by gangsters. In a related incident in Tokyo, a man slashed a cinema screen during the showing of another of Itami's films.

Misery (1990)
Dir: Rob Reiner /USA
Writer Paul Sheldon (James Caan) crashes his car off a mountain road during a blizzard. He is later pulled from the wreckage by his number one fan, Annie Wilkes (Kathy Bates). She takes him back to her secluded home and begins nursing him back to health. However, Annie is emotionally unstable and has a violent temper. She could also have been responsible for the deaths of young children who were in her care

in her former career as a nurse. And when Annie learns that Paul has killed off her favourite fictional character, she burns his manuscript and forces the bed-ridden writer to start again from scratch. *Misery* is one of the best adaptations of Stephen King source material (the book is also one of King's best). It takes a long, dark look at the price of fame and the nuttiest realms of fandom, and is at times wickedly funny. The film's central premise is perhaps the notion of control – or, in this case, the sudden loss of it – and the film charts the psychological conflict between the two main characters. Annie is a writer's worst nightmare; she is stifling and controlling and anti-intellectual; she is ignorant at the top of her voice; she acquaints morality with a hatred of profanity, and exudes a homicidal rage for anything that doesn't fit into her narrow world view. As a film which examines the relationship between the artist, the critics and the fans, *Misery* has no equal.

Mongrel (1982)
Dir: Robert A. Burns /USA

The directorial debut of Robert A. Burns, the set designer on *The Texas Chain Saw Massacre* (1975) and *The Hills Have Eyes* (1977). After a vicious dog is shot dead during an attack, a young man has recurring dreams about the beast coming back to life and attacking the residents of a run down guest house. And when the dreams turn out to be somewhat true, the remaining guests club together in their efforts to kill the pest. *Mongrel* is the kind of film that is populated with so many annoying characters, it's a joy to watch the dog snap and tear them to pieces. Even the main protagonist is a lumbering dangle-mouth. And things are not helped with the casting of an obviously timid dog, who – despite all the posturing and dubbed 'growling' sound effects – looks like it's just dying to roll over so you can tickle its belly. That useless fucking mutt will never work in Hollywood again. This isn't *Lassie*! You're supposed to be mean! Grrrrrr!

The Monster Squad (1987)
Dir: Fred Dekker /USA

A charming, big-budget attempt to revitalise the Universal monster cycle of the 1930s. This film sees an assortment of gothic ghouls (Count Dracula, Frankenstein's monster, the creature from the black lagoon, the wolfman, the mummy, and others) transported via a magical portal to a modern-day small American town. It's up to a gang of tree-house kids – who call themselves 'The Monster Squad' – to slay the ghouls and save the day, with a little help from a reclusive 'scary German guy' who turns out to be a Van Helsing-like vampire slayer, just like Roddy McDowell in *Fright Night* (1985).

Mum & Dad (2008)
Dir: Steven Sheil /UK

A young Polish cleaner is abducted by a crazy English 'family' who live in a house of horrors under the Heathrow flight path. It's not an entirely convincing scenario, and there are problems with clunky dialogue, but the film at least attempts to update the 'crazy family' horrors of old, like *The Texas Chain Saw Massacre* (1974), *Parents* (1989) and T*he People Under the Stairs* (1991). The end result will surely give viewers an idea of what it must have been like to live with Fred and Rosemary West. *Mum & Dad* should also be commended for giving the viewers the choice of how they would like to see it; the film was released simultaneously in the cinema, on DVD, on pay-per-view TV, legitimate download, and for streaming on your phone. So while Hollywood was still in a huff about combating piracy, this independent British horror flick simply gave the viewers the choice of watching it in any way they wanted. And the film made a decent profit, too. It set a nice example for other production companies to follow.

Murder By Numbers (2002)
Dir: Barbet Schroeder /USA

Murder By Numbers (2002) is part of a spate of post-*Scream* 'clever clogs' slasher movies in which arrogant high school losers plot murders and taunt the investigators. See also *Ripper* (2001) and *Dead Man's Curve* (1998). Here we have two students commit the 'perfect crime' by murdering a girl and framing the dope-selling janitor. As the title suggests, this is basically a routine, by-the-numbers murder investigation movie posing as some kind of 'hip,' smarty-pants, postmodern slasher. Amusingly, the characters try their best to ignore the peculiar, bulbous bollock that squats in the middle of Sandra Bullock's face. Call that a nose? It looks as if her DNA couldn't work out if it was supposed to be a snout or a kneecap, and so made it a bit of both. As with other films in this tradition, the characters are poor rich white kids with money to burn and no responsibilities; the monstrous middle-class, where murder is seen as an intellectual pursuit rather than outright psychopathy. But, of course, the killer's here are far from sane. They plan their crimes down to the smallest detail, but – perhaps owing to their egotism and narcissism – never pause to consider the consequences of being caught. Such is the arrogance of youth.

Mutant (1984)
(aka *Night Shadows*)
Dir: John 'Bud' Cardos /USA
A pair of knucklehead brothers visit a small country town and are run off the road by a truck-full of hostile rednecks. To make matters worse, the town is overrun with mutants, transformed by a chemical spill at a local corporate plant. The remaining brother teams up with a hot blonde barmaid, and together they hold up in a hardware store and fend off the ghouls. *Mutants* is a typical, join-the-dots monster movie in the 50s tradition, and is enjoyable for what it is. It is also infused with the post-*Night of the Living Dead* tradition, meaning the mutants are grey-skinned and prone to gurgling and traipsing the streets in mobs, just like the zombies in George Romero's films.

Mute Witness (1995)
Dir: Anthony Waller /USA
Mute Witness takes the paranoia of the 'snuff-movie-within-the-set-of-a-legitimate-film' scenario of *Effects*, and ramps up the tension like never before, offering a nerve-shredding nightmare on film. When director Anthony Waller was given the go-ahead to make his feature, he switched locations from Chicago to Moscow where he discovered sets and labour would be much cheaper. Moscow also seemed to be an

appropriate location for a snuff-based movie considering the unsettled social situation in Russia after the dismantling of the Soviet state. Organised crime was rampant in that part of the world at the time, and much shady goings on were happening while the country was finding its feet once again. And American director Waller plays up to the panic and paranoia of those times. *Mute Witness* is a genuine 'edge of your seat' horror movie about a mute make-up artist who inadvertently stumbles upon the making of a snuff porn film in the studio. A thrilling chase begins when she is spotted and then targeted by the murderers. And her plight is made all the more terrifying by her inability to scream for help. Director Waller turns the constraints of a low budget to his advantage, using limited locations to claustrophobic effect. And, like other films discussed in this book – *Effects, Snuff-Movie, Special Effects, The Last Horror Horror Movie*, etc – the film effectively toys with both your mind and the blurred line between reality and films within a film. The late great, Alec Guiness, makes an uncredited appearance as a very sinister snuff movie dealer ("Did it go smoothly?"), which was filmed nine years before the rest of the picture. He was billed as 'Mystery Guest Star.' Variety magazine accurately described *Mute Witness* as "A seductive piece of real filmmaking that should keep audiences hyperventilating to the last reel."

My Little Eye (2002)
Dir: Marc Evans /UK/ USA
My Little Eye plays like a slasher version of the *Big Brother* reality show in which six contestants must live in a house for six months under constant web-cam surveillance under the promise that they will each pick up $1 million in prize money. Of course, things turn very sinister and the contestants are not clear as to what's going on. It's a better film than I expected, but is let down by a lack of social commentary. It has its moments but the 'zombies-in-the-Big-Brother-house' variant, *Dead Set* (2008), managed to touch on all the points that *My Little Eye* glossed over. It would have been nice to see the original four-hour cut of *My Little Eye* – the producers panicked after it bombed at test screenings, and hastily shredded it down to 95 minutes. But as it stands,

the film feels quite hollow and trails many loose ends in its current form.

Mysterious Skin (2004)
Dir: Gregg Araki /USA /Holland

Two teenage boys in a small Kansas town discover that their childhood memories of alien abduction are in fact blocking out real memories of sexual abuse. This is a disturbing look at paedophilia and its effects on the victims, told in a calm, graphic way which led the BBC to comment "The only thing *Mysterious Skin* will do is make yours crawl." For all the controversy surrounding this film, it's definitely a step-up for director Gregg Araki who had matured considerably since his earlier, chaotic shockers like *Totally Fucked Up* and *The Doom Generation*. It's a brave piece of filmmaking, even if it makes for some very uncomfortable viewing.

Mysterious Two (1982)
Dir: Gary Sherman /USA

An intrepid journalist follows a mysterious couple who claim to be evangelists. Turns out they're cult leaders who have convinced their followers that they're from another galaxy. They then encourage the faithful to join them on a spaceship and journey back to their home planet. The unquestioning followers are soon selling all of their possessions in preparations for the 'trip,' while the journalist and local Sheriff investigate why people are disappearing. This TV movie was written and directed by the underrated Gary Sherman – of *Death Line* (1972) and *Dead and Buried* (1981) fame – and is far better than expected and still largely unseen by horror fans. The film does a fine job of exploring the mindsets of those who are suckered in by charismatic leaders, and does a lot to foreshadow the tragedies of real-life cult suicides. The film is loosely inspired by Marshall Applewhite and Bonnie Nettles, also known as 'The Two,' a couple of supposed UFO contactees who built a considerable following in California in the 1970s before disappearing. Applewhite showed up again in the early 90s (Bonnie died of a brain tumour in the 80s), as the leader of

Heaven's Gate, surgically castrated and claiming that a spaceship was awaiting him and his followers behind the Hale Bopp comet to take them to a better world. When the police broke into their commune-like home in March 1997, they discovered the cult members' bodies laying in their beds. All had killed themselves by drinking a poisonous concoction.

Naked (1993)
Dir: Mike Leigh /UK
Fleeing from Manchester after raping a woman, a jobless, talkative misogynist visits an ex-girlfriend in London and moves in with her. Bleak and despairing, *Naked* has a real sourness to it as it presents its unlovely people with an emotional viciousness rarely seen on screen. Gavin Smith of Film Comment called it "a neorealist monster movie, and the monster won't lie down and die - he just keeps coming." David Thewlis won the award for Best Actor and Mike Leigh for Best Director at Cannes in 1993.

Necromancer (1988)
Dir: Dusty Nelson /USA
A supernatural rape/revenge flick in which a young blonde college graduate is raped, then unwittingly utilises the help of a demon to get her own back on her aggressors and anyone else she happens to be upset with. The attacks are all bloodless and depicted in the same way: red creature growls and shows its teeth, and the victim's screams echo into the next scene, that sort of thing. The video box claims "A special effects extravaganza in the tradition of *Serpent and the Rainbow*," but actually this is crude and amateurish, and the laughs are all unintentional. It's akin to a real shitty Troma movie, minus the deliberate humour.

Necronomicon (1993)
Dir: Brian Yuzna, Christophe Gans & Shusuke Kaneko /USA /France
HP Lovecraft (played by Jeffrey Combs) enters a gothic library at night for a spot of research and 'fact checking' for his latest story. He finds

the original occult text, the necronomicon (Lovecraft's own fictional devising), and begins writing a short trilogy of tales which forms this anthology film. The first story, *The Drawned*, is perhaps the weakest, in which a man in an old dark house uses the text to perform Satanic rites and resurrect his dead relatives, but the results go by way of *The Monkey's Paw*. In the second story, *The Cold*, a Boston journalist visits a strange girl in an unusually chilly house as part of his investigation into a spate of unsolved murders, only to be told the story of Dr. Maden (David Warner), a man afflicted with a rare skin condition which can only be controlled in a cold environment. And finally, *Whispers* is set in modern-day Boston with a female cop in pursuit of a criminal into an abandoned industrial building which contains a hellish pit full of skeletons and evil flying creatures. *Necronomicon* is a pretty solid anthology horror, but considering the talent behind the camera, it doesn't quite live up to its promise. *The Cold* is the most satisfying story, as it enters *Re-Animator* territory as spinal fluid is stolen from victims to keep one's immortality going. And in the wraparound at the end, Lovecraft is forced to slay one of his own tentacled creations and skin the head of a monk.

Needful Things (1993)
Dir: Fraser C. Heston /USA

The Devil incarnate moves into the sleepy New England town of Castle Rock and opens an antique store, Needful Things, gifting the local residents with their heart's desires. All he asks in return is a little favour. Turns out that each of his customers are merely pawns in his evil game in which he sets out to spread his destructive chaos throughout the town. It's up to the local Sheriff, Ed Harris, to save the day. This film has its moments of flair and some memorable characters - such as J.T. Walsh as a crooked politician/degenerate gambler, Amanda Plummer as a meek cafe waitress, and Max Von Sydow as Old Scratch himself – but it fails to string together the complex chain-link of mayhem which involves all of the characters, as portrayed in Stephen King's source novel. However, scriptwriter W.D. Richter does a fine job of packing this epic story into two hours (the TV version runs for three hours but I haven't seen that version, dammit). Viewers are rewarded with a panoramic view of how evil spreads due to misplaced anger, resentments and prejudices.

New Year's Evil (1981)
Dir: Emmett Alston /USA
Typical 80s slasher nonsense about a misogynistic maniac in various disguises who targets a television station broadcasting a musical showcase on the countdown to midnight. The slashings are fairly graphic and bloody, but none of the characters are particularly likeable. The film is worth watching if only for the roster of forgotten punk bands (including Made in Japan), and the lift sequence at the end is exceptionally well done. Director Emmett Alston's only other credit of note is the underrated video gem, *Demonwarp* (1988).

Night of the Comet (1984)
Dir: Thom Eberhardt /USA
A passing comet turns most of the population of earth into crumpled cloth bodies. A cinema projectionist and an usherette, Regina (Catherine Mary Stewart) have survived the apocalypse by spending the night in the projection booth with steel walls. The man is soon beaten to death outside by a mutant beastie, so Regina escapes on a motorcycle and sees that the entire city of Los Angeles looks to be deserted of people, and the skies are glowing a hellish red. She finds that her sister Samantha (Kelli Maroney) has also survived, and, together with a trucker they meet at a radio station, they battle for survival against the mutants and the underground coven of scientists who are on a mission to suck the blood of survivors to ensure their own survival... *Night of the Comet* is a cult classic that takes its cue from an assortment of sci-fi and horror movies of the 50s and 60s (chiefly *Target: Earth* (1953) and *The Day of the Triffids* (1962)), while also borrowing elements from Richard Matheson's *I Am Legend*/*Last Man On Earth*/*Omega Man*. Eberhardt's witty script also has the survivors indulge in some *Dawn of the Dead*-type fun in a deserted shopping mall, and somehow making the post-apocalyptic fantasy seem like utopia. We also get a constant

barrage of cheesy 80s pop music and Mary Woronov as a suicidal scientist. Personally, although I like this film, I think it could have been so much better; it lacks the all-out mutant mayhem, and instead concentrates on the evil scientists and their immoral behaviour. There are also loose ends here and there; it is never made clear why some people were vaporised and others were transformed into mutants.

The Night Evelyn Came Out of the Grave (1971)
(Orig title: *La notte che Evelyn usci dalla tomba*)
After suffering a mental breakdown and spending time in a psychiatric hospital, a degenerate English Lord, Alan (Anthony Steffen) procures redhead prostitutes to torture and murder in his own private dungeon. He seems to act in this way in order to soil the memory of his deceased wife (who was also a ginge), as he believes she was having an affair before she died. Alan's doctor suggests he should get remarried, and this he does. Then both he and his new bride see Evelyn's ghost. And meanwhile, the bodies continue to pile up... A guilty pleasure for fans of Eurohorror, *The Night* sets up an interesting premise as a psychological character study before shifting into sub-par giallo territory (those paying attention should spot who the killer is quite early on). Like other gialli of the time, this remains utterly unconvincing in its English setting and English characters (see also *Cold Eyes of Fear* – supposedly set in London). But nevertheless, the film is put together quite well with good production values and a plethora of memorable set-pieces. Look out for the fox cage scene.

Night of the Living Dead (1990)
Dir: Tom Savini /USA
Tom Savini's respectable remake of Romero's zombie classic brings changes on expectations from the very beginning. The first zombie attack in the graveyard is nicely done, and the follow up of a recently risen corpse dressed in a funeral suit, cut down the back; it slips off and reveals the autopsy wounds on its chest. Nice touch. At the farmhouse, Barbara doesn't slip into catatonia this time, she remains logical, gazes through the window, notices how slow the ghouls are, and suggests

escaping from the house. Ben (Tony Todd) agrees, but convinces her that they should stay overnight before making a move. Stupidly, they draw much attention to the house by loudly hammering doors and tables across the windows – if this was *The Walking Dead* (2010-) these characters wouldn't last five minutes. When the zombies do besiege the property, Barbara turns into a shotgun-blasting badass, in keeping with the tough heroine characters dating back to Ripley in *Alien* (1979) (she even wears a white vest with a strap of ammo across her shoulder, like Ripley).

We get more stupidity at the gas station. In the original, we never actually saw what happened there, as Tom (William Butler) decides to shoot the petrol pumps, turning him and his girlfriend into fresh barbeque for the flatliners. Tom Towles portrays the bad guy, Harry Cooper, as even more reckless and aggressive this time around, even going as far as taking pot-shots at Ben when his zombified daughter is about to be brained. The ending is almost as shocking as the 1968 version, and also very different. The updates and unexpected twists on the familiar story may not seem all that important, but they toy effectively with viewer expectations, and continually keep us off-centre throughout.

This remake also contains interesting references to the other films in Romero's series, such as Barbara visiting the redneck picnic – perhaps the very same picnic the characters in *Dawn of the Dead* (1978) fly over in a helicopter on their way to the shopping mall. The helicopter is even visible in one shot. Also, the zombie cage fight in the remake was later expanded upon in Romero's *Land of the Dead* (2005), in which humans are forced to battle the stinkers for lurid entertainment purposes (a similar idea also crops up in *The Walking Dead* season 3).

Night Screams (1987)
Dir: Allen Plone /USA

A pair of homicidal prison escapees hide out in the basement of a college football jock, David (Joe Manno), who throws a party at his home to celebrate his scholarship and to bid farewell to his buddies. However, David is also prone to mental instability when he hasn't taken his meds. And when dead bodies start piling up nearby, there are more than enough red herrings to keep viewers guessing on the culprit's identity to the end. This is a badly made, poorly scripted, and fairly bloodless slasher movie of interest to completists only. See also *Graduation Day* (1981).

Night Skies (2007)
Dir: Roy Knyrim /USA

Based on events surrounding the 'Phoenix Lights' incident of March 1997, this tells the story of a group of annoying youngsters in a camper van in the wilderness who are abducted and experimented on by extraterrestrials. Much of the running time is spent on the characters and their predicament as one of their friends disappears, but their bitching and squealing and all-round douchiness leaves viewer sympathy thin on the ground. Instead, by the hour mark, the average viewer will be hoping that the aliens insert huge, fire extinguisher-sized probes into their rectums. We get all the usual abduction phenomena: isolated areas, missing time, public and press scepticism, regression/hypnosis therapy, the story based on 'real transcripts,' which turns out to be almost entirely fictional, etc. There are no surprises on the alien front, either; the 'Greys' are smart enough to have figured out anti-gravity and wormhole travel, and yet are constantly out-smarted by numptoid college kid earthlings. However, for all the film's shortcomings, the finale on board the organic spacecraft is very weird, and the experiments are particularly ghoulish to behold.

Night Slaves (1970)
Dir: Ted Post /USA

Aliens of an different type show up in *Night Slaves* (1970), in which James Franciscus deals with sinister body snatchers. After recovering from a near-fatal car accident, Franciscus moves with his wife to a – literally – sleepy town where the locals are constantly yawning and nodding off. After a bit of sleuthing, he discovers that the town is surrounded by an invisible force field, a solid shell that makes it impossible for anyone to leave. Turns out that a 'psychokinetic' race of space aliens, disguised in human form, have colonised the town, enslaving the locals in nocturnal hard labour. To make matters worse, the populace doesn't seem to mind their exploitation, and they walk around espousing their mindless, stupidly proud, self-congratulatory work ethic of being unthinking drones (Jeez, sound familiar?). *Night Slaves* is an interesting little TV movie which is perfect for watching in bed while in a drowsy state of mind. There seems to be a conservative stance here about the perceived dangers of trade unions and organised labour, in keeping with the commie witch-hunt subtext of this film's biggest inspiration, Don Siegels' classic, *Invasion of the Body Snatchers* (1955).

Nightbreed (1990)
Dir: Clive Barker /USA
Based on Clive Barker's own novella, *Cabal*, *Nightbreed* was an unmitigated disaster. Originally intended as a two-and-a-half-hour epic monster fantasy, 20th Century-Fox aggressively cut the film down to 102 minutes and marketed it as a typical slasher movie. What was left of Barker's ambitious vision flopped dead at the box-office, alienated much of its audience, and sidelined Barker as a director. The plot is about a young man, Boone (Craig Sheffer), who is accused by his psychiatrist, Decker (David Cronenberg), of murdering six families. However, the doc is actually a cold-blooded psychopath, and he arranges for Boone to be executed by the Gestapo-like police. So Boone heads for Midian, a subterranean city of monsters, with Decker and the police in hot pursuit... *Nightbreed* is a study on bigotry and on the acceptance of one's true nature, even if that nature goes against the 'mores' of society. The 'monsters' in Midian are good and kind hearted, while Decker and his all-too-human accomplices reveal themselves to be the truly monstrous. The director's cut of this film is long overdue.

Nightmares and Dreamscapes: From the Stories of Stephen King (2006)
Dir: -Various- /Australia /USA
An 8 part mini-series, based on short stories by Stephen King,

Nightmares and Dreamscapes offers up a combination of fantasy and action, but sadly very little all-out horror. The first episode is the best; entitled *Battleground*, it's about a hired assassin who is targeted by killer toy soldiers after he shoots dead their manufacturer. Unlike the other episodes in the series, this one manages to sustain a degree of mystery and tension, despite the ludicrous premise. *Battleground* owes much to an episode of *Darkroom*, entitled *Siege of 31 August*, in which a child's toy soldiers come to life and attack the family farm house. *Battleground* is also amusing, especially with its deadpan protagonist firing back against the plastic miniatures, and eventually resorting to burning, stomping and beating them with a hammer. The hitman's swanky apartment becomes a full-on war zone, and he is forced to climb out of his high-rise window and walk along the precipice ledge above the city, just like Robert Hays in *Cat's Eye* (1987) and John Cussack in *1408* (2007), other King-based movies.

Crouch End sees a yuppie couple take a taxi ride to a fictional borough of London where they run across freaks, ghouls and cosmic portals. It's basically an unfocused tribute to HP Lovecraft. *Umney's Last Case* starts out as a pulpy parody of old skool detective and gangster flicks. William H. Macy is Clive, a private eye who is visited in his hotel room by Samuel D. Landry (also played by Macy), the man who owns the building. Landry turns out to be an author, and Clive is simply a character in his novels. Landry is obviously based on King himself, and this tale serves as his own take on the *New Nightmare*-like exploration of postmodern themes – stories within stories and fiction vs reality.

In *The End of the Whole Mess*, a documentary filmmaker tells the story of his younger brother, an inventor, mathematician and all-round child prodigy who grew up to invent a serum which pacified humanity. He slipped the concoction into the Texas water supply in what he referred to as "calm bombs," to bring about peace on earth. However, there was a side effect; after three years the entire population of the planet developed alzheimer's. In *The Road Virus Heads North*, best selling horror author, Richard Kinnell (Tom Berenger), buys a painting that is possessed by the evil spirit of something or other. This is one of the weakest entries in the set, rehashing themes that were previously explored to death in duds like *Amityville 1992: It's About Time* (1992) and *Amityville Dollhouse* (1996).

T*he Fifth Quarter* stars Jeremy Sisto as a newly-released prisoner who goes on a treasure hunt for his share of robbed loot. However, he soon comes into conflict with his old acquaintances who have the same idea. What? You mean to tell me there's no loyalty among thieves? *Autopsy Room Four* is clearly inspired by Aldo Lado's classic giallo weirdy, *Short Night of the Glass Dolls* (1972), and is about a golfer who is bitten by a spider. The poison paralyses his body while he remains fully conscious of his surroundings. Doctors declare him dead, so he is wheeled into the autopsy room. And while the pathologists are preparing to cut him open, the golfer figures that if he can get a hardon, the pathologists will realise he is still alive. And so he tries to think of happy thoughts... A similar story appeared in the 80s horror anthology film, *Freakshow* (1989). And finally there's *You Know They Got a Hell of a Band*, in which a bickering couple on the road stop by at a small town called 'Rock 'n' Roll Heaven' that is populated by dead rock stars, including Janis Joplin as a diner waitress, Roy Orbison, Buddy Holly, Jimi Hendrix, Otis Redding as a cop and Elvis Presley as Mayor.

976-Evil (1989)
Dir: Robert Englund /USA
Trailer quote: "A real man has the nerves to take what he deserves." A victimised nerd, Hoax (Stephen Geoffreys), who is obsessed with his cousin, Spike, finds himself drawn to an evil phone line that can change the future of its callers. Hoax then becomes empowered with the forces of darkness, and his megalomania comes to the fore as he dispatches the bullies who made his life hell. *976-Evil* is the directorial debut of *A Nightmare On Elm Street*'s Robert Englund, and he delivers a pretty decent – if formulaic – slice of late 80s American horror.

976-Evil II: The Astral Factor (1992)
Dir: Jim Wynorski /USA
The evil phone line is pushed more towards the background in this

sequel, as we see a school principle held on suspicion of a spate of killings. But while in custody, the killings continue, and the police have no idea what to do. Turns out that the evildoer is using astral projection to free his spirit from the cell and carry on his evil plan. However, a leather-clad burk called Spike and his bimbo blonde sidekick, Robin, discover what he is up to and put a stop to this nonsense. Basically a remake of *Psychic Killer* (1975), *976-Evil II* dresses up the hackneyed script with amusing sequences such as the 'mirror' scene in the motel and the part where one of the characters is somehow sucked into a TV set showing *It's a Wonderful Life*; but while she's there with the characters, they suddenly turn into zombies from *Night of the Living Dead*! Also, Robin wears her jeans so tight they're slowly being sucked up into her vagina. Forget 'camel's toe,' this is more like 'Hippo's yawn'!

No Mercy, No Future (1981)
(aka *The Heiress*; Orig title: *Die Beruhrte*)
Dir: Helma Sanders-Brahms /West Germany
A suicidal schizophrenic wanders through the streets of Berlin looking for Jesus and having sex with strangers until she is eventually institutionalised. Based on the true story of 'Rita G', a schizophrenic woman who is said to have written letters to director Sanders-Brahms pleading with her to make a film about her plight, *No Mercy, No Future* is a bleak docu-drama that offers a superb performance from Elisabeth Stepanek as the doomed Veronika. Viewers are taken on a dark journey alongside the protagonist as she finds herself trapped in a miserable cycle of abuse, self-abuse and the psychiatric clinic. She seeks love but finds sex; she wants acceptance but gets exploited; she wants to find solace in God but instead finds a collective of downtrodden, broken people. In the end, she decides she wants to escape life entirely, and she cuts her own throat in the shower. Her parents find her and send her back the hospital, and when she is released, the bleak cycle continues all over again... This is a little-seen film that will be hell to sit through for fans of mainstream cinema, but for those with an interest in downbeat, disturbing films with an edge, *No Mercy, No Future* offers a fiercely uncompromising study on insanity that presents a plethora of

shocking images and a cold, detached directorial style.

No Retreat, No Surrender 4 (1990)
(aka *The Kickboxer*; aka *The King of Kickboxers*)
Dir: Lucas Lowe /USA
Martial arts romp with a sinister snuff movie edge. Jake, a policeman and retired kickboxing champion, is sent over to Thailand to investigate a group of shady filmmakers who murder their actors on the sets. Turns out that one of the men responsible for the films had killed Jake's brother ten years earlier. The film is basically a carbon copy of the Jean-Claude Van Damme vehicle, *Kickboxer* (1989) with a darker, more depraved snuff undertone.

Nowhere (1997)
Dir: Gregg Araki /USA /France
A wicked send-up of high school movies, *Nowhere* follows a group of friends as they indulge in a variety of sexual experiences. One of the characters turns into a giant cockroach and the other alienated teens find themselves mixed up in polymorphous perversities. Includes sex, drugs, debauchery, alien abduction and death by soup can. It's perhaps Araki's most accessible films to date.

The Nun and The Devil (1973)
(Orig title: *Monache di Saint'Arcengelo*)
Dir: Domenico Paolella /Italy /France
Set in an Italian convent in the 1570s, a sister uses devious means to become Mother Superior. But despite providing lots of the usual in sex and death which proliferate the nunsploitation sub-genre, and also a steady directorial hand with nice compositions and photography, *The Nun and The Devil* is ultimately let down by a lack of dramatic drive.

The Oblong Box (1969)
Dir: Gordon Hessler /UK
In this tale of witchcraft, disfigurement, murder and grave-robbing, aristocrat Julian (Vincent Price) keeps his mutilated brother, Edward

(Alister Williamson), hidden in the attic. And when Edward instructs his lawyer to bring to England the African sorcerer responsible for his disfigurement, Julian refuses to allow them to meet. So, to get round this problem, the lawyer pretends that Edward has died, and the 'body' is removed from the house in an 'oblong box,' a coffin. However, a real dead body comes into the possession of a research pathologist (Christopher Lee). In a panic, Edward pays a doctor to live in the attic and pretend to be him while wearing scarlet mask to conceal his face. Edward then goes on a killing spree in the nearby town, and things become even *more* convoluted for the final third... *The Oblong Box* is remembered today primarily as the first film which paired Vincent Price and Christopher Lee together in the same scene. It also has a sombre tone as scriptwriter, Lawrence Huntington, died not long after he completed the screenplay, and the film's original director, Michael Reeves (of *The Sorcerers* and *Witchfinder General*), committed suicide. Gordon Hessler took over the project as producer/director, and he brought in Christopher Wicking to re-write the script. The result is an interesting – if flawed – entry in the British horror tradition of its time that also marks an ambitious attempt to keep the tragedy-stricken project afloat.

The Old Dark House (1932)
Dir: James Whale /USA
"No beds. You can't have the beds!" Three stranded travellers, who have narrowly avoided being crushed to death in a mudslide due to torrential downpours, stop by at an old dark house to seek shelter for the night. Inside, they meet a family of creepy eccentrics headed by Horace Femm (Ernest Thesiger), who, along with his aggressive sister, Rebecca (Eva Moore), and the mongoloid servant, Morgan (Boris Karloff), host an awkward dinner in which the lights seem to have a mind of their own. Shortly after, another pair enter the house seeking shelter, and things become even more sinister when characters go walkabout, the mongoloid downs a bottle of gin, and the psychotic, pyromaniac brother is released from the attic... *The Old Dark House* was Universal's affectionate lampooning of British manners. The script

was based on J.B. Priestley's novel, *The Benighted* (1927), with all the philosophical elements scrapped in favour of colourful characters and mordant humour. The result isn't as memorable or as iconic as the other Universal hits of the time, like *Frankenstein* (1932), *Dracula* (1931) and *The Invisible Man* (1932), but is an off-beat classic in its own right, and has influenced dozens of 'crazy family' pictures and TV shows over the decades, among them *Eraserhead* (1976), *Spider Baby* (1964), *The Texas Chain Saw Massacre* (1974), *The Munsters* (1964-66), *The Adams Family* (1964-66), *The 'Burbs* (1989), *Calvaire* (2004), and even the eccentric British sitcom, *The League of Gentlemen* (1999-2002).

One Dark Night (1982)
Dir: Tom McLoughlin /USA
A young Meg Tilly is so keen to join 'The Sisters,' a high school girl gang, that she agrees to spend the night in a crypt at the local funeral home as part of her initiation. However, a recently deceased telekinetic practitioner has been entombed there, and he returns from the dead, unleashing a horde of 'zombie' minions from their coffins to terrorise the girls. *One Dark Night* is a slow-paced, damp squid of a movie which is worth a watch if only for the final 20-minutes when the re-animated corpses are unleashed. Crucially, these aren't zombies in the traditional sense of running on some deep primal instincts, but literally dead meat puppeteered by telekinesis. The upright coffins open up like mummy's tombs, and the bodies – dressed in funeral suits and with stitched up, yellowy eyes – clamber out at the terrified girls. Fans of *Children Shouldn't Play With Dead Things* (1972) should lap it up.

100 Years Of Horror (1996)
Dir: Ted Newsom /USA
Horror documentary hosted by Christopher Lee. The horror icon takes viewers on a jumbled tour through the ages, starting at the beginning with the early trick films of Georges Melies, before taking a look at cinema's dark side with Universal monster movies, Hammer, early werewolf movies, maniac movies, gialli, William Castle's promotional gimmicks, and the slasher boom of the late 70s/early 80s. Along the

way, Jimmy Sangster claims that *Les Diaboliques* (1955) so horrified his wife that she almost miscarried their baby, while also admitting that he used the film as a template for his own work in *Paranoiac* (1963). Elsewhere, the godfather of gore, Herschell Gordon Lewis, talks about audience and censor reactions to *Blood Feast* (1963), while Boris Karloff discusses the difficulties of wearing the iconic Frankenstein's monster make up. As with most overview documentaries, this is mostly entry-level stuff, and the format skips from one movie to the next, and from random era to random era, with very little linking the films together. The clips are mostly taken from trailers, which always seems to annoy fans of horror documentaries, but I thought it worked quite well. Lee talks about the genre with seriousness and respect, and admirably avoids saying things like 'don't forget to turn out the light!' or 'pray the monster doesn't get you!' the sort of silly lines that crop up from time to time in this kind of fare. Also included are some very funny Abbott and Costello blooper reels, and John Carpenter comparing Dario Argento's work with Luis Bunuel as they both gained inspiration for their films by focusing on their dreams. Other talking heads include Roger Corman, Hugh Hefner, Robert De Niro, Dick Miller, Vincent Price, Ray Bradbury and Rachel Welsh. *100 Years of Horror* was originally made as a thirteen-part TV series, but I've been unable to source the whole series. The VHS release discussed here contains just two episodes pasted together.

Onibaba (1964)
(aka *The Hole*)
Dir: Kaneto Shindo /Japan
On remote marshland during medieval times, a mother and daughter survive by murdering stray soldiers and selling their armour, until the daughter gets into a sexual relationship with one, and the mother becomes extremely jealous. *Onibaba* is the re-telling of a classic horror story of Japanese legend, presented here as a strange fable punctuated with moments of nastiness. It's a film which also explores sex from both sides of the laws of desire, from the ecstasies of fulfilment to the tortures of frustration.

Other Worlds: A Journey To the Heart of Shipibo Shamanism (2004)

(Orig title: *D'autres mondes*)
Dir: Jan Kounen /France
Documentary by Dutch-born filmmaker, Jan Kounen, which looks at the seldom explored world of Ayahuasca ceremonies led by the shamans in the Amazon jungle. Lots of familiar faces from psychedelic culture – Pablo Amaringo, Kary Mullis, Alex Grey, Moebius – contribute lots of information while Kounen tries to engage with the culture. Whether the Ayahuasca medicine is simply an intense hallucinogen (all in the mind), or – as many believe – a way of shifting your consciousness to another dimension, isn't explored in any depth. But lots of effort went in to trying to put those terrifying visions up on the screen. Another astonishing phenomena about Ayahuasca is that the shaman can share the subject's visions as if telepathically, and can warn them about any potentially dangerous beings (or 'entities') they come in contact with and who could be attempting to do harm (indeed, there's a whole sub-culture in South America of evil shamans who enter a dosed state so that they can physically harm others by sending 'poison darts' into their enemies, telepathically – The Ayahuasca vine hasn't been studied nearly enough in the West). *Other Worlds* is perhaps the finest film ever made on the subject.

Out of the Body (1989)

Dir: Brian Trenchard-Smith /Australia
Tessa Humphries returns again after the similarly-themed *Cassandra* (1986), for another *Eyes of Laura Mars*-inspired psychic killer movie. This is also directed by Brian Trenchard-Smith, who co-wrote *Cassandra*. After a spate of killings in which the victim's eyeballs are removed, musician David Gaze believes he may share psychic links with the lunatic who commits his deadly deeds via astral projection. His attempts to inform the police of the killer's plans and his warnings to future victims leaves him labelled as both a weirdo and prime suspect. However, as the killings continue and Gaze's 'predictions' are proven correct, he feels he has no alternative but to track down the killer

himself. *Out of the Body* is a decently made film, but anyone familiar with those films mentioned above will know exactly how the narrative will pan out within the first ten minutes. On the plus side, the film does have a nice giallo feel to it, sharing links with Argento's *Deep Red* (1975) and Lamberto Bava's *A Blade in the Dark* (1983), films in which musicians are drawn into solving murder mysteries. For an even stranger twist on the theme, check out *Spasms* (1983), in which Oliver Reed shares psychic links with a demonic killer snake.

The Pack (2010)
(Orig title: *La meute*)
Dir: Franck Richard /France /Belgium
A French/Belgian co-production about a young woman who falls victim to a group of cannibals/zombies at a run down restaurant. Directed by first-time helmer, Franck Richard, who seems to enjoy toying with genre conventions just as much as creeping out his audience, *The Pack* is more of a playful pastiche of French (and American) backwoods horrors, rather than a serious horror movie, but is worth watching if only for Phillipe Nahon's performance as a perverted policeman.

The People (1972)
Dir: John Korty /USA
A dull, boring teacher enters a dull, boring town in the wilderness to start a dull, boring job of teaching dull, boring kids about dull, boring subjects until a bunch of dull, boring levitating space invaders – who look just like humans – come along to kill off the last stoic viewer with an onslaught of sheer uneventful tedium. With William Shatner.

Phantom Brother (1988)
Dir: William Szarka /USA
An extremely annoying mulleted prick and his friends visit a spooky old house to get laid, but little do they know that in the house dwells a quartet of fancy dressed killers. This is a total lame-brained attempt at horror comedy with a basic slasher movie template and sub-standard everything else.

Phantoms (1998)
Dir: Joe Chappelle /USA
A mid-budget monster horror based on a story by Dean Koontz (who also wrote the script). The small community of Snowfield, Colorado, has disappeared off the face of the earth. Who, or what, is responsible? A group of good-looking youngsters show up and decide to investigate, and soon learn that a disgusting underground monster from the beginning of time could be responsible. Delivering its fair share of spooky atmospherics and a talented cast – which includes Peter O'Toole, Ben Affleck and Rose McGowan – fans of *The X-Files* will lap it up.

The Pig Farm (2010)
Dir: *Director not credited* /Canada
Documentary on serial killer, Willie Pikton, whose reign of terror among the down and outs in Vancouver in the late 90s exposed serious deficiencies in the underfunded police department. Pikton ran a farm, and employed crack heads and other addicts to help out. Many turned a blind eye to his evil deeds to ensure their drug supplies. This is a powerful documentary that explores some of the scummiest behaviour humans are capable of. Even years later, one of the former crack heads who was on the farm at the time, doesn't show any remorse for not cooperating with the investigators – Her eye witness testimony would have ensured a search warrant for the premises, and chances are Pikton would have been stopped much sooner than he was. But instead, she kept her mouth shut, and dozens of other girls were strung up and butchered in the barn, just because she had a spat with the police years earlier and didn't like them. Her name is Lisa Yelds, and even in retrospect, she doesn't regret the fact that she could have saved the lives of others. What a cunt. No shame, no sorrow, no apology. The police finally got their warrant as late as 2002 after an anonymous tip-off about illegal firearms on the farm. After a thorough search, the police found belongings of the victims as well as human remains. Pikton was charged with 26 murders and will never be released from prison.

Planetary Evacuation Recruitment Tape (1996)
Dir: N/A /USA

Documentaries about Heaven's Gate have proliferated since the mass suicide of its members in the late 90s. Mostly television documentaries. The American ones tend to be made with a religious slant of their own; a Christian angle ("Hey, don't believe the Heaven's Gate bullshit. Believe *our* bullshit instead!"). In the American documentaries, there tends to be an underlying condemnation of the suicides as an anti-Christian thing. The British take on the subject - most notably the one made for the BBC's *Inside Story* series, entitled *Heaven's Gate* - offers a more rational, scientific condemnation: spaceships don't exist and the cult members were poorly led sheep, guided by a leader who was probably a tortured, closet-case homosexual. Even for the supposedly 'objective' BBC, the 'truth' about Heaven's Gate must be sugar-coated in a propaganda-like manufacture of opinion for its viewers, to send them away not with a greater understanding of the cult, but a creeped-out revulsion at the mere thought of Heaven's Gate and its beliefs.

If the curious want to get a real feel for the cult, one must go directly to the horses mouth and watch the videos made by Applegate himself. In *Planetary Evacuation Recruitment Tape*, Applegate (now known as 'Do') claims that his former partner, Bonnie (who died in the 80s, and is now dubbed 'Ti'), has already returned to the kingdom of heaven, and that she is actually God, his father and teacher. Do claims to be God's representation on earth. In other words, he's the second coming. The kingdom of heaven, referred to in the bible, is actually the evolutionary plain higher than man, located on a distant planet. Planet earth is about to be 'recycled,' and a new civilisation will arise shortly. Accordingly, in order to avoid this grand inconvenience, viewers are encouraged to leave their 'flesh vehicles' behind and join the group in an evacuation of earth. Do addresses the viewers directly to camera. He gives it the hard sell, like an over-animated Jehova's Witness on a doorstep. He presses on the urgency of the situation, and like any preacher worth his salt, uses biblical quotes as unimpeachable evidence.

The Possessed (1977)
Dir: Jerry Thorpe /USA

Alcoholic priest James Farentino shows up at a girl's Catholic boarding school to conduct an exorcism on Joan Hacket. There's no scepticism here; as soon as a couple of things catch fire – including Joan's dress – the exorcist is called in immediately. The highlight for me is undoubtedly the scene in which Harrison Ford's legs are set on fire and he proceeds with a slow and awkward tap dance of the damned. In fact, there are so many fire outbreaks in this film, the staff would have been wiser to call the fire brigade instead of a priest.

Progeny (1999)
Dir: Brian Yuzna /USA

A psychologically unstable doctor is shocked when his wife falls pregnant with a slimy red creature. After all, his sperm count was so low it could barely pass for cabbage water. Turns out that space aliens have been humping the missus, inseminating her, and hubby must perform an emergency caesarean section to get the little fucker out. *Progeny* contains lots of lurid gyenocological details, an attempted DIY abortion with a coat hanger, and Brad Dourif as a writer of the paranormal and alien abductions. But sadly, the talents of the usually great special effects artist, Screaming Mad George, are underused here. This is perhaps Brian Yuzna's most serious attempt at a horror film. The ending, set in a locked operating room, is particularly horrific.

Prom Night (1980)
Dir: Paul Lynch /Canada

Starting with a prologue in which children cause a fatal accident while playing in an abandoned building, the film cuts to six years later with Jamie Lee Curtis and her high school buddies preparing for the prom. Meanwhile, a detective hunts for a maniac whom he believes will strike again. With its Haddonfield-like suburban setting, *Prom Night* is a shameless Canadian cash-in on the success of John Carpenter's *Halloween* (1978), and features a godawful shit disco soundtrack and a bunch of mediocre, spazmoid characters. *Prom Night* is a real chore to sit through; the first killing (after the death in the prologue) doesn't occur until the hour mark, and is a disappointingly bloodless throat slashing. In the meantime we have to put up with time-padded dance scenes in which the mediocre students spaz around like desperate animals on the dance floor, and the girls get bitchy with each other in their bathroom mirror congregations. Turns out the killer's psychosis was brought on by the guilt of witnessing the death of the child in the prologue. Pfft! *Prom Night* was followed by two sequels, *Hello Mary Lou: Prom Night II* (1987) and *Prom Night III: The Last Kiss* (1990). A disastrous remake appeared in 2008.

Pumpkinhead (1988)
(aka *Vengeance: The Demon*)
Dir: Stan Winston /USA
A late-80s classic starring Lance Henriksen as a farmer who summons an earth demon to get revenge on the teenagers who accidentally killed his son. But, to do this, he must first head deep into the woods and seek the blessing of old lady Haggis, a reclusive witch who advises him against such drastic action. And sure enough, once Pumpkinhead – a ten foot tall scaly killing machine – is unleashed and begins slaughtering the terrified teens, the distraught father must face up to the consequences of his decision. *Pumpkinhead* is a marvel; a sort of dark fairytale brought to life on screen. It is also beautifully crafted, and director Stan Winston should be commended for never allowing the bloodshed to overshadow the unforgettable storyline.

Pumpkinhead II: Bloodwings (1993)
(aka *The Revenge of Pumpkinhead*)
Dir: Jeff Burr /USA
Small-town Sheriff (*Hellraiser*'s Andrew Robinson) is upset that his teenage daughter Jenny (Ami Dolenz) has befriended a group of degenerates who hang around smoking dope all day. She has a crush on the denim-clad donger of the group, and sneaks out after dark to hang out with them. However, while speeding recklessly on the road, they hit an old woman who turns out to be Haggis. The teens dig something up

at a strange, *Pet Sematary 2*-like burial ground, and wind up resurrecting old Pumpkinhead. The teens also inadvertently set fire to Haggis' house. And while she burns to death, she uses an incantation to raise the vengeful monster – and her murdered son, Tommy, seems to be part of the creature. *Bloodwings* is a respectable sequel to *Pumpkinhead*, and much more bloody than the first film. This time the demon is much less discriminating on its vengeance spree; it seems anyone who gets in its way is a legitimate target. The only downside is that whenever Pumpkinhead shows up, we get an excessive amount of strobe lights which get very annoying very quickly. The film shares similarities with *Friday the 13th*, with the mother avenging college boys for the death of her mongoloid son. Oh, and Linea Quigley rides Pumpkinhead's pole, apparently.

Pumpkinhead: Ashes to Ashes (2006)
Dir: Jake West /USA
This second sequel stars *Hellraiser*'s Doug Bradley as a burk (as in Burke & Hare), a grave-robbing doctor who takes the skin and organs of dead bodies to sell on the medical black market. The doc's team of errand boys handle and dispose of the corpses. When the bodies are discovered, however, along comes Haggis to reclaim her son's body that got mixed up with all the other ones. She drags it back into the woods, and the relatives of other victims follow and plead with her to unleash Pumpkinhead's vengeance on the scumbags. The old witch does her thing, and hey presto, the demon returns (while embodying the spirit of Lance Henriksen), and the bloody payback begins all over again. Despite the over-reliance on CGI monster effects this time around, *Ashes To Ashes* is a watchable sequel which is basically just a re-run of part one with a different set-up. The hillbilly kid from the original film, Bunt Wallace (Doug Roberts) returns as an adult, and it seems to be his job to explain the legend and fill the doc in on the back-story. And Doug Bradley gets sent to hell, which nicely sets up *Pinhead Vs. Pumpkinhead*. We can only dream... A fourth sequel followed, *Pumpkinhead: Blood Feud* (2007).

Rag and Bone (1997)
Dir: Robert Lieberman /USA

A supernatural TV movie based on a story by acclaimed horror author Anne Rice (*Interview With the Vampire*). It tells the story of a New Orleans cop, Dean Cain, who is puzzled by a mysterious ghostly figure that leads him to new clues in an unsolved murder case. Made as a pilot for a TV series, none of the networks picked it up, so it was re-packaged onto DVD and dumped in the bargain bins. As a stand alone film, it leaves a few loose ends but is worth a watch.

The Rats (2002)
Dir: John Lafia /USA

Tagline: 'The City's rat race just got deadly.' A TV movie which teams up a department store manager (Madchen Amick) and a jolly exterminator (Vincent Spano) to wage war against mutated lab rats. It starts off slow, despite a janitor losing an ear, but gets better for the finale in which Amick almost drowns in a pool full of raging rodents. With a confident, unpretentious direction from John Lafia, and a script which gives the underrated leads much to do, this fun film is only let down by the unconvincing CGI shitstorm of jibbering rats.

Razorback (1984)
Dir: Russell Mulcahy /Australia

One of the great horror debuts of the 80s which saw director Russell Mulcahy signed up to Hollywood almost immediately after the film was released in the States. *Razorback* starts with a man standing trial for the murder of his grandson. He is adamant that the child was carried away by a wild boar. Meanwhile, an American television journalist catches wind of the story and heads over to Australia to get the scoop. However, she soon falls victim to the creature. Next, her husband Carl (Gregory Harrison) arrives in town looking for her, and he ends up teaming up with a couple of locals to track down the elusive beast... Inspired by the Dingo baby case, *Razorback* is a stylish treat for horror fans, boasting strange backlighting effects, arresting images (a car stuck in the branches of a tree, a man watching TV has half of his house torn

177

away), and a marvellous score by Iva Davis which is a throwback to 50s monster and disaster movies punctuated with synths and piano. The scenes where Carl falls into the lake from the windmill tower, and his hallucinatory trip through the desert, pre-dates the slapstick weirdness inflicted on Ash in *Evil Dead II* (1987) and *Army of Darkness* (1992). Screenwriter, Everett de Roche (of *Long Weekend*, 1977), continued to churn out movie scripts based on killer animals – *Frog Dreaming* (1985) and *Link* (1986) – but none of them are in the same league as *Razorback*.

[Rec] (2007)
Dir: Juame Balaguero & Paco Plaza /Spain
A reality TV crew is caught up in a rabid virus/zombie outbreak while accompanying firemen on a routine call to a rundown apartment block. All they can do is record the unfolding nightmare as the violence and hysteria reach fever pitch. Similar to *The Blair Wicth Project* in terms of its gritty hand-held style, *[Rec]* has an urgent, alarming aesthetic, no doubt equally inspired by news coverage on shaky cams of post-9/11 events, and includes some genuinely hair-raising moments. It was remade less successfully as *Quarantine* in America.

Reign In Darkness (2003)
Dir: David W. Allen & Kelly Dolen /Australia
Made in Australia, *Reign In Darkness* is another of those godawful 'let's-dress-in-black-leather-and-pose-with-guns' movies that were shat out in the wake of *Blade* (1998). Here we have a pair of vampire hunters who put on fake American accents while wandering around deserted warehouse settings doing nothing beyond pointing their weapons and pulling earnest, heroic faces any chance they get. This is barely above an amateur home movie, and the filmmakers even cast themselves in the lead roles. Somebody slap them, please.

The Rejuvenator (1988)
Dir: Brian Thomas Jones /USA
A scientist in the closing stages of perfecting a youth-preserving agent,

is pressured by his financial backer – an ageing actress desperate to get back into the limelight – to rush through his research and bring immediate results... The serum is administered intravenously and seems to be a success at first. However, there is also the undesired side-effect of an acceleration of the ageing process once the dosage has worn off. Thus, the user must be continuously dosed up like a junky to avoid becoming an ugly, putrefied Andrew Lloyd Webber lookalike. *The Rejuvinator* has its roots in the 'mad scientist' movie, but here the doctor is the sanest, most level-headed character in the film. Instead, it's the madness of our youth-obsessed, brain dead vanity culture that hijacks scientific research for a short, sharp fix, with disastrous results. An underrated curio.

Relentless (1989)
Dir: William Lustig /USA
A New York cop relocates to L.A. and his first assignment is to help track down a vicious serial killer who seems to be selecting his victims at random from the phone book. The killer turns out to be the son of a legendary tough guy cop who had so traumatised his boy by bullying him into a psychotic mess. He now talks to his father's picture, and continues to carry out 'orders' through the voices in his head. This film is disappointingly ordinary from the director of the notorious slasher, *Maniac* (1980). Perhaps director Lustig was aiming more towards the mainstream this time around. But despite the off-beat humour and east coast/west coast rivalries, *Relentless* is a routine police procedural picture.

The Relic (1997)
Dir: Peter Hyams /USA
A cargo ship delivers something very menacing from the Amazon rainforest and deposits it in Chicago's Natural History Museum. This strange creature has already chowed down on the ship's crew, munched on a security guard and now threatens to wreak havoc at the opening of a new exhibition. Sweet boffin Penelope Ann Miller joins up with tough cop Tom Sizemore to pursue the monster that is rampaging

through the galleries. What you see is what you get in this well-crafted horror. There's no 'knowing' humour or trendy hand-held camera work here, just efficient atmospherics, spooky chase sequences and lots of mood and suspense. And the monster is shown mostly in the shadows. An above-average creature feature.

The Remake (2006)
Dir: Tommy Brunswick /USA

The Remake is a decent little pic about a crazed horror movie fan who shows up on the set of a remake and begins offing the cast and crew in bloody fashion. If nothing else, this film can be commended for its anti-remake spirit and its stance as a feature which favours craft over cash, originality over imitation, and solid chills and atmosphere over T&A. Director Tommy Brunswick later returned to the snuff horror theme with *Jingles the Clown* (2009). By the way, if there are any gullible maniacs reading this who are open to suggestions, may I point your attention to people like Samuel Bayer and John Moore, the men responsible for such awful remakes as *A Nightmare On Elm Street* (2010) and *The Omen* (2006). I don't want to plant any bad ideas in your head, and I appreciate your fragile mental state, but wouldn't it be nice if they were brutally murdered and decapitated? It would make great art, wouldn't it? Just think of the statement that would make. Why don't you find those men responsible. Sharpen your sharp things and go find them. Kill your partners and give us Channel 83. Go on, sport, you can do it.

Requiem For a Dream (2000)
Dir: Darren Aronofsky /USA

Co-written by Hubert Selby Jr, and based on his novel, *Requiem For a Dream* is a nightmarish visual experience, especially for those who have ever had to deal with speed psychosis. The film links two distinct story lines on the nature of drug addiction, from a young man and his girlfriend who are addicted to heroin and do all they can to secure their next fix, to the man's mother who orders diet pills but quickly becomes addicted to them, and spirals downward into a hallucinatory, paranoid hell. Some have claimed it to be a masterpiece but I wouldn't go that far. It's certainly well worth watching but the cliché characters makes it feel like territory you have roamed many times before in the movies, especially the predictable moments of the characters trying and failing to go cold turkey, their 'love conquers all' attitudes, and so on. Worth watching if only for the sequence in which Ellen Burstyn's television comes to life with a delirious interactive quiz show. The BBC described it as "brutal, stark, stomach-churning and unglamorous."

Resurrecting the Street Walker (2009)
Dir: Ozgur Uyanik /UK

Another faux-documentary. This time it's about a runner for a small production company who discovers a few reels of film while clearing out an old basement storage area. The reels contain footage of an unfinished film called 'The Street Walker' about a man who tortures and murders women. The runner's curiosity gets the better of him, and he decides to complete the movie while his buddy records his progress... Like *The Last Broadcast* (1998), *Resurrecting the Street Walker* is put together entirely with documentary techniques, including talking head sequences, movie clips and video diary footage, and is quite well put together despite the twist ending that can be spotted quite early on (especially for those familiar with *The Last Broadcast*). Most intriguingly, this film has several layers of 'reality' reflecting into infinity like the reflections of opposing mirrors. Abel Ferrara tackled similar themes in *Dangerous Game* (1993). A reviewer on IMDb summed it up best: "You have the real director of the film making a movie about a director of a film who is inspired to complete the production of a film where the 'real' director of the 'real' (movie world) film was making a movie about a director who used movie-making as a pretext for trapping and killing his victims." You got that?

Resurrection (1999)
Dir: Russell Mulcahy /USA

Director Russell Mulcahy and actor Christopher Lambert teamed up again for the first time since *Highlander* (1986) for this dark and gruesome thriller. A cross between *Frankenstein* and *Seven*, the plot follows a cop's pursuit of a serial killer who removes a limb from each of his victims, and leaves the massage "he is coming." Eventually we discover that the killer is a deranged religious fanatic who is methodically piecing together a new Messiah from the body parts of his victims. Tense and atmospheric at times, *Resurrection* is recommended to those who appreciate dark and disturbing horror.

Return of the Fly (1959)
Dir: Edward Bernds /USA
This rather silly sequel to the 1958 classic isn't a patch on the original. This time it's the turn of Andre's son, Brett Halsey to meddle with things he doesn't understand. And despite his father's grotesque mutation at the end of the first film, he can't resist tinkering with the old man's teleportation chamber. Horror fans may get a kick out of the scene where a man is transformed literally into a human guinea pig, but otherwise this really isn't up to much. Another sequel, *Curse of the Fly*, followed in 1965.

Return of the Killer Tomatoes! (1988)
Dir: John De Bello /USA
The killer tomatoes are back with lots of footage from the first film in another plot to win the hearts of B-movie fans. This time the tomatoes take on human form (which saves the 'special effects' team a lot of effort), and a pizza delivery guy must save the day when the mad Dr. Gangreen engineers the deadly tomato assault. Some of the gags actually work this time but still, it's a real clunker. It was followed by *Killer Tomatoes Strike Back* (1990).

Revenge of the Stepford Wives (1980)
(aka *Terror in New York*)
Dir: Robert Fuest /USA
TV journalist Kay Forster moves into the town of Stepford to investigate why it has the lowest crime and divorce rates in America. There she befriends Megan, another outsider of the town whose

husband is there on a work assignment. And it isn't long before Kay encounters the weirdness when she is almost run over by a droid-like, mechanized lady, who later has no memory of the incident. Kay digs deeper and discovers a populace of servile women (or, as she puts it, "an empty-headed bunch of plastics") who are obsessed with cleaning, and tuppaware, appliances and domesticity. And if everything's a little out of whack in the strange town, things only get worse when she is attacked with a meat cleaver, and, to her horror, sees that the usually witty and no-nonsense Megan has become just another bubble-headed part of the community. Kay then sets out to rescue Megan from the white-washed suburban hell. Although it feels like a TV movie and is quite predictable, this is actually a decent sequel to the mid-70s classic, *The Stepford Wives*, that continues the original's theme of how people in affluent neighbourhoods become monstrous snobs.

Ring of Darkness (1979)
(aka *Satan's Wife*; aka *Un'ombra nell'ombra*)
Dir: 'Peter Karp' [Pier Carpi] /Italy /UK
Carlotta (Anne Heywood) is a member of a secretive Satanic sect. She and other members of the cult become increasingly worried by the exploits of Daria (Lara Wendel), Carlotta's teenage daughter, who has developed terrifying powers, and thinks nothing of casting evil spells on those around her whom she is upset with, including members of the sect. Carlotta and others renounce their pacts with Satan, and in desperation seek the assistance of a Priest to help rid Daria of the evil that has consumed her soul... *Ring of Darkness* is better than the usual *Exorcist* rip-offs, even though the performances are a little stilted at times. The film has a cold, gloomy, paranoid vibe to it, and Stelvio Cipriani provides the Goblin-esque, prog-rock score that works wonders at enlivening what is essentially a cheap exploitation pic. The film is shrouded in controversy to this for the casting of Lara Wendel; she also appeared in the notorious *Maladolescenza* – both films were shot in 1977 when she was just thirteen-years-old, and both films contain scenes in which she is naked for much of the time. *Ring of Darkness*, in particular, includes the outrageous scene in which mother

and daughter have a fight in the middle of a pentagram in a church, in the nude.

Ritual (2002)
Dir: Avi Nesher /USA
Not released on DVD until 2006, *Ritual* was originally made as the third film spin-off of the popular *Tales From the Crypt* TV series after *Demon Knight* (1995) and *Bordello of Blood* (1996). The producers were unsure how to proceed with the film as the TV show had long been over. They cut out all the Cryptkeeper scenes and sat on it for a few years before finally releasing it with those scenes reinstated. And thank goodness they did because *Ritual* is the finest film of the loose trilogy. The story follows Dr. Alice Dodgson who looses her medical license after the death of a patient in her care. Desperate for work, she accepts the job as a nurse for a young man afflicted with cephalitis. And before long, she finds herself embroiled in voodoo and zombies during a visit to Jamaica. With such a long delay in release, horror fans were expecting a disaster, but *Ritual* is actually a smooth-sailing slice of twisted fun.

Road Rage (1999)
Dir: Deran Sarafian /USA
Former *Baywatch* babe Yasmine Bleeth stars in this middle-of-the-road stalker thriller made for TV. The curvaceous star makes the big mistake of cutting off a delivery driver on the road. He then spends the rest of the film vengefully terrorising her. This type of thing has been done many times before in the movies – most notably in Spielberg's *Duel*, for example – and much better.

Roberto Succo (2001)
Dir: Cedric Kahn /France /Switzerland
Based on the exploits of Italian serial killer, Roberto Succo, this film explores his compulsive lying and Walter Mitty-like fantasy life moreso than his killings, and boasts a superb controlled performance by first-time actor, Stefano Casetti. It's an intimate portrait, with director Kahn

holding back somewhat with the more explosive and sensationalist elements of the story. He also admirably keeps things nicely balanced by refusing to glorify or pass judgement on any of the characters, whether it be Succo, his unsuspecting girlfriend or his pursuers.

Rock 'n' Roll Nightmare (1987)

(aka *The Edge of Hell*)
Dir: John Fasano /Canada
This film spends no less than 15 minutes on the title sequence and initial establishing shots of an 80s hair metal band arriving at a large house to record a single. And while the band – real band, The Tritons – rehearse their racket, the groupies and engineers are ravaged by hand puppet beasties and shape-shifting demons. For the most part meandering and nonsensical. As far as guilty pleasures go, I'd rather watch Jess Franco's *Killer Barbys* (1996) any day. Now there's a *real* rock 'n' roll nightmare!

Rocktober Blood (1984)

Dir:Beverly Sebastian /USA
Rock singer, Billy, loses his mind and goes on a killing spree, murdering his manager and others in the recording studio. Two years after his execution, Billy's ex-girlfriend, Lynne, attempts to rebuild her life by joining a new group called Headmistress. However, the trauma of having escaped death is too much for her to bear. And when Billy returns from the dead to stalk and harass her with obscene phone calls ("I want your hot, steaming pussy blood all over my face, ha ha ha ha ha!!!"), her friends fear that she could be losing her mind, too. That is, until the finale when Billy shows up at a Headmistress gig with murder in mind... The first and final ten minutes of this video are glorious snippets of bad movie heaven – we get silly death scenes, half-arsed line deliveries, abysmal songs, and cat screams that go on and on forever. The middle chunk of the film sits in a much more ordinary bad movie realm, but is still entertaining. If you want to remind yourself of how awful the 80s were, there's no alternative.

Romance (1998)

(aka *Romance X*)

Dir: Catherine Breillat /France

Frustrated by her boyfriend's disinterest in having sex with her, a school teacher embarks on series of affairs, including an excursion into sadomasochism. The scenes of explicit sexuality caused much controversy at the time of its release, especially the hardcore shots featuring the well-endowed adult film star, Rocco Siffredi. However, at its core, *Romance* is actually a very typical French film of its time in that a woman's quest for sexual freedom causes her to be abused by men. The biggest problem with the film is that it's ultimately boring, as Kenneth Turan of the Los Angeles Times put it, "who could have imagined that sex on screen could be so unbearably dull?"

Rose Red (2002)

Dir: Craig R. Baxley /USA /Canada

A Stephen King-scripted, three part mini-series for television. Taking the bulk of its premise from Robert Wise's *The Haunting* (1963), episode one sets up the story of a team of psychics arriving at a mansion called Rose Red, an impressive haunted house; episode two puts the psychic investigators (Melanie Lynskey, Julian Sands, Nancy Travis) under attack from the ghostly apparitions; and episode three unleashes all the usual hell of screaming, ghosts and strobe lighting. With smart, snappy dialogue and long-fingered, creepy looking ghouls, *Rose Red* is quite fun to watch, but can never really get going quick enough due to its stop-start narrative which is dictated by the intrusion of commercial ad breaks.

Route 666 (2001)

Dir: William Wesley /USA

A couple of cops, Lou Diamond Phillips and Lori Petty, turn off the main highway to elude the hitmen who are intent on killing a snitching witness in their custody. They head down a disused stretch of road, known locally as 'Route 666,' and come up against a horde of concrete-faced zombie convicts who are charged with extra power every time blood is spilled on the road. The impressive ghouls brandish roadworks tools to pound their victims into the asphalt. But, in order to bring the film up to feature length, a further menace later shows up to augment the zombies, and this leads to a last-reel cameo appearance from L.Q. Jones who plays a 70s-era, redneck Sheriff. *Route 666* is a far better movie than anyone could have expected.

Ruby (1977)
Dir: Curtis Harrington /USA

One of the great benefits of sifting through thousands of horror movies is that, occasionally, you come across gems that have been all but ignored by fans and critics. And for me, *Ruby* is one of those gems, a supernatural shocker starring Piper Laurie as an ex-gangster's moll. Sixteen years previously, she betrayed her lover to the merciless guns of his gangster rivals. And now their daughter, who hasn't spoken a word since birth, is behaving very oddly. It soon becomes clear that the dead man has returned in ghostly form and is using their child as a vehicle for vengeance. This is downright eerie stuff, with much of the content filmed at twilight in a decrepit drive-in movie theatre which is owned by Laurie's character. The plot shares similarities with Mario Bava's classic, *Shock* (1977), which was made at the same time. A remastered Blu-Ray release would be a dream come true.

Rumpelstilskin (1996)
Dir: Mark Jones /USA

A routine, predictable monster movie which is at least more watchable than any of the *Leprechaun* series. Rumpelstilstin is a child thief who is basically immortal. The only way to stop it is to guess its name – which is no easy task. It's an ugly little fuck, too, with ego problems – a bit like Leo Sayer. It shows up in L.A. in the mid-90s after being consigned to the ocean since medieval times. Widow Shelly (Kim Johnston Ulrich) teams up with her neighbour and an obnoxious TV personality to track down the evil troll and get her baby back, and this leads to a seemingly never-ending road chase with no style or suspense, nor much incident.

Run! Bitch! Run! (2009)

Dir: Joseph Guzman /USA

A rape-revenge movie that attempts to hark back to the glory days of the grindhouses but gets it all wrong. Two Catholic school girls go door-to-door selling bibles and wind up knocking on the door of a gang of deviants. Director Joseph Guzman claims to be a fan of 70s exploitation films but *Run! Bitch! Run!* has much more in common with the politically correct, well-behaved remakes of *Last House On the Left* (2009) and *I Spit On Your Grave* (2010) rather than the ugly, unruly grubbiness of the grindhouse originals.

Saint Sinner (2002)

Dir: Joshua Butler /Canada /USA

An overwrought, silly sci-fi/horror TV movie derived from Clive Barker. It's about a time-travelling monk and an atheist cop who team up to track down soul-sucking sexual succubi disguised as hookers. Made for the Sci-Fi Channel (or Syfy, or whatever the fuck it's called nowadays), this flick skimps on sex, blood and nudity due to network regulations, but offers shit-loads of gel lighting, creaky sets, predictable plot-lines and hammy performances.

Salon Kitty (1976)

Dir: Tinto Brass /Italy /West Germany /France

In the late 1930s, a Nazi army officer commandeers a Berlin brothel and installs bugging devices and prostitutes loyal to the party to report on any insubordination among the visiting troops and other clients. This is the film that kick-started the short-lived 'Nazisploitation' sub-genre which flourished in the late 70s, and *Salon Kitty* remains one of the best and most competently made of them all.

S&Man (2006)

Dir: J.T. Petty /USA

S&Man (pronounced 'sandman', apparently) mixes documentary segments about voyeurism and the underground horror and fetish scenes with a fictionalized sub-plot which involves the film's director

(J.T. Petty) suspecting a fellow director of making torture-snuff movies. Underground horror filmmakers Fred Vogel and Bill Zebub are interviewed, and even feminist academic, Carol Clover – author of *Men, Women and Chainsaws* – makes an appearance, too. Those looking for a factual documentary about underground horror fandom will get what they're looking for provided they can put up with the fictionalized stuff. It's clear that Petty wanted to creep out his viewers with this film, and the only way he could achieve his goal was to insert the story of Eric Rost and his deviant films. When *S&Man* was screened at festivals, it actually worked on many audiences and often helped to create an uneasy atmosphere. It was only when Petty took to the stage after screenings and informed audiences of the fictionalized Rost could people relax in the knowledge that Rost was a fictional character.

The Satanic Rites of Dracula (1973)
Dir: Alan Gibson /UK

A Satanic cult revives Count Dracula (Lee again, in the last time he ever donned the cape for Hammer) who blends into the community by posing as a wealthy property developer. However, when Scotland Yard finds evidence of vampiric murders, Peter Cushing's Van Helsing is called in to help with the investigation and dissolve Dracula one last time. *The Satanic Rites* is one of the few Hammer horrors set in the modern day, and relies heavily on a 'scientific' approach to telling the story, and borrows many of its narrative contraptions from action capers, like Bond movies which were very popular at the time. And Dracula also finds a modern, scientific way of spreading his deadly plague.

Satan's Slave (1976)
(aka *Evil Heritage*)
Dir: Norman J. Warren /UK

A young woman, Catherine (Candace Glendenning), is horrified to learn that she was born into a Devil-worshipping cult. Her uncle and cousin try their damndest to ease her into his Satanic Majesty's service in their plans to resurrect a long-dead relative, but Catherine has other plans... This is perhaps Norman J. Warren's weakest horror effort of the 70s and early 80s (which also includes *Terror* (1978), *Prey* (1981) and *Inseminoid* (1981)). The production values are impressive, but it plays like a bad soap opera with the added bonus of bizarre Satanic visions, incest and graphic gore. For a more interesting take on a similar theme, see the obscure American TV movie, *The Devil's Daughter* (1973). Here, the daughter turns the tables on her Satanist guardians by embracing the darkside much more than anyone around her had dared. As for *Satan's Slave*, in an interview with *Flesh & Blood* magazine in 1995, Warren confirmed rumours that there was a bloodier cut of the film made for the Japanese market. That version included a flashback sequence in which the blonde girl tied to the tree is stabbed to death. Horror fans immediately went on the hunt in the Far East and rescued the only print known to exist of that version. It was later issued on DVD.

Savage Weekend (1976)
(aka *The Killer Behind the Mask*)
Dir: David Paulsen & Jason Mason Kirby /USA
A group of couples head for the wilderness of upstate New York for a fishing trip while one of them also uses the opportunity to fix his boat. While there, they employ the services of local farmhand, Otis (*Fight For Your Life*'s William Sanderson), to carry out menial tasks. Otis is also known to have a violent past, and of course, it isn't long before a masked maniac begins offing the tourists with a variety of farmyard implements and stringing them up in a nearby barn... *Savage Weekend* was made primarily to cash-in on the success of grindhouse hits like *Last House on the Left* (1972) and *The Texas Chain Saw Massacre* (1974), complete with isolated setting and an excessive banjo soundtrack. The difference here is that the filmmakers attempt to add some depth to the characters by giving them lots of extraneous dialogue, but all this does is set up the usual roster of red herrings while the actual murders are postponed until the 50-minute mark. This isn't the worst of the backwoods slasher movies, but the sluggish pace and

technical shortcomings sure make it feel that way. The film was released in 1979 but was actually completed three years earlier under the working title, *The Killer Behind the Mask*.

Scalps (1983)
Dir: Fred Olen Ray /USA
A group of college students take a field trip out to the California desert plains for a spot of artefact hunting. However, one of the them disturbs an old burial ground near to the sacred 'black trees,' and he is possessed by 'black claw,' the vengeful spirit of a native American. And when night falls, he sets about slashing and scalping his classmates... With its effectively doomy synth score, isolated setting, and grisly death scenes, *Scalps* is a must-see for fans of early 80s slasher flicks. It boasts a lurid 'video nasty' appeal and a strange, otherworldly atmosphere in some parts. And even the teens aren't as annoying as usual, and viewers can enjoy their company as they trek their way to oblivion without wishing death upon them from the outset. Forrest J. Ackerman makes an early cameo appearance as a professor chastised for reading monster mags. An unofficial sequel followed, *Dream Warrior* (1988).

Scarecrows (1988)
Dir: William Wesley /USA
Double-crossing criminals in search of a box of stolen money trek through the woods after dark. The area is also guarded by huge scarecrows that come to life and pick off the crummy humans, one by one, EC comics style. *Scarecrows* has much in common with the – then - fading slasher movie tradition, in that it shares with those films a puritan vibe in which the monster seems to feed on sin while the innocent ones are spared. Michael Simms as Curry is the Captain Rhodes of the group, a sinister scumbag whose fate is disappointingly bloodless. The crux of the story could have fit into an episode of *Tales From the Crypt*, but by spreading things out over the course of 83 minutes, the characters are given the chance to dig their holes even deeper, making the pay-off that much more satisfying. A late-80s classic.

Scary Movie 4 (2006)
Dir: David Zucker /USA

An absolute rancid bum-spill posing as a movie. This series just gets worse. We get more lame jokes on *Saw*, with Dr. Phil as his usual, twatty self. More J-Horror nonsense. Mike Tyson appears in a boxing skit and bites off lots of ears. Ha ha ha, Mike Tyson bites ears off! I've never heard *that* one before! Characters accidentally bash their heads on things, which isn't funny the first time, and this non-gag is then repeated dozens of times throughout the film, and doesn't get any funnier. Most of the running time concentrates on *War of the Worlds*, Spielberg's epic remake, and none of the supposed 'spoofings' have anything to do with that film. I've never seen such a crude, cynical, shallow series of films in all my life. This is fucking abysmal. By this point in the series, Hitler's 'final solution' to the Jew problem doesn't seem like such a barbaric idea anymore. Tut tut. Curiously, the filmmakers here play up the stereotypes of black car thieves, effeminate homos, dumb politicians and Muslim terrorists, while failing to acknowledge that, with movies like this, they're in fact playing up to their own Jewish stereotype of the huckster parasites squatting on Western culture and taking a great big steamy turd all over it.

Scary Movie 5 (2013)
Dir: Malcolm D. Lee [and David Zucker, uncredited] /USA

Just when you thought it was safe to go back to the multiplex, along comes another in the *Scary Movie* franchise. And yes, *Scary Movie 5* is just as bloody awful as we have come to expect in this series. Charlie Sheen shows up again for a *Paranormal Activity* skit involving viagra; Snoop Dogg appears in a *Cabin in the Woods* bit involving a massive blunt; more characters bump their heads on things, *ad nauseam*. Ugh. Surely the point of making fun of something is to capture a certain truth about it; that's where the humour comes from! But here, the jokes have nothing to do with the films they're supposedly spoofing on. In the first *Scary Movie* (2000), this is achieved somewhat in the scene where the Ghostface killer is seen hiding behind the sofa after supposedly doing a Michael Myers disappearing act. The joke worked because Myers in

Halloween would disappear from view in a short space of time, so we knew he couldn't have gotten far! However, in *Scary Movie 5* we're supposed to find gas masks funny because they were used in a scene in *Insidious* (2010), and the *Black Swan* (2010) segments are supposed to be funny because the characters here are bad at ballet. Where's the connection? There aren't any! The result is a string of unfunny, off-target gags which not only fail as spoof, but sucks monstrous Jabba the Hutt balls at the same time. Ah, but what do the filmmakers care, they made their millions out of it. Mission accomplished, I guess.

Scream of the Wolf (1974)
Dir: Dan Curtis /USA
Writer Peter Graves investigates a series of vicious killings in the woods. Hey, if you're in the mood for a werewolf movie that doesn't actually contain any werewolf action, this is it! Instead, what we get is a shit load of 70s era clichés, such as the grey-haired hero, the funky porno chic wah-wah guitars, and corduroy flares. And if you can't spot who the 'werewolf' is within the first twenty minutes, you're an idiot.

Scream And Scream Again (1969)
Dir: Gordon Hessler /UK
The police trace a spate of bloody murders to Vincent Price, a mad scientist suspected of creating a Frankenstein-like race of super-humans constructed from stolen body parts. Set in modern-day London, *Scream And Scream Again* contains lots of action, weird science, super-long car chases and shady bad guys, all designed to cash-in on the Bond craze which was at full-swing at the time. This atypical Brit horror sees the re-teaming of scriptwriter Christopher Wicking and director Gordon Hessler (the pair also collaborated on the troubled *The Oblong Box* in the same year). Here they serve up another complicated tale of madness, murder and body-snatching. Those accustomed to Hammer horrors of old may be less than impressed with the idea of their beloved horror heroes engaging in such modern-day tomfoolery, but others will appreciate the film as an ambitious attempt to keep the slow death of British horror at bay. The producers were not impressed with such

modern-day material, and they oversaw a drastic re-cut which the filmmakers were deeply unhappy with.

Screamtime (1983)
Dir: 'Al Beresford' [Michael Armstrong & Stanley Long] /UK
Screamtime is a horror anthology comprising of three short films that were cobbled together with a wraparound plot shot in New York. The film starts with two youths stealing a bunch of video tapes from a store. They later show up at a girl's apartment and play the tapes. The first tape is about a middle-aged man who runs a Punch & Judy show on Brighton beach. His family doesn't share the same enthusiasm for the puppets as he does. And after his son burns down the theatre stand, a slightly charred Mr. Punch goes on a killing spree, beating people to death with a plank of wood...On the second tape, a married couple move into a new house, and the wife sees strange, ghostly figures in and around the place. The husband becomes concerned for her mental health, and even the local ghost whisperer think she's nuts. And when she is finally sent to the nuthouse, viewers will find that perhaps she isn't insane after all (this second segment was released as a stand alone short film entitled *Dreamhouse* in 1982). And in the third tape, a young motorcross enthusiast, who needs money to repair his bike, accepts the job of handyman for a pair of kooky old ladies who believe in fairies. One night, he takes his brother and mechanic friend to the house. They break in with the intention of stealing a treasure-trove of silver and cash. However, the garden gnomes and fairies come to life and murder the intruders, one by one... *Screamtime* was an attempt to recapture the glory days of the British anthology horror as popularised by Amicus and *Hammer House of Horror.* The film is partly successful – the *Dreamhouse* segment manages to sustain a sense of uneasiness and suspense – but the low budget and lack of directorial skill ensured that this feature will be forever languishing in video hell, where only the most rabid of horror fans will get to see it.

The Secret of Seagull Island (1981)
(aka *Seagull Island*; Orig title: *L'isola del gabbiano*)

PHENOMENA

Dir: Nestore Ungaro /UK /Italy

A five-part mini-series made for cable TV. A British woman, Barbara (Prunella Ransome), heads to Rome in search of her blind sister, Marianne, who has mysteriously vanished. After alerting the police, the body of a blind woman is discovered on a rubber dinghy adrift at sea. But when it comes to identifying the body, Barbara is relieved to find that it isn't that of her sister. However, when she learns that the boat victim was murdered, she suspects that the killer may also have something to do with Marianne's disappearance. And so she does a bit of giallo sleuthing, and all clues lead to a mysterious island... This lightweight mystery has nothing going for it beyond the splendid underwater photography and early 80s fashion atrocities. The performances are lacklustre, as is the script, and the direction by the unknown Nestore Ungaro only comes to life when scenes take place below the ocean surface (I suspect underwater photography was Ungaro's day job, and the main reason he got this gig). Beyond that, the 'mystery' takes all of ten minutes to solve, and the heroine pretends to be blind so that she can get close to the sight-phobic maniac and save the day. Okay, so there's slightly *more* to the story than that, but the revelations really aren't worth sticking around for. Recommended only to die-hard giallo completists.

Secretary (2002)

Dir: Steven Shainberg /USA

Tagline: 'A comedy for everybody who's been tied up at work.' Absolute garbage. Posy, self-conscious, trend-following nonsense featuring a couple of leads (James Spader and Maggie Gyllenhaal) who really should've known better than agreeing to this shit. A self-harmer gets involved in a sadomasochistic relationship with her new boss. It isn't "smart" or "daring" or "provocative" or any of the things the critics said at the time in their efforts to blow smoke up its arse. *Secretary* is simply a crashing bore; it's nothing more than a typically safe drama that 'tastefully' touches on its kinky themes, conveniently released in an era when such subject-matter as this rarely raises an eyebrow.

Session 9 (2001)

Dir: Brad Anderson /USA

One of the best straight-to-video horror movies released in the early 00s, *Session 9* is superior to much of the swill that makes it onto the big screen. It's a curious blending of *The Blair Witch Project, Cube* and John Carpenter's *The Thing*, as a team of workers are sent to remove asbestos from an old lunatic asylum, with seriously creepy consequences. The predictable ending is a bit of a let down, but the build-up tension, spectacular location and excellent cast – which includes Peter Mullan, Josh Lucas and David Caruso – more than make up for the film's routine finale. There are no CGI ghouls or hammy psychos here, just slow-building fear and skin-crawling creepiness, especially in the moments where Mullan plays back those old tape recordings.

Seven in Darkness (1969)

Dir: Michael Caffey /USA

A group of blind folks on a plane heading for a convention crash land in a stormy wilderness and have to make their way back to civilization. Not only do they have to navigate the hostile terrain, but they are also being picked off by a pack of wolves. This film is absolutely riveting for all the wrong reasons; we have blind people tapping around with their sticks, slipping and rolling down hills, walking into trees and falling through the gaps on railroad bridges. It's played completely straight but feels like a politically incorrect slapstick comedy. I'm surprised it doesn't have more of a cult following among fans of wrong-headed cinema. Maybe it would have if more people actually saw it.

Shadow People (2013)

(aka *The Door*)

Dir: Matthew Arnold /USA

A late-night radio host, Charlie Crowe (Dallas Roberts), receives phone calls and a package from a listener who fears he will be the victim of 'the shadow people.' Initially sceptical until the caller later dies, Charlie then does some research and uncovers a supernatural, *Ring*-like curse that has been covered up by medical officials for the public's own safety... *Shadow people* is inspired by 'true events' – a medical study in the early 70s in which patients died in their sleep after claiming that 'shadow people' were out to get them. This intriguing film is better than expected; the story grips quite early on, and by the hour mark you'll find yourself genuinely concerned about what is fact and what is fiction. Director Matthew Arnold presents his film as a 'dramatic reconstruction,' similar to the type you see in true crime TV shows like *Crimewatch*. He also breaks up the narrative by inserting short YouTube clips and home video recordings of people discussing the events, and even the real Charlie Crowe being interviewed on tape (but whether these clips are genuine or all part of the illusion of reality is difficult to tell). Casual horror fans may be put off by this unorthodox approach to telling a story, but this is a subtle masterclass in how to carefully blend fact and fiction in such a way that many viewers will find themselves with a head-full of uneasy thoughts as the end credits roll.

Shocker (1989)
Dir: Wes Craven /USA
Serial Killer, Horace Pinker (Mitch Pileggi), is executed by electric chair and returns in the form of an electric power source to continue on his killing spree. A college football kid, equipped with psychic abilities after bumping his head on a goalpost, teams up with a detective to somehow put an end to the killings. But it's far from easy as Pinker now has the power to shift his being from person to person, literally possessing the bodies of anyone in contact to carry out his evil deeds... *Shocker* is an enjoyable if unremarkable flick. It's lively and action-packed, and moves from one absurd sequence to the next with no concern for practicalities or logic. In one sequence, the teenage hero is pursued by Pinker (in the guise of a cop) through a park, and he is shot at at least two dozen times with a handgun – Of course, every shot misses him while bystanders are picked off with ease. Anyway, minor annoyances aside, *Shocker* is a fun little film if you go in with low expectations. There's a streak of goofy humour throughout, and the film

shares the surreal, 'plastic reality' dream-world style with Craven's earlier *A Nightmare On Elm Street* (1984). And, for once, here is a Craven film that doesn't attempt to turn an entire sub-genre on its head in an 'oh so clever, Mr. Craven' sort of way. How modest of him. Look out for bit-parts and cameos from Craven, Heather Langenkamp and Ted Raimi.

Short Cuts (1993)
Dir: Robert Altman /USA
The lives of nine dysfunctional suburban couples in L.A. are intertwined. A fascinating three-hour examination of people living on the edge. Based on the stories of Raymond Carver, and offering superb performances from the likes of Andie McDowell, Jack Lemmon, Julianne Moore, Matthew Modine, Jennifer Jason Leigh, Chris Penn, Robert Downey Jr, Madeline Stowe, Tim Robbins, Tom Waits and Frances McDormand. Similar in style to *Magnolia*, *Crash* and *Happiness*, in the way it presents a panorama of life's problems, and is expertly weaved together with an assured hand by director Altman. It's a 188-minute masterpiece which never puts a foot wrong, despite its long running-time and daring performances.

Sick: The Life and Death of Bob Flanagan, Supermasochist (1997)
Dir: Kirby Dick /USA
Documentary on Bob Flanagan, the artist who learned to deal with the agony of cystic fibrosis by becoming a self-styled 'supermasochist'. He used suffering as the basis of his life and was involved in a sadomasochistic relationship. Flanagan famously appeared in the notorious NIN music video for *Broken* (1993) as the man in the torture chair having his genitals clawed by the metallic talons. But despite his good humour throughout *Sick*, this is a difficult film to watch. The final moments of his life were captured on camera and presented on screen, along with still photographs.

Sinister (2012)
Dir: Scott Derrickson /USA

One of the better films in this book is *Sinister* (2012), a creepy, supernatural tale grounded in the grittiness of true crime. Writer Ethan Hawke moves his family into a house that has a dark past. He finds some old 8mm films in the attic which show ritualized murders. And rather than inform the police about his discovery, he decides to investigate alone with the aim of writing a true crime best seller. However, his obsession with the case causes strange behaviour in his children and the collapse of his marriage. The snuff footage is very well crafted and unsettling; the family hanging from the tree has a 'lynched by the klan' quality to it. There are also slashed throats, burnings and drownings. As the plot unfolds, we discover that the snuff films are the extension of a Pagan deity (the 'eater of children'), and this makes for an interesting alternative to the usual found footage scenarios.

Sinister isn't perfect. There are some routine, predictable moments throughout, and the sinister ghoul at the centre of it all is stripped of much of its mystery, and as such, pushes the narrative very close to all-out silliness. The monster is in danger of becoming a Freddy Krueger-like boogeyman. To make the transition into farce complete, this deity could have spouted villainous lines like "You're all my children now," but thankfully that doesn't happen. I do get the impression that the filmmakers were pressured into including a boogeyman character in order to get the green light. I can imagine the execs' rationale for this: "Well, we love the script and all, but our market research tells us that all the popular horror movies of late had a boogeyman in them. So, in order for us to give the green light, we're going to need a monster... C'mon guys, what's wrong with you? This is a horror movie! Where's the monster?" etc, etc. And as a result, the mystery about the origin of the films, and the ambiguity of how they came to be – the balance between true crime and the otherworldly - is swept aside in favour of keeping the movie in line with such contemporary drivel as *Cabin In the Woods* and *Innkeepers*.

Slash Dance (1989)
Dir: James Shyman /USA
A woman undercover, whose "tits are too nice to be a cop," tracks

down a serial killer who has been picking off auditionees for a musical. This is an extremely low-budget rehash of Mario Bava's *Blood and Black Lace* (1964), and suffers badly from extraneous exposition, blatant time-padding sequences and spandex overload.

Slashers (2001)
Dir: Maurice Devereaux /Canada

By the early 00s, it wasn't long before the internet age crept its way into the snuff realm with a series of films which focused on evil websites and live streaming death. The first in this area was *Muzan-e* (1999), the Japanese AV shocker which blurred the line between fact and fiction by presenting it as a faux-documentary. It was later followed by *Slashers*, a narrative-based – but equally eccentric - take on the snuff genre which comes on like a cross between *Takashi's Castle* and *The Running Man* (1987). Six contestants have volunteered for a Japanese game show in which they have to pass through a maze while being pursued by maniacs, and the show is broadcast live across the globe. It's an interesting concept for a horror movie, and there are some fun moments here and there (including one character who is cut in half with a chainsaw), but it's ultimately forgettable and unremarkable, and isn't helped by the crappy performances, unconvincing characters and inane dialogue.

Slaughter Disc (2005)
Dir: David Kwitmire /USA

A porn addict orders a XXX DVD online only to find that it's actually a snuff movie featuring people he knew. It's a good idea for a film but is let down by the overlong graphic sex scenes which run for around fifteen minutes each and do nothing but obstruct the story line. The result is similar to *Amateur Porn Star Killer* in that the audience is expected to 'get off' on the mixture of sex and suffering. Forgive my cock for remaining unerect, but that's not my idea of fun.

Slaughterhouse (1987)
Dir: Rick Roesseler /USA

An old man, whose slaughterhouse business faces foreclosure, encourages his huge, retarded, pig-loving son to slaughter the locals as a way of settling his grudge against the Sheriff and court officials whom he blames for his destitution... *Slaughterhouse* is a low-budget 80s rehash of *The Texas Chain Saw Massacre* (1974) which expands on the premise of a family being forced to adapt to the industrial upheaval as the corporate bigwigs squeeze them out of the market, damaging their livelihoods and ensuring a violent reaction (as also seen in Tobe Hooper's classic). The film is quite well made, with lots of dark humour and a professional sheen that is rare in 80s cheapjack video swill. However, the death scenes – though certainly bloody enough – lack a certain panache; there's barely any musical accompaniment or anything to put an exclamation point on the scenes to separate them from the rest of the picture. Those not paying attention will miss the scenes of the Sheriff's deputy having his hand cut off, and another guy getting his head squashed by the maniac. 80s slasher freaks should get a kick out of it though.

The Slayer (1982)
Dir: J. S. Cardone /USA
A surrealist painter, Kay (Sarah Kendall), endures recurring nightmares about a demon killing her friends. And when her husband arranges a vacation for them and their buddies, Kay's protests against the trip fall on deaf ears. And, sure enough, not long after they arrive on the fishing island, someone – or some*thing* – begins wiping out the cats members, one by one... The concept of a dream demon coming to life and murdering the heroine's friends while she desperately tries to stay awake to avoid confronting the ghoul, may seem hokey nowadays, but *The Slayer* pre-dates Wes Craven's *A Nightmare on Elm Street* (1984) by a couple of years. The film can be commended for having adult characters instead of the usual teens, and for adding a supernatural twist to the 'slasher' movie template. Memorable death scenes include one character getting his head trapped and slowly decapitated by his own bodyweight, and a pitchfork murder which rivals the ones seen in *The Bogey Man* (1980) and *Friday the 13th Part 2* (1981).

Sleepstalker (1995)

Dir: Turi Meyer /USA

Journalist Jay Underwood is relieved to report on the execution of a serial killer known as 'The Sandman.' After all, the maniac did kill his family. However, a voodoo priest who is given access to the killer to read him his last rites, is actually in cahoots with him, and instead gives the maniac immortality as a shape-shifting demon intent on wreaking more havoc on the world. Owing much to Wes Craven's *Shocker* and *A Nightmare On Elm Street*, but also armed with some unique ideas of its own – such as the Sandman appearing in the form of sand that can pursue its victims even through locked doors by literally pouring itself through key holes, etc – but ultimately, the low-budget doesn't allow for a wholly effective telling of the story.

Slugs (1988)

(aka *Slugs: The Movie*; Orig title: *Slugs, muerte viscosa*)
Dir: Juan Piquer Simon /Spain /USA

A perpetually pissed-off health inspector tries to convince politicians that his town has been invaded by giant killer slugs. They think he's insane and ignore his pleas until the bodies start piling up... *Slugs* is a low-budget gem and a triumph for fans of creepy bug movies. It takes a while for the action to pick up, but once it does it never falters. We get the usual B-movie characters, such as the sceptical Sheriff, the all-knowing scientist and the teenage lovers joined at the genitals. The slugs themselves are long, black and repulsive, and there are literally *thousands* of them that have been breeding in the sewage pipes. And, unlike normal slugs, these things also have razor sharp teeth and devour flesh while they slither through the eye-sockets of their victims, slowly nibbling away at their internal organs. Mutated bug movies of the 50s and 60s put the blame on radiation (see giant radioactive ants in *Them!* (1954) and radioactive leeches in *Attack of the Giant Leeches* (1960)), and in the 70s it was pollution (see the mutant cockroaches of *Bug* (1975)). But here in the 80s, it's toxic waste that is to blame for the mutations as it is discovered that there is a secret waste dump in town. Gooey moments include a gardener hacking off his own hand with an axe, a man's head exploding in the middle of a restaurant, sending blood and bugs flying across the room, and another character is shredded alive in the sewers. *Slugs* would sit nicely on a tripple-bill with *Kingdom of the Spiders* (1977) and *The Deadly Spawn* (1983).

Snuff: A Documentary About Killing On Camera (2008)
Dir: Paul Von Stoetzel /USA

A cynical and offensive take on the supposed snuff documentary format is *Snuff: A Documentary About Killing On Camera.* Played entirely straight, it purports to be a factual report with 'academics', 'FBI profilers' and 'film experts' discussing whether or not snuff films actually exist. I noticed numerous factual errors while watching this, such as the claims that *The Texas Chain Saw Massacre* was based on a true story (it wasn't; it was actually very loosely based on the exploits of Ed Gein, who, although he did make masks out of human skin, he never chased teenagers around Texas with a chainsaw), and the Russian snuff-gang crime ring reeks of bullshit; only TWO articles were ever written about it in the whole world? Really? Much of this so-called documentary is so utterly fabricated as a cynical selling point, and anyone with even a passing interest in the subject will see it for what it is. At one point, one of the talking heads tries to qualify *Bowling For Columbine* as a snuff movie because it includes CCTV footage of the massacre, and the clearly political internet beheadings by Al Quaeda fanatics are also passed off as snuff. Not only are those claims wrong, but then we're actually *shown* that sickening footage for no other reason than to gain kudos with fans of *True Gore* and *Traces of Death*. For a more credible documentary on the subject, there's the episode of *The Dark Side of Porn* entitled *Does Snuff Exist?* (2006). It's a TV programme which inevitably leaves more questions than answers, but rightly acknowledges that the advance in readily available technology has made the whole snuff nightmare pretty much inevitable.

Snuff Killer: La morte in diretta (2003)
(aka *Snuff Trap*)
Dir: 'Pierre le Blanc' [Bruno Mattei] /Italy

Directed by Bruno Mattei, who, at 73 years old at the time, could barely direct his own bowel movements, much less a horror film. *Snuff Killer* is an Italian variant on *Hardcore* and *8mm*, but this time it's a woman trying to track down her kidnapped daughter through the murky underbelly of Europe's porno underground. And before long she finds herself roped into the hell of prostitution as a way of gaining some clues as to her girl's whereabouts. She eventually discovers that the snuff organisation responsible for the kidnapping is ruled over by an evil woman appropriately named Dr. Hades, and sure enough she finds herself in grave danger. This film is disappointingly sleaze-less for a Bruno Mattei movie. It left me longing for the glory days of *Blade Violent* and *The Other Hell*. Mattei died in 2007 after a frenzy of cheapjack productions late in life, including the sloppy *Cannibal Ferox 3*, the nonsensical *Cannibal Holocaust 2* and the downright appalling *Island of the Living Dead*. He will be sadly missed by, um, his kids. Probably.

Snuff-Movie (2005)
(aka *Man With a Movie Camera*)
Dir: Bernard Rose /UK
Bernard Rose, of *Paperhouse* and *Candyman* fame, entered the fray with *Snuff-Movie* (2005) which remains perhaps the finest web-based snuff film to date. Also known as *Man With a Movie Camera*, this film sees a group of actors arrive at an old mansion to make a mysterious movie, but little do they know that the house has a dark past. The house is fitted with hundreds of mini cameras, and the footage is relayed live on the internet. And before you know it, there are Mansonite gangs, severed heads, internet snuff, crucifixions and Satanic rites. *Snuff-Movie* is similar to *Last House On Dead Street* with its angle on snuff-as-performance-art; victims are martyred, literally crucified for a cause. Human sacrifice for the digital age. Rose purposely blurs the line between art and reality, and also targets the media, from its sensationalist reporting of the Tate/La Bianca murders to modern-day exploitation; how people mistreat each other (and how some even volunteer for it) out of greed and a hunger for fame, and how the media

are happy to pander to whatever cause for exactly the same reasons.

Snuff Perversions: Bizarre Cases of Death (1999)
Dir: D. J. Kary & Marcus Koch /USA
A cheesy comedy about a cop and a psychologist who watch a bunch of unconvincing snuff movies starring a few familiar faces from the Z-budget horror scene (including Tina Krause) before a pair of maniacs storm the studio and murder them so that they can get their hands on the incriminating tapes. A sequel followed the next year, *Snuff Perversions 2: More Bizarre Cases of Death* (aka *Shock 2000*).

Songs From The Second Floor (2000)
Dir: Roy Anderson /Sweden /France /Denmark /Norway /Germany
In an unknown European city, a man sets fire to his own furniture store for the insurance payout, while other characters find themselves in bizarre situations. A darkly funny set of jagged vignettes on the themes of personal despair and middle class alienation, *Songs From The Second Floor* comes on like a series of comedy sketches with a dark and morbid edge, and includes sequences in which a magician accidentally saws open one of his volunteers, and a young child is pushed off a cliff in a bizarre ritual.

Spasms (1983)
Dir: William Fruet /Canada
Western anthropologists argue over whether or not to destroy a demonic monster that was summoned by African tribesmen. Millionaire Oliver Reed wants to keep it alive for research purposes, while Reed's wife and psychologist Peter Fonda set out to destroy it before any more people are killed. Of course, Satanic forces are also at work, and after a spate of *Omen*-inspired fatal 'accidents,' the demon escapes and rampages through the city. Meanwhile, a group of Satanists also want to be in possession of 'the great serpent' for their own sinister purposes. *Spasms* is a watchable, if disastrous, production which ran out of money before many of the key sequences were shot. The filmmakers had to make do with padding things out with extraneous footage and

outtakes. Had the film been completed in its intended form we may have had a minor gem on our hands. But as it stands, it often gets branded with 'worst movie ever' stigma on IMDb. It certainly isn't the worst. Nowhere near the worst. Only today I watched *Slash Dance*, and that's a hell of a lot worse than this, believe me.

Special Effects (1984)
Dir: Larry Cohen/USA

A recurring theme in fictional snuff-based movies is the megalomaniac filmmaker; from Terry Hawkins in *Last House On Dead End Street*, Boris Arkardin in *Snuff-Movie*, Vukmir in *A Serbian Film*, Brauth in *Melancholie der Angel*, Bill in *The Great American Snuff Film*, Jefe in *The Counselor*, 'The Wall Street Butcher' in *The Poughkeepsie Tapes*, and many others. These characters may vary in their backgrounds and outward aggression, but they're united by a common attitude which places themselves above everyone else: They harbour Sadean philosophies and hold their fellow humans in outright contempt. Many of these types of characters also view their filmmaking as ongoing artistic projects and view everyone who doesn't share the same opinions as weak and dumb. Larry Cohen's *Special Effects,* a hitchcockian B-movie, focuses on a reclusive sicko filmmaker who is obsessed with the meaning of reality. Zapruder happens to be his favourite 'director'. And when runaway wife, Maryjean (*Ms.45*'s Zoe Tamerlis) breaks away from softcore films to work with him, he murders her in his bed while covertly filming the crime through a one-way mirror. The police suspect Maryjean's redneck husband of killing her, and when the filmmaker decides to make a movie about her death, those involved in the production soon begin to learn what a sly, manipulative scumbag he is.

Species (1995)
Dir: Roger Donaldson /USA

Scientists receive a message from outer space informing them how to construct alien DNA. Like idiots, they do it, and this results in the beautiful blonde, Natasha Henstridge (if they all look like her, why not make more?). The downside is that whenever she gets horny or upset she transforms into a ferocious killing machine and goes on the rampage. Ex-model Henstridge is fantastic as the sexy alien in this amusing and silly sci-fi horror. Michael Madsen and Ben Kingsley do all they can to not to smirk while they deliver their lines.

Species II (1998)
(aka *Species II: Offspring*)
Dir: Peter Medak /USA
An astronaut on the first manned mission to Mars gets infected by an alien and begins to mutate. Back on earth, he makes a beeline for sexy Henstridge for a matter of urgent, uncontrollable reproduction. Panned by the critics on its release, this sequel continues the campy fun of part one, but is not quite as good. Still, it's worth watching for the slimy alien sex.

Species III (2004)
Dir: Brad Turner /USA
With this third entry in the series, things drop to TV movie quality. This time, Eve's daughter breaks out of the science facility where she has been brought up and hits the streets for more bloody mayhem. The plot is also expanded somewhat to deal with the 'half breeds,' half human/half alien outcasts who often succumb to death and disease. As straight-to-DVD sequels go, it's not too bad.

Species: The Awakening (2007)
Dir: Nick Lyon /USA
This fourth and final instalment in the *Species* saga sees a DNA specialist take his half breed daughter to Mexico to undergo a reversal of the alien side of her genetic make-up. However, things go wrong, and she manages to break free and take to the streets in a destructive rampage in her efforts to – yep, you guessed it – find someone to pro-create with! The producers decided to appease fans this time by embracing HR Giger's alien designs to the full (they were more or less dropped from *Species III*), but still, this is a tame, lukewarm effort

compared with the earlier entries, and often feels like a space-age re-telling of Mary Shelley's *Frankenstein*.

The Spiral (1998)
(aka *Ringu: Anthology of Terror;* aka *Ring 4: The Spiral*)
(Orig title: *Rasen*)
Dir: Joji Iida /Japan
Released on DVD in the UK during a slew of Japanese weirdies being churned out at the time (*Hiruko The Goblin*, *Princess Blade*, *Uzumaki*, etc), *The Spiral* shouldn't be confused with *Uzumaki* (which translates as 'spiral'). It's a confusing sequel to Hideo Nakata's *Ringu* which is just as silly and over-the-top as *Exorcist II: The Heretic*. After the mysterious death of a friend, a young pathologist comes across the cursed video tape haunted by the child ghost, Sadako. The film proved so unpopular in Japan that the production company made *Ringu 2* in order to erase it from memory. Dull, sprawling and lethargic rather than terrifying, *The Spiral* was later re-released on DVD under the title *Ring 4: The Spiral*, implying that it was a distant cash-in rather than the direct sequel, which it originally was.

Spontaneous Combustion (1990)
Dir: Tobe Hooper /USA
In 1955, a young couple, Brian and Peggy, volunteer to sit in an underground state-of-the-art bomb shelter in the Nevada desert while scientists carry out hydrogen bomb tests right above them. The couple emerge unscathed, and, thanks to newsreel footage of their days underground, they become national heroes. Peggy later gives birth to a boy they call David. However, the parents burn to death in the maternity ward for no apparent reason. The orphaned baby is re-named Sam, and he grows up to be a struggling actor and divorcee (Brad Dourif), and people around him begin burning to death in mysterious circumstances. Turns out that, not only is Sam responsible for the burnings through some kind of psychic pyromania, but the bomb tests his parents were involved with may also have something to do with it... This film starts off well enough but sags quite badly after the hour mark

and never recovers. *Spontaneous Combustion* came along after director Tobe Hooper delivered the late 80s duds like *Invaders From Mars* (1986) and *Texas Chainsaw Massacre 2* (1986), and the rut only continued with turds like *I'm Dangerous Tonight* (1990), *Night Terrors* (1993) and others. This film kind of sits in the middle; it isn't the complete disaster that many have claimed, but nor is it on a par with his better works, like *Death Trap* (1976), *'Salem's Lot* (1979) and *Lifeforce* (1985). Taken on its own merits, *Spontaneous Combustion* is your typical direct-to-video horror fare of the early 90s. In its favour, Dourif offers a decent performance as the tortured protagonist, the action comes thick and fast, and almost every character ends up burning to death. Look out for cameo appearances by Hooper, along with John Landis (who is burned to death in a radio studio), and cult legend, 'Buck' Flowers, in a radio voice-over part as a preacher.

Stephen King's Sleepwalkers (1992)
Dir: Mick Garris /USA
Two shape-shifting monsters disguised as a mother and son terrorize a small town in their search for the blood of virgins. But feisty Madchen Amick refuses to give in so easily. A disappointing effort which nonetheless contains its fair share of gruesomeness (cat lovers will be dismayed at the number of dead and mutilated felines on display). Hardcore genre fans will spot familiar faces like Joe Dante, Tobe Hooper, Clive Barker, John Landis and Stephen King (who also wrote the screenplay) in cameo roles.

St. John's Wort (2001)
(Orig title: *Otogiriso*)
Dir: Ten Shimoyama /Japan
The influence of *The Blair Witch Project* had soon crept its way over to Japan in the early 00s for *St. John's Wort*, a creepy shocker in which characters foolishly head off in search of an isolated house which is surrounded by the eponymous herb, and are terrorized by an evil twin in the attic. The heroine creates bizarre artwork for video games, and this is a good excuse to decorate the look of the film in a visual style of

hi-tech glossiness added in post-production. The ending is quite a surprise.

Strange Days (1995)
Dir: Kathryn Bigelow /USA

With *Videodrome* (1982), the snuff-themed movie entered the sci-fi realm when a television entrepreneur discovered a pirate satellite signal that caused brain tumours to develop in the viewers. Writer/director David Cronenberg used the hallucinatory visuals and far-out themes to fashion an allegorical tale about censorship and government control. More than a decade later, sci-fi snuff hit the screens once again with *Strange Days* (1995), but this time the filmmakers chickened out of delivering the subversive goods. Set during the last few days of 1999 in L.A., *Strange Days* is about an ex-cop, Lenny (Ralph Fiennes), who runs a dealership in 'clips' – movies recorded from people's memories and sold on the black market to those who wish to experience them. Lenny sees himself as an ethical dealer because he refuses to push snuff (or 'blackjack' clips). These contraband recordings are taken from those equipped with a Superconducting Quantum Interference Device (SQUID), a device easily concealed under a hat or wig. Lenny uses the technology on himself to re-live moments from his past and to ease his broken heart after his split from Faith (Juliette Lewis), a rising pop star under the control of a menacing record label owner (Michael Wincott). Before long, Lenny is shown a brutal snuff clip of a woman being raped and murdered. And, as he investigates those responsible for the clip, he and his friends are caught up in a murder conspiracy that could bring about an apocalyptic race war.

This future-phobic thriller is fascinating and annoying in equal measure. On the one hand, it attempts to update *Peeping Tom* with its angle on voyeurism and killer's eye camera work. It's also visually stunning and sustains an atmosphere of dread and paranoia. It offers a bleak, noir-ish vision of the (then) near-future like *Blade Runner* before it. Some complained that the plot is overly convoluted and crammed in to the point where the narrative spills over into confusion, but I disagree. I found it quite easy to follow, despite the clunky exposition through dialogue. For me, the problem is that too much of the story and the character's motivations are given away through needless exposition. Just look at the scene after Lenny and Max (Tom Sizemore) have watched the snuff clip, for example. While they try to ascertain who could make such a clip, the viewers are given details about the switching of signals while they're at it:

Lenny – He stalks her, he rapes her and he kills her...

Max – And he records it. It's a thrill, right?

Lenny – Yeah.

Max – He wants to see it again and again and again.

Lenny – He records himself raping and killing her.

Max – But at the same time he's sending a signal to her...

Lenny - ...So she feels what he feels while he's inside her. The thrill, while he's killing her, is sent to her, hightening her fear, which in turn hightens the turn-on for him... He makes her see her own death and feeds on her reaction. He records it all. Everything.

But the most annoying thing about *Strange Days* is its attempts to restore faith in (white) police authority. The film is a cultural by-product of the Rodney King beating, and yet it also serves as a calculated Hollywood propaganda piece. Director Kathryn Bigelow and co-author James Cameron posit their film as a meaningful statement about the racial and socio/economic implications of the Rodney King video and the subsequent riots, and yet the L.A. Police are ultimately let off the hook here. What we're left with is a 'Hey look! We have a white man and a black woman falling in love! Aww, what sweet racial harmony!' The questions this film raises are finally swept aside and replaced with confetti and pyrotechnics. It's downright insulting.

The Strangeness (1980)

Dir: David Michael Hillman /USA

An exploration party visits an old mine, Gold Spike, that has been closed for almost a hundred years. And while they explore the dark maze of rocks and tunnels, they spook each other with tales of urban legend about a creature that is said to have lived in the cave and killed dozens of miners back in the days of the gold rush. And in the final reel, the impressive monster makes an appearance... Released on VHS in Europe and North America in the mid to late 80s, *The Strangeness* was actually completed as early as 1980. It isn't the greatest monster movie ever made, but, considering how few people have seen it, this is well worth a watch, especially since it was re-issued on DVD. It boasts good characterisation, heavy atmospherics, and a Giger-esque clay-motion creature complete with a phallic-like head, creepy tentacles and a large, meaty vagina for a face.

The Strangler (1964)

Dir: Burt Topper /USA

A serial killer thriller which was released when Boston was still reeling from a string of headline-grabbing (and then unsolved) stranglings. It's a much maligned, low-budget offering with the talented Victor Buono - who first starred in *What Ever Happened To Baby Jane?* (1962) - as a deeply damaged psycho killer who preys on nurses as a form of revenge for being abused by his appalling mother. It's exploitative, indebted to Hitchcock's *Psycho* (1960) – which means that no Freudian cliché is left unturned – but it's also gritty and surprisingly nasty for its time.

Soul Survivors (2001)

Dir: Stephen Carpenter /USA

The producers of *I Know What You Did Last Summer* and *Urban Legend* tried their hands once again at a teen terror flick, and failed miserably as we get a pretty student who loses her boyfriend in a car wreck and then finds herself spooked by discomforting hallucinations. Talented up-and-comers Wes Bentley and Casey Affleck were completely wasted in this, and the silly visuals – which are supposed to represent the dark dimension between life and death – are incredibly silly. Plus, the twist ending is one of the worst in memory.

Suffer, Little Children (1983)
Dir: Alan Briggs /UK
A mysterious mute girl shows up at a children's home and causes demonic havoc among the other children and staff before Jesus Christ makes an appearance to magically banish her back to hell. *Suffer, Little Children* (1983) is a 'home movie' shot on video at a London drama school. The 'direction' is non-existent; the camera is almost completely static in every shot, the performances are generally terrible, etc. Nonetheless, it got a video release in the 80s, and was available to rent up and down the country. The video even got caught up in the 'video nasties' panic when police raided the offices of distribution company, Films Galore, and seized the tapes. The company hit back by threatening to sue the OPA's Public Prosecutions' goons for £3000 a day, arguing that the police had acted beyond their powers by purposely misinterpreting the Video Recordings Act (VRA) and acting on a film before the BBFC cuts were made. The tapes were not available to the public at the time of the raid, so Films Galore had every right to sue. Unsurprisingly, neither the police nor the Director of Public Prosecutions would comment on the matter, though James Ferman (who was head of the BBFC at the time) admitted in a letter to the company that there were inadequacies in interpreting the VRA. The Meg Shanks drama school was immediately closed down as a direct result of the negative press (headlines included 'School of video nasties'). Oh, feel that rush of pipsqueak power coursing through your veins. Congratulations, you quashed a bit of fun!

Superstition (1982)
(aka *The Witch*)
Dir: James W. Roberson /Canada
The evil spirit of a witch that was drowned to death by the Church in 1692, returns to the 'black pond' almost three centuries later to dish out

some revenge on the descendants of the original townfolk... Anyone familiar with movies like *Black Sunday* (1960), *Mark of the Witch* (1972) and *Burned at the Stake* (1981) will have seen it all before. But in its favour, *Superstition* takes the hokey theme and delivers the story with an urgent, action-packed appeal. Barely a minute passes without a character revelation or the lead-up to a vicious death scene. And the production values are very impressive for a low-budget fright flick of its time, and looks wonderful on DVD all these years later. Gory highlights include a human head exploding in a microwave, a body torn in half on a window pane, a Priest having his chest ripped open by a runaway circular saw, and a young woman graphically staked through the forehead.

Surf II (1984)
Dir: Randall Badat /USA

A zombie punk infection spreads through a beach party after a vengeful chemistry nerd (*Grease*'s Eddie Deezen) contaminates the Buzz cola drinks. Before you know it, the revellers are scoffing down garbage, rioting, and have somehow grown multi-coloured mohawks and are suddenly clad in spikes and pins and leather. It's the kind of film that defies all synopsis' and criticism, but if you enjoyed *Street Trash* (1987), then chances are you'll like this too. The video cover sums it up best: "Menlo Schwartzer – the geekiest mad scientist of all – wants to rid the world of surfers by transforming them into garbage-ingesting zombie punks! But no way dude can he stop their most awesome party!" A timeless classic that was never released on DVD.

Taboo (2002)
Dir: Max Makowski /USA

Shot in Romania, *Taboo* is a typical youth-appeal, old dark house story which borrows elements from *April Fool's Day* (1986). A group of college buddies spend New Years Eve in an old mansion during a thunderstorm. Murders take place, but this turns out to be a planned hoax to expose a blackmailer. And that's when the real murders begin... This is routine silliness all the way; the smart dialogue and bitchy characters are utterly overshadowed by the sense that this film was created as a made-for-market generic slasher template.

Tales From the Crypt (1972)

Dir: Freddie Francis /UK

An Amicus compendium of tongue-in-cheek horror stories based on the famous EC comic strips. This film throws several British character actors into horrifying situations. In the most memorable of the five tales, Joan Collins is attacked by an evil Santa Claus, while Peter Cushing, Ian Hendry, Patrick Magee and Richard Greene have to deal with all kinds of spooky goings-on. A quintet of ghoulish fun.

Tales From the Crypt (1989-1996)

(aka *HBO's Tales From the Crypt*)

Dir: -Various- /USA

An American horror anthology series made for the HBO cable channel. Running for seven seasons totalling 93 episodes, the show was based on the gory EC comics from the 50s of the same name (plus a range of other comics, including *The Vault of Horror, Crypt of Terror,* and *Haunt of Fear*). Each show was presented by the 'Cryptkeeper', a cackling skull-faced puppet that introduced tales in which characters made bad decisions which inevitably led to their gruesome deaths. Memorable episodes include '*You, Murderer*' (season 6, episode 15) in which Humphrey Bogart, and Alfred Hitchcock made 'cameo' appearances thanks to the magic of digital technology. It was also directed by co-producer Robert Zemeckis. Other memorable episodes include '*Cutting Cards*', '*The Switch*' and '*Carrion Death*'. The show's broadcast on cable allowed it to be exempt from the strict censorship of regular network television, and this meant that things like graphic violence, bad language and nudity could flourish (though re-runs on regular networks were often censored). Episodes were sometimes directed by established horror filmmakers like John Frankenheimer, William Friedkin, Walter Hill, Tobe Hooper and Freddie Francis (Francis also directed the Amicus film, *Tales From the Crypt* in 1972).

Special guest directors also showed up, including Michael J. Fox,

Tom Hanks and Arnold Schwarzenegger, the latter two even making a cameo appearances in the show. Numerous spin-offs were made, including movies (*Demon Kinight* (1995), *Bordello of Blood* (1996) and *Ritual* (2002)), a Saturday morning cartoon (*Tales From the Cryptkeeper*, 1993), a kiddies game show (*Secrets of the Cryptkeeper's Haunted House*, 1996-1997), a sci-fi variant of the original show (*Perversions of Science*, 1997) and even a radio series.

First broadcast in the summer of 1989, season one gets off to a frying start with Walter Hill's *The Man Who Was Death*, in which Bill Saddler stars as a State executioner whose job it is to pull the lever on the electric chair. When the death penalty is abolished, he loses his job, and he sees the justice system go to pot with murderers walking free from court. Outraged at what he sees as judicial weakness, he resorts to vigilante action, electrocuting to death those he feels have escaped justice. However, karma eventually catches up with him ("Don't worry, boys and girls, I'm sure he never knew watt hit him. Hee hee")... In the seasonal farce, *And All Through the Night* – directed by Zemeckis from a script by Fred Dekker – a woman kills her husband on Christmas Eve by smashing his head in with a fire poker. She plans on fleeing the scene and meeting up with her illicit lover. However, an evil Sanata Claus shows up wielding an axe... This episode was based on the same *Vault of Horror* comic that formed the basis of the Joan Collins segment of Freddie Francis' 70s version of *Tales From the Crypt*. The best episode of season one is undoubtedly Richard Donner's *Dig That Cat... He's Real Gone*, in which a meddling scientist conducts experiments on a homeless man and succeeds in giving him nine lives by transfusing his mortality with a cat. Together they hit the road to fortune as part of a macabre carnival act, astounding audiences with death-defying stunts – drowning, hanging, electrocution, etc - ("Maybe this dying shit's taking years off my life"). However, it isn't long before greed and literal backstabbing muddies his count of how many lives he actually has left... In the Faustian *Only Sin Deep*, a street hooker called Miss Vane is desperate to live the high life. So she robs and murders her pimp. And when she tries to sell his gold, the owner of the pawn shop instead gives her $10,000 to 'capture' her beauty in a wax cast of her face. And as she spends a few months in the lap of luxury with the man of her dreams, she notices that her pretty looks are fading fast... In Tom Holland's *Lover Come Hack To Me*, newly-weds Amanda Plummer and Stephen Shellen spend a rain-soaked honeymoon evening stuck in an old dark house where competing murder plots go head to head with a large inheritance at stake... And finally, in Mary Lambert's *Collection Completed*, M. Emmet Walsh stars as a recently retired grumpy old man who finds himself a new hobby to deal with his wife's fondness for taking in stray pets...

Season two (1990) gets off to a great start with *Dead Right* in which Demi Moore stars as a hot barmaid. She allows herself to be 'wooed' into a relationship with a large, overweight man after her psychic assures her that he will come into a fortune. And though she finds him repulsive, she sticks around, spurred on by the psychic's vision that he will die a violent death shortly after they marry. However, destiny doesn't quite go according to her wishes... Arnold Schwarzenegger pops up next to direct *The Switch* – he also makes a cameo appearance in the intro – in which an old millionaire takes drastic measures to restore his youth so that he can win the heart of a much younger woman, with disastrous consequences... Walter Hill returns with *Cutting Cards*, a classic episode starring Lance Henriksen and Kevin Tighe as a pair of stubborn old gamblers who agree to settle their differences with intense games of Russian Roulette and 'chop poker.' This episode was the inspiration for the Tarantino segment in the anthology film, *Four Rooms* (1995), and also includes an appearance from *Crypt* regular, Roy Brocksmith as a bartender. Chris Walas' *'Til Death* sees a wealthy landowner use a voodoo potion to win the lust of a highly-strung English aristocrat. However, when he causes her to overdose on the horny potion, her corpse breaks out of the ground and molests him. The bumbling fool does all he can to destroy the ghoul, but even when she catches fire, her charred corpse still wants nookie ("So much for 'burning desire,'" hee hee)... In *Three's a Crowd,* a man feels that he is losing his wife to his rich best friend. The three of them go on holiday together, and the paranoia brings him to breaking point. The ending of this episode is especially horrific. Next up, Fred Dekker takes to the director's chair for *The Thing From the Grave*, in which a fashion photographer finds himself attracted to a beautiful model. She's attracted to him too, but the problem is she's already in a relationship with her manager, an uber-arsehole. However, their passion for each other is so great that they end up fucking anyway, and so the boyfriend lures the photographer into a death trap and a shallow grave. He then sets up an even more elaborate revenge for the girl who betrayed him. But little does he know that he's in for a ghoulish surprise of his own... In *The Sacrifice*, an insurance agent murders an arrogant client so that he can collect the money and steal his wife. And all seems to be running smoothly until Michael Ironside shows up to blackmail him... In *For Cryin' Out Loud*, the owner of a rock club attempts to steal $1 million in cash from a charity concert fund. He even commits murder to cover his tracks. However, his conscience – voiced by comedian Sam Kinison – delights in tormenting him every step of the way... Tom Holland's *Four-Sided Triangle* sees a young Patricia Arquette as a confused farm girl who is in love with a scarecrow, and is forced to defend herself against her lecherous boss and his wife... Richard Donner's *The Ventriloquist's Dummy* - written for the screen by Frank Darabont – stars Bobcat Goldthwait as an aspiring showman who seeks the advice of a retired master. However, the old man holds a dark secret under his glove... The first weak entry in the series is *Judy, You're Not Yourself Today*, in which a vain housewife has her body stolen by a doorstep cosmetics rep via a magic necklace... Much better is Jack Sholder's blackly funny *Fitting Punishment* which stars Moses Gunn as an evil, penny-pinching mortician whose orphaned nephew comes to stay with him. The old man shows the kid how to cut corners to keep the business running, but his evil ways eventually come back to haunt him... In *Korman's Kalamity*, male fertility pills work wonders at firing up the imagination of a comic book artist. But there also happens to be monstrous side-effects... *Lower Berth* is another below average episode that centres on a carnival freak show host who is duped into buying the cursed remains of a 4000-year-old Egyptian mummy... Much better is *Mute Witness To Murder*, in which Patricia Clarkson witnesses a husband murder his wife in the opposite building. She immediately collapses in a mute and catatonic state. Her husband finds her on the balcony and calls for a doctor. And when the doc shoes up, he turns out to be the same man who has just killed his wife... The last three episodes of season two are rather silly schedule-fillers – *Television Terror* is about a reality TV show broadcast live from a haunted house, *My Brother's Keeper* charts the fall-out of siamese twins, with very distinct personalities, who go to war over their surgical separation, and in *The Secret*, an orphaned child is sent to live with a weird, childless couple in a huge mansion.

Broadcast throughout the summer of 1991, season three contains fourteen episodes starting with *Loved To Death* - which echoes an earlier episode, *'Til Death* – in which a screenwriter uses a magic potion to win the heart of an attractive neighbour he's obsessed with ("Miranda, I'm fucked-out!"). It was followed by another classic episode, *Carrion Death*, which stars Kyle MacLachlan as an armed robber fleeing to Mexico with a motorcycle cop in close pursuit. Without giving away any spoilers, it's worth noting here that the criminal makes some incredibly dumb decisions in his efforts to be free, but that's perhaps the whole point; he fashions a DIY axe, but uses it to strike the wrong area. And also, the key to freedom is right there the whole time in the dead guy's gut... Anyway, next up Michael J. Fox serves as guest director on *The Trap*, a tale in which an obnoxious man fakes his own death with the help of his wife and brother in order to collect the $500,000 life insurance payout. However, the wife and brother have a thing for each other, and plot a very different outcome... Another great episode is *Abra Cadaver* which opens with a brilliant practical joke in an autopsy room. But the laughs soon turn to horror when the victim suffers a heart attack. Cut to years later, and we learn that the prankster and the victim are brothers who both work in medical research. And the victim decides to get some payback on his little bro... In *Top Billing,* a struggling actor hits rock bottom when he is evicted from his apartment and his girlfriend moves in with another man. He auditions for the role of Hamlet in a run-down theatre, but snaps and becomes a mad murderer when his acting rival lands the part instead of him... In Tobe Hooper's *Dead Wait*, a tale of greed, voodoo and double-crossing, a petty thug (James Remar) gains the trust of a wealthy plantation owner (John Rhys-Davis). The thug manages to steal a valuable black pearl, but a voodoo sorceress (Whoopi Goldberg) leads him into a deadly trap... Elliot Silverstein's spoofy *The Reluctant Vampire* stars Malcolm McDowell as an age-old bloodsucker with a heart. He passes the time by working the night shift as a security officer at a blood bank, and helps himself to the bags of plasma which he drinks from a cocktail glass. Mr. Longtooth's morality, however, is put to the test when the secretary comes onto him... This episode, for all its silliness, has some good ideas, such as the holy water pistols, Michael Berryman as a bumbling vampire hunter, and McDowell's fangs which jut out like pointy erections every time the secretary embraces him... John Harrison's *Easel Kill Ya* stars Tim Roth as a struggling painter who accidentally kills a noisy neighbour. The death inspires a painting which he sells for $20,000, and so for further inspiration he engineers a few more fatal mishaps. But when he tries to save the life of an art student friend, he makes a grave mistake ("Now *that's* a still life, hee hee")... In *Undertaking Palor*, a group of teens break into a mortuary to film a dead body. However, they also stumble upon a murder conspiracy and a mad mortician who beats the corpses with a mallet. The following day, one of the boy's fathers is killed by the crooks, so they grab a video camera and head back to the mortuary with the intention of securing some video evidence. But it isn't easy as the deranged mortician thinks nothing of pouring embalming fluid into the chest cavities of victims that aren't even dead yet... In *Mournin' Mess*, a womanising journalist investigates a spate of killings among the city's homeless. And while digging for clues, he falls into a literal underground conspiracy run by bloodthirsty, bald-headed ghouls that pose as members of a homeless charity organisation... Russell Mulcahy's *Split Second* – written for the screen by Richard Matheson – concerns the boss of a logging firm (Brion James) whose jealous streak gets out of control when his attractive wife turns the heads of his lumberjack workers. A new employee is seduced by the bored wife, and when the boss catches them together he beats the man with an axe, blinding him. After his recovery, the young man's workmates help him to get bloody revenge on the couple in a macabre stunt at a log-cutting tournament... In Walter Hill's *Deadline*, an alcoholic reporter meets a mysterious woman called Vicky in a bar. He quits drinking to show her how serious he is, but she insists on keeping their relationship as a casual fling. One night he witnesses a cafe owner murder his wife, and after listening to the murderer's story of how his wife would pick up random guys from bars for one-night-stands, he realises that the victim is Vicky. But he also realises that she's not quite dead. And his sense of betrayal overwhelms him as he reaches for her throat ("What some people won't do for a good 'stiff one,' hee hee")... In *Spoiled*, a mad scientist who has been working on reanimating a rabbit, discovers that his fantasist wife has been shagging the cable guy. So he subjects them both to a prolonged surgical procedure in the basement whereby he swaps their heads around and brings them back to life so that they can marvel at his handywork... The final episode of season three is *Yellow* – it's also longer than usual at 38 minutes – set in France in World War 1. The son of a general (Eric Douglas) is sent on a risky mission to prove that he isn't a coward. However, his cowardly conduct leads to his fellow soldiers being killed. He is court marshalled and sentenced to death by firing squad. However, on the eve of his execution, his father visits him with a cunning plan... *Yellow* also stars Lance Henriksen as an ill-fated soldier, Dan Ackroyd as the General's right hand man, and Kirk Douglas as the father who is determined that his son will be remembered as a gallant man. This episode is different in tone from the usual *Crypt* fare; the tongue-in-cheek style is nowhere to be seen, and instead we get a poignant and sobering tale that ends the season on a sombre note.

The disappointing season 4 (1992) sees the rot setting in with stories watered-down with toothless scripts and weak endings to make the show more palatable for mainstream audiences. Things get off to a choppy start with Tom Hanks' *None But the Lonely Heart*, about an evil man who has made his fortune by bumping off his wives for the inheritance money. He sets his sights on a new companion, a rich elderly widow. He worms his way into her life, and she falls head over heels for him. And after they marry, he puts his murderous plan into place, but comes to a sticky end in a mausoleum. Look out for cameos from Hank's himself as a victim who has his head rammed into a television screen, and Sugar Ray Leonard as a gravedigger... In the disappointing *This'll Kill Ya*, Dylan McDermott takes revenge on his colleagues after they inject him with an experimental virus that has no antidote... Not much better is William Friedkin's *On a Deadman's Chest*, which sees a rock singer (in a band called 'Exorcist') head to the rough side of town to get a tattoo. However, he hates it. And when he undergoes surgery to have it removed, it just comes back. In the end, the awful tattoo drives him to madness and murder... The rut continues with *Seance*, a tale in which con artists end up killing one of their marks, so they turn their attentions onto the victim's blind wife instead... Slightly better is *Beauty Rest*, in which an actress (Mimi Rogers), jealous of her roommate's success at landing roles, accidentally kills her. She then develops a taste for murder, and bumps off another rival before landing a dream job that soon becomes a nightmare... In *What's Cookin'*, Christopher Reeve serves up his mean landlord's (Meat Loaf's) remains as steaks so that he can keep his struggling diner in business ("The restaurant business is a little hard to swallow")... In Peter Medak's *New Arrival*, David Warner stars as a radio psychologist who visits the home of a mother (Zelda Rubinstein) whose mentally disturbed daughter leads him to a grim discovery in the attic... Richard Donner's western-themed *Showdown* – adapted to the screen by Frank Darabont – follows an outlaw as he shoots dead a Texas ranger and meets a strange Irishman in a bar who offers him a 'medical tonic' that he is assured will quicken his gun-drawing reflexes. However, as soon as he drinks it, his deceased victims appear around him and send him to hell... Tom Holland returns to the director's seat with the lacklustre *King of the Road*, in which Brad Pitt plays a cocky young road racer who meets his match when he messes with the daughter of a road cop, who is also legendary himself behind the wheel. And all leads to a fiery finale ("Now that's what *I* call 'burning rubber,' hee hee")... Next up, John Frankenheimer joins the fray with *Maniac At Large*, in which Blythe Danner plays a nervous librarian who believes that she will be the next victim of a serial killer that has been making the local headlines... In *Split Personality*, Joe Pesci stars as a con man who gets more than he bargains for when he attempts to scam a couple of reclusive billionaire twins... *Strung Along* sees a puppeteer with heart problems – and who also communicates with his doll – suspect his wife of cheating on him. The final image of this episode is brilliantly creepy... In *Werewolf Concerto*, a lycanthrope is on the loose on the grounds of a luxury hotel, and the guests – which include Charles Fleischer, Timothy Dalton, Beverly D'Angelo and Dennis Farina – have to work out who among them is the beastie... And finally, in Elliot Silverstein's *Curiosity Killed*, a bickering old couple (Kevin McCarthy and Margot Kidder) are camping in the woods. Another couple on the trip lets the old man into a secret concerning a youth potion, and Kidder suspects the men of murder...

Broadcast in the winter of 1993, season five sees a return to form for the series, and includes a couple of gems. First up is *Death of Some Salesmen*, in which Ed Begley, Jr stars as a con man who goes around scamming grieving relatives, and eventually targets the wrong house. This episode is perhaps most notable for the appearance of Tim Curry who plays three roles as members of the redneck family... In Kyle MacLachlan's *As Ye Sow*, a man employs the services of private detectives to snoop on his wife as he is convinced she is having an affair. The investigation leads to a Catholic Priest, and when the husband pays to have him whacked, he soon comes to regret it. This one also features Patsy Kensit as the wife trying – and failing – to perform with an 'Irish' accent... One of the gems of season five is *Forever Ambergis*, which stars Roger Daltery as a combat photographer who ropes a talented young colleague (Steve Buscemi) into joining him on a dangerous assignment in Central America. However, it turns out to be all a ruse so that he can return home and steal the young man's girlfriend... In *Food For Thought*, another character loses his head over a pretty girl when a jealous carnival clown discovers that the psychic lady is in love with the fire-swallower... Next up is Russell Mulcahy's *People Who Live in Brass Hearses*. Perhaps the most memorable episode of season five, this stars Bill Paxton as a foul-tempered thug who ropes his younger brother (Brad Dourif) into helping him get revenge on the ice cream man whose testimony put him behind bars years earlier. However, he doesn't take into account his little brother's trigger-happy ways, and the ice cream man's peculiar secret... In *Two For the Show*, a man tries to dispose of his wife's body after stabbing her to death. A cop shows up on the doorstep after receiving reports of a scream. And after a quick look around the house, the cop thinks all is well and leaves. However, the two men meet again later that night at a train station where the murderous husband is transporting a large, suspicious package... In *House of Horror*, fraternity initiates are challenged to make it to the top floor of a haunted house. However, when they fail to return, the sadistic leader of the club (Kevin Bacon) heads up there only to find that the sorority girls have a nasty little surprise of their own to dish out... In *Well Cooked Hams*, Billy Zane stars as a failing magician who murders a grand illusionist and steals his 'box of death' idea, only to find his work sabotaged when trying to perform the death-defying stunt himself... In *Creep Course*, a high school football player attempts to steal exam questions from the home of his teacher with the aid of a nerdy bookworm. However, once at the teacher's house, the girl is betrayed and locked in the basement with an immortal mummy ("Ewww, I guess that's a wrap for Findlay, hee hee")... Uli Edel's *Came the Dawn* stars Perry King as an outwardly mild-mannered man who picks up a woman in a rainstorm as her truck has broken down. He drives her back to his country cabin for some *Dressed To Kill*-style mayhem... The worst episode of season five is probably *Oil's Well That Ends Well,* which stars Lou Diamond Phillips and Priscilla Presley as con artists who convince a bunch of old men to invest in 'recently-discovered crude oil' found beneath a cemetery. This episode also features John Kassir, who provides the voice of the Cryptkeeper, in a supporting role... Clancy Brown stars in *Half-Way Horrible* as the owner of a chemical corporation with links to macumba voodoo. His colleagues are being killed off by a mysterious assailant. And when he returns home one night to find threatening graffiti on his living room wall, he suspects he could be next on the hit list... And the season ends on a tribute to Amrose Bierce's short story, *An Occurrence at Owl Creek Bridge*, as a young woman imagines her possible future before she is executed by her treacherous gangster lover...

Season six (1994-1995) brings on a surreal, nightmarish quality to many episodes, with strange, oversized, architecturally-improbable rooms, and a bizarre 'plastic reality.' Russell Mulcahy's *Let the Punishment Fit the Crime* is about an injury lawyer who finds herself trapped in a Kafka-esque bureaucratic hell where her past sins come back to bite her on the arse... William Malone's *Only Skin Deep* centres on a man who picks up a mysterious blonde at a fancy dress party. Back at her place, their sexual fling hits the skids when the woman refuses to remove her 'mask'... Next up, Mick Garris chips in with *Whirlpool*, a tale about a comic book artist who is fired and has recurring dreams about shooting dead her editor... In *Operation Friendship*, a computer programmer is tormented by his destructive, *Drop Dead Fred*-like imaginary friend while dating a beautiful neighbour... In *Revenge is the Nuts*, the residents of a home for the blind take sweet revenge on the scumbag owner of the place... Next up, *The Stepfather* himself, Terry O'Quinn, stars in *The Bribe* as a health and safety inspector who makes a deal with a sleazy night club owner to help pay for his daughter's college tuition... In the awful episode, *The Pit*, two martial artists are manipulated by their wives into competing in a no-hold-barred death match in a cage... Bill Saddler returns as the Grim Reaper in *The Assassin*, in which a group of killers terrorize a housewife while searching for her husband who once worked for the US government... *Staired In Horror* stars D. B. Sweeney as a fugitive who hides out in an old lady's house that has a cursed stairway... In Vincent Spano's *In the Groove*, a struggling radio DJ attempts to boost his career by committing murder... In *Surprise Party*, a man inherits an old burned-out building after strangling his father. However, when he shows up he finds the place has been invaded by ghoulish revellers... In *Doctor of Horror*, a deranged 'Dr. Orloff' steals corpses with the aid of a couple of dim-witted security guards so that he can dissect them and 'find their souls'... Next up, Michael Ironside and Bruce Payne star in *Comes the Dawn* as a pair of Army poachers who use a young woman to catch a bear. However, the hunters soon become the hunted when they stumble into a den of vampires. This is a decent episode that was perhaps the inspiration for *30 Days of Night* (2007)... In *99&44/100% Pure Horror*, a pompous, self-absorbed artist murders her rich husband and turns him into soap. She later comes to a sticky end in the shower... And finally, *You, Murderer* stars Humphrey Bogart as a company executive with a violent past whose wife (Isabella Rossellini) threatens to expose his identity.

Season 7 (1996) strays across the Atlantic with 13 episodes set and shot in the UK, and featuring many familiar faces from British film and television. And though there are no masterpieces here, the episodes are consistently good throughout, offering the best tales since season 3. First up is *Fatal Caper*, in which an aristocrat nearing retirement is faced with a dilemma: He wants to pass on his estate to his sons, but they're a pair of irresponsible dunces. Before he dies, he creates a will that includes a clause that states that unless the sons can track down their long lost brother, the inheritance will be donated to charity. This is a strong opening episode with a great twist at the end... Next up, Freddie Francis returns with *Last Respects*, which is basically a re-telling of W.W. Jacob's classic tale, *The Monkey's Paw*. This time, the story is set in an antique gift shop where the three sisters who work there come into contact with a monkey's paw that grants them wishes... In *A Slight Case of Murder*, a novelist is bothered by house callers, including her estranged husband who plans on burying her alive... Martin Kemp stars in *Escape*, a World War II drama about a German POW who also operates as a spy for the British. When a fellow German he had betrayed ends up in the same camp as him, he feels he must make a daring escape before his cover is blown... In Russell Mulcahy's *Horror in the Night*, a wounded diamond thief hides out in a spooky hotel... In *Cold War*, Ewen McGregor and Jane Horrocks show up at a service station to rob the place, only to find that it is already being robbed by a Chinese motorcycle gang. After a shoot-out, they flee to a hotel and are attacked by a vampire... *The Kidnapper* stars Steve Coogan as a lonely proprietor of a pawn shop who allows a pregnant homeless woman (Julia Sawalha) to live with him. After she gives birth, they get into a romantic relationship, but the man becomes jealous of the attention the baby gets. One day, the baby is snatched in the park, and the pawn broker may have had something to do with it... In William Malone's *Report From the Grave*, a scientist violates the tomb of a long dead corpse in his attempts to conduct experimental research, but accidentally kills his girlfriend in the process. Thus, he becomes obsessed with the idea of resurrecting her from the grave... In *Smoke Wrings*, Daniel Craig saunters into an advertising company and blags himself a job. However, the impressed executive has no idea that he is there on behalf of her disgruntled ex partner who is looking for revenge... *About Face* stars Anthony Andrews as a seedy Priest who learns that he has fathered twins, one of whom is a deformed fundamentalist Christian with a murderous streak. This one shares a similar twist ending with an earlier episode, *People Who Live In Brass Hearses*. *Confession* stars Eddie Izzard as the prime suspect in a serial killer case in which hookers have been decapitated. Detectives oversee his interrogation at the hands of a master criminal psychologist... In *Ear Today... Gone Tomorrow*, a gangster's moll lures a safe cracker into robbing her partner's private vault. However, he is hard of hearing, so before getting to work, he undergoes an operation to fine-tune his hearing to that of an owl... And the final episode, *The Third Pig*, is an amusing and gruesome animation narrated by the Cryptkeeper throughout. It's about three pigs who are targeted by a big bad wolf who has a habit of fluffing his lines. And that's it, boils and ghouls.

Tales From the Crypt: Demon Knight (1995)
Dir: Ernest Dickerson /USA
Here's yet another villainous role for Billy Zane after his devilish turns in *Dead Calm* (1989), *The Case of the Hillside Strangler* (1989) and an episode of *Tales From the Crypt* (*Well Cooked Hams*, season 5). In this average horror flick he plays a demonic charmer trying to worm his way into an isolated Texas boarding house whose guests are protecting a talisman that he's eager to get his evil hands on. William Saddler plays the mysterious dude who leads the battle against him. It's darkly comic and bloody in places, but annoyingly predictable too.

Tales From the Crypt Presents Bordello of Blood (1996)
Dir: Gilbert Adler /USA

A preacher opens a brothel run by vampires beneath a funeral home. A gory, tongue-in-cheek caper which shares similarities with Robert Rodriquez's *From Dusk till Dawn*, which was made around the same time. Includes lots of gratuitous gore and nudity which will offend many, but is also a guilty pleasure in some less demanding horror fan circles.

Taxidermia (2006)
Dir: Gyorgy Palfi /France /Hungary /Austria

Three male generations in a troubled Hungarian family each appear in a trilogy of tales exploring raw human activities of sex, consumption and death. An often repulsive and darkly amusing slap in the face for audiences, as this film seems all-out to shock, horrify and churn stomachs using surreal, grotesque imagery and hardcore sex. Critics attacked the film, accusing it of being extremely gross and shocking for no apparent reason.

Taxi To The Darkside (2007)
Dir: Alex Gibney /USA

With the death in custody of an innocent Afghan taxi driver, this documentary analyses the brutal, even illegal interrogation techniques employed by the American government since 9/11. It's an illuminating and horrifying account of torture, and the way it is used routinely in the name of freedom. The Observer called it "one of the most important films of the past five years."

The 10th Victim (1965)
(Orig title: *La decima vittima*)
Dir: Elio Petri /Italy /France

Perhaps the closest thing to a snuff theme in 60s cinema was *The 10th Victim,* an Italian/French co-production set in the near future where the Big Hunt is a popular form of televised entertainment. Contestants are given weapons to hunt victims, with the opportunity – for both the hunters and the surviving victims – to earn a fortune. Ten years later and Paul Bartel took a similar theme of televised murder entertainment and added a welcome dose of graphic gore and satire in the cult classic *Death Race 2000* (1975). And the hunting theme was later updated in minor gems like *The Running Man* (1987), *Hard Target* (1993), *Battle Royale* (2000), *Slashers* (2001), *The Condemned* (2007) and *Series 7: The Contenders* (2001), the latter updating the reality TV satire to great effect.

Terror on the Beach (1973)
Dir: Paul Wendkos /USA

Duel's Denis Weaver takes his family on vacation in a camper van where they're initially mocked by a group of degenerate low-lives. When the family ignores them, the teasing turns to all-out hostility as their RV is vandalised and bugged through a PA system where loud animal noises are played all night, keeping the family awake. They are then terrorised by the thugs on dune buggies. Like *Duel*, Neil (Weaver) is subjected to an unprovoked series of attacks in the American wilderness. And like *The Hills Have Eyes* (1977), Weaver plays the confused pacifist at a loss as to why anyone would get pleasure out of tormenting a lone family. And also like *Hills* (and *Straw Dogs*, 1972), the mild-mannered family man is gradually drawn into a savage battle with the low-lives, becoming a bloodthirsty homicidal maniac to protect his loved ones. The film's status as a TV movie ensured it could never compete with *Hills* or *Straw Dogs* in terms of sheer visceral horror and bloodshed, but *Terror on the Beach* is a decent little pic – save for the cop-out ending – which hit the screens almost half a decade before Wes Craven's film.

Terror Tract (2000)
(aka *House on Terror Tract*)
Dir: Lance W. Dreesen & Clint Hutchison /USA

Horror anthology in which a suburban real estate agent tells three gruesome tales about the house's previous owners to potential buyers. The first story, '*Nightmare*,' is about a cheating wife and her lover who kill her husband and dispose of his body, only to suspect that he may not be dead... The second story, '*Bobo*,' stars *Breaking Bad*'s Bryan Cranston, as a father who becomes concerned with his daughter's relationship with an over-protective pet monkey, and resorts to hilarious extremes to in order to rid the house of the pest (you can imagine Walter White would have behaved in the same way). And finally, in '*Come To Granny*,' a psychic teen visits a psychiatrist to warn her that she will be the next victim of 'Granny,' a vicious, cleaver-wielding serial killer who wears a granny mask... *Terror Tract* is a fun yet highly derivative horror trilogy. It's well made but thoroughly cliché-ridden. It owes a lot to movies like *Les Diaboliques* (1955), *The House That Dripped Blood* (1970), *Monkey Shines* (1988) and *Out of the Body* (1989), but is watchable if you're in the right mood.

TerrorVision (1986)
Dir: Ted Nicolaou /USA
The Putterman family has trouble with their newly-installed satellite dish. And no sooner is the problem 'fixed' when a one-eyed space monster is beamed through their television screen to cause havoc in the household... *TerrorVision* is a fun little flick aimed at teens, and became a cult item on VHS. It's rare for an intentionally campy movie to work, but this one hits the ground running. Everyone on screen delivers the campy goods in spades; Mary Woronov and Gerrit Graham play the swinging parents whose double-date with a suave Greek man and his wife doesn't go quite to plan. There's also Diane Franklin as the teenage daughter, Suzie, a monolith of brightly-coloured hair dye and spandex. Her metal-head boyfriend, O.D., is played by Jon Gries (who also played the legendary arcade maniac, 'King Vidiot,' in *Joysticks* (1983)), here in a slightly more subdued mode. A young Chad Allen is marvellous as the younger brother, Sherman, a resourceful kid who struggles to convince his family of the truth. And then there's grandpa, played by former Robert Altman regular, Bert Remsen, a keen survivalist who has his own underground bunker stock-piled with a shit-load of military hardware. Grandpa also delivers the best line ("Well, do something, you ugly bastard!"). As for the space monster

itself, it looks like a giant scrotum dipped in acid, or a slime-drenched gloopy mess, sort of like a cross between Jabba the Hutt and the alien creatures of *The Deadly Spawn* (1983). And its voice sounds like it's talking and burping at the same time.

The Texas Chainsaw Massacre 3 (1990)
(aka *Leatherface: The Texas Chainsaw Massacre 3*)
Dir: Jeff Burr /USA
By the time *Texas Chainsaw Massacre 3* came along, New Line Cinema wanted to turn the films into a franchise in the same vein as the *Halloween* and *Friday the 13th* series'. To do this, they hired splatter punk writer, David J. Schow to pen the script which was to be unashamedly gruesome as an L.A. Girl, Michelle, has to endure a night of horror in the Sawyer's farmhouse. And like David in *Straw Dogs* (1971), Michelle has to learn that pacifism is for pussies, and that violence is the only answer... Entertaining if uninspired, again the filmmakers ignore everything that made the original such a classic, and seem content to heap on the brutal killings. On the up side, there is a particularly ghoulish scene in which a victim is strung upside down while the crazy family members stand around casually discussing which parts of him they would like to eat while the poor guy is still alive and conscious.

Theatre of Blood (1973)
Dir: Douglas Hickox /UK
Refreshingly gruesome for its day while managing to maintain an air of early 70s camp, *Theatre of Blood* sees Vincent Price at his hammiest as a sour actor who embarks on a dramatic murder spree. Having been the butt of many critics' jokes throughout his career, Price murders his detractors using Shakespeare as a bloody template. One scribe donates a pound of flesh, *Merchant of Venice*-style; another is repeatedly stabbed, a la *Julius Caesar.* Other murders include tributes to *Cymbeline* (nocturnal decapitation) and *Titus Andronicus* (the poodles scene). The film doesn't quite share the same madcap vibe as the earlier *Dr Phibes* movies but still, it boasts a 'knowing' humour which pre-

dates *Scream* (1996) by more than 20 years.

Theatre of Death (1967)
(aka *Blood Fiend*)
Dir: Samuel Gallu /UK
A Paris-set mystery which offers one of Christopher Lee's finest performances. The grumbly-voiced actor plays a theatre director who puts on macabre, *grand guignol*-type shows about the occult. When a wave of vampiric murders sweeps the city with bodies turning up drained of all their blood, Lee and his team fall under instant suspicion. *Theatre of Death* has been a cult favourite for decades, a film which soaks up every tired cliché of the horror genre and then turns them on their heads for the spectacular finale. It isn't as bloody or as delirious as Herschell Gordon Lewis' similarly themed *The Wizard of Gore* (1967), which was made around the same time, but it has its own camp charms all of its own.

Them! (1954)
Dir: Gordon Douglas /USA
An influential 50s creature feature which begins in the desert with a decimated caravan, a stink of formic acid, stolen sugar and a traumatized little girl afraid of "them." The FBI and insect experts arrive on the scene and trace a mysterious footprint to a nest of giant radioactive ants that have mutated thanks to A-bomb tests. *Them* is a superb documentary-style horror flick which charts America's defence against the commie ants, and features an unforgettable finale set in the L.A. Storm drains. It's one of the very best creature features of its time, and was Warner Bros' biggest box-office draw of that year. With savvy dialogue, restrained performances and sharp photography embellished with a newsreel documentary feel, the crazy proceedings nonetheless have an alarming air of authenticity. The only let down is Dick Smith's 15-foot-long model ants, which – though cutting edge for the time – look incredibly silly six decades on.

PHENOMENA

They Crawl (2001)
Dir: John Allardice /USA
Another TV movie made for the Sci-Fi Channel. This time we get a government-sponsored research project that transforms cockroaches into top secret bio-weapons. And the research falls into the hands of a body mutilation cult called Trillion. Mickey Rourke appears in a 'blink-and-you'll-miss-it' cameo role, purely for the quick pay cheque. And the creature at the end is hilariously bad. The script offers up howlers, such as "You have a kind heart. I know people who'd like to have it in their icebox." The 'special effects' are beyond ridiculous, and there's probably a joke somewhere about a film attempting to mimic *Mimic*, but I can't be arsed thinking of one.

13 Tzameti (2005)
Dir: Gela Babulani /France
Not as shocking or disturbing as other movies in this book, *13 Tzameti* is mentioned here only because it is regularly noted on lists of 'extreme' movies, and also because it's a low-budget, black and white gem which is very difficult to talk about without spoilers, but basically it's about a young man who steals an envelope containing a train ticket and hotel reservations. He is eventually given instructions to arrive at an isolated meeting place and finds himself drawn into a very dangerous game. Indeed, I can't even mention the titles of films that could've influenced this for fear of giving things away, but this is an incredible debut feature by the French-Georgian writer/director, Gela Babulani, and is a nerve-shredding thriller of the highest order. It's just a shame that Babulani still hasn't managed to capitalise on the early promise shown here. You could call it the *Clerks* of micro-budget thrillers, only it's much less known.

Thundercrack! (1975)
Dir: Curt McDowell /USA
A cheap porn version of a haunted house tale, *Thundercrack!* centres on a group of characters who are stranded in a creepy old house for the night during a fierce thunderstorm. And in between lots of sex scenes,

233

the characters set out on their various plot strands, such as a zoo keeper in search of a gorilla, his lost love. But despite the decent script, some interesting sound effects and a haunting piano score, the film suffers from its grubby cheapness and wretched performances of the cast who were hired for their willingness to bugger each other on camera, rather than for their acting abilities.

Tied in Blood (2012)
Dir: Matthew Laurence /UK
A distressed man calls on a medium to help exorcise his home of an evil spirit that has slaughtered his family. This intriguing premise is let down by the usual low-budget problems – namely, poor acting, a listless script, a bleary shot-on-video look, and lack of all-out horror. Director Matthew Laurence and writer David Ross spend too much time on the inconsequentials; instead of tightening things up for a more engaging viewing experience, they delve into the tiresome fall-out of a dysfunctional family. Can't see the woods for the trees.

A Time For Drunken Horses (2000)
(Orig title: *Zamani Baraye Masti Asbha*)
Dir: Bahman Ghobadi /Iran
A young Kurdish orphan joins a group of smugglers in order to make money to pay for treatment for his disabled, dying mother. A harsh, emotionally-charged documentary-style pic of hardship and poverty. The title refers to the alcohol-laced water given to the mules so that they can endure the long, hard snowbound journeys. It's a deeply moving film told without sentimentality and utilises a superb cast of non-professional actors.

Together (2000)
Dir: Lukas Moodysson /Sweden /Denmark /Italy
In the mid-70s, a mother leaves her abusive husband and joins a disorganised vegetarian commune with her children. This film starts off as a glowing endorsement for *laissez-faire*, liberal, hippy-drippy values of soft drugs and a rejection of the evils of capitalist society. However,

that initial impression is turned upside down, and the film presents the problems of sustaining such an idealistic lifestyle when ego-centric human worms get together in all their greedy and selfish glory, and how our very nature as human animals will inevitably destroy any attempts at harmony. The result is a finely-honed, all-too-believable social comedy that could be read as an allegory on the collapse of Communism (Karl Marx never once took into account how much the human race loves to compete with each other and are obsessed with 'keeping up with the Jones's', and all that). Fucking failing species. Writer/director Lukas Moodysson does an excellent job of illustrating the self-centred narcissism that exists at the core of any kind of human interaction and organisation. And he somehow manages to convey all of this without a single polemical word.

Torched (2004)
(aka *Hell Hath No Fury*)
Dir: Ryan Nicholson /Canada
A short, 45-minute rape-revenge flick featuring some of the most excruciating dick torture you'll ever see. The story centres on a young nurse who has been raped, but has no idea who is responsible. In the end she decides to take brutal action against all five of the suspects who live in her apartment building. With an abrasive soundtrack which throws up expletive-laden hip hop and jibbering death metal, *Torched* was the directorial debut of special effects artist, Ryan Nicholson, who went on to make *Live Feed* (2006) and *Gutterballs* (2008). Recommended to fans of underground horror and graphic buzz-saw butchery.

Totally Fucked Up (1993)
Dir: Gregg Araki /USA
An episodic account of six gay teens living in L.A., which ends tragically when one of them commits suicide. Made in a semi-documentary style, and starring James Duval, who later returned in Araki's next film, *The Doom Generation*.

The Tower (1993)
Dir: Richard Kletter /USA
The Intercorp Tower is a hi-tech building with a Hal-9000-like central computer in charge of everything from making the coffee, watering the plants and 'deleting' those who breach the security parameters. And when new employee, Paul Reiser, makes a few fuck-ups on his first day on the job, the system deems him eligible for termination. *The Tower* is a TV remake of the 1985 Canadian movie of the same title. This film pits its protagonist against the dangers of faceless corporate monstrosities (and also pre-dates similarly-themed movies like *Gremlins 2: The New Batch* (1990) and *Cube* (1997)). The film has much to say on the ant-like humans who contribute to the development of ice-cold, inhuman technologies that have a monopoly on life and death, creating a runaway menace in which no one is in control. Fun little film.

Tower Block (2012)
Dir: Ronnie Thompson & James Nunn /UK
The residents of a soon-to-be-demolished tower block come under attack from a deadly accurate sniper hidden away in the opposite building. An enjoyable if unremarkable thriller with a bunch of cliché characters (with both token goodies and baddies) who must club together out of necessity, just like in *Night of the Living Dead* and *Cube* and countless others. The motivation for the sniping is not convincing, but this is an often tense and gripping movie which comes with a message about the collapse of community spirit in the wake of Thatcherism.

Trapped (1973)
Dir: Frank DeFelitta /USA
In this TV movie by Universal, James Brolin is mugged and beaten unconscious by two men in the toilets of a department store. When he awakens in the middle of the night, he discovers that the security guards have unleashed a pack of killer dogs to roam free throughout the store. So Brolin spends the rest of the night trying to keep the feeding

frenzy away from his protein-packed genitals. *Trapped* is a fun but little-seen movie that would make for a great double-bill with Jim Wynorski's *Chopping Mall* (1986). As far as I'm aware, this hasn't been released on DVD, but catch it if you can. Also check out another TV movie of the same name, Fred Walton's *Trapped* (1989), in which Kathleen Quinlan is locked overnight in her work place, and is pursued through 40 floors of bland office space by a knife – and bat – wielding nut job.

Trash Humpers (2009)
Dir: Harmony Korine /USA

Recorded on an old video camera, *Trash Humpers* portrays the activities of a group of destructive, sociopathic geriatrics. They vandalise property, cackle endlessly, perform fellatio on random objects and hump trash cans. Oh, and they also record themselves decapitating, slashing throats and suffocating strangers, too. A lot of people strongly dislike this film (just take a look at the scathing reviews on the IMDb), and it isn't difficult to see why. Anyone renting this expecting a 'normal' independent movie will be outraged. *Trash Humpers* is deliberately abrasive with its VHS aesthetic (it was edited together at random on two VCRs) and the fact that there is no plot to follow, no character development, or anything like that. However, those looking for a change from the norm may find it amusing. *Trash Humpers* is often compared to Werner Herzog's *Even Dwarfs Started Small* and Lars Von Trier's *The Idiots*, and there are doubtless similarities there, but Korine's film is actually closer in spirit to stunt shows like *Jackass, Dirty Sanchez* and *The Dudesons*, etc (Johnny Knoxville even wore the same body suit for his old man stunts on an episode of *Jackass*). It has a free spirit to it, much like those shows. It isn't great art, nor is it pretending to be. It's a film which embraces the spontaneity of fucking a mail box for no other reason than having the freedom to do so. And the joy in knowing that it will annoy a lot of people. And let's face it, old people being obscene can be quite funny. The old guy improvising the tune on an acoustic guitar almost killed me. It's hilarious. I think the lyrics go something like, "you girls sure suck a large fat penis." It's a song that has been stuck in my head for days now. If I still had the band going, we would have done a fuzzed-up rock cover of it.

I'll leave you with this memorable quote: "Heads. It would be nice to live without a head. Think of how much money you would save on shampoo and hats. Models would be judged by their shoulders. And your ears would be in your armpits. And everyone would look like a stump. Sweaters, they would fit like socks. Boxers would have to rely on body-blows. Dandruff would be obsolete. No more zits! No more tea-bagging! Lower Ceilings! Chest hair will replace the need for beards. People would buy less tables; they'd eat off the table like stumps. People would weigh eight to eleven pounds less. And best of all, no one would get dizzy again."

Trip With the Teacher (1975)
Dir: Earl Barton /USA
An old grindhouse exploitation fave, *Trip With the Teacher* sees four girls and their teacher terrorised and molested by biker thugs out in the Arizona wilderness. The leader of the bad guys is Al (Zalman King), a hook-nosed, snickering sadist who sports a Syd Barrett hairdo. He's no Krug, but he's a nasty piece of work, nonetheless. The film was made ultimately to cash-in on the success of *Last House on the Left* (1972). *Trip* also has much in common with *Weekend of Terrors* (1970), in which three nuns travelling on a desert road are terrorised by crooks when their car breaks down.

Tombs of the Blind Dead (1972)
(aka *The Blind Dead*; Orig title: *La noche del terror ciego*)
Dir: Amando de Ossorio /Spain /Portugal
During a trip to Portugal, Spanish friends investigate the disappearance of Virginia (Maria Elena Arpon), who had stormed off in a huff, and learn that she was killed by 'the Knight's Templar,' blind zombies on horseback, after she had awoken them from their tombs in the ancient ruins of a monastery. And, soon enough, the Knights target the friends – and anyone else who gets in their way – as they saunter on through the plains using their swords and teeth to finish their victims... *Tombs of the*

Blind Dead is a slow-moving but haunting and stylish little zombie flick, but beware of the censored version which has all the bloody stuff cut out, including the torture scene in the opening prologue. Fans of 70s Eurohorror – and Jean Rollin in particular – should find much to savour here. It was followed by three loose sequels; *Return of the Evil Dead* (1973), *The Ghost Galleon* (1975) and *Night of the Seagulls* (1976).

The Tortured (2010)
Dir: Robert Lieberman /USA /Canada
Tagline: 'The only way to ease the pain is to inflict some.' Parents get revenge on the sick maniac who had kidnapped and murdered their six-year-old son. They commandeer the prison truck he was travelling in, take him to a deserted house, cut him and burn him cigarettes, inject him with some kind of drug which causes his muscles to cramp up in excruciating pain, and use other medical supplies to prolong his agony. Then comes the 'little elephant' KGB techniques, and the inevitable twist (or twisted) ending. *The Tortured* shares a very similar storyline with the French-Canadian revenge shocker, *Les 7 jours du talion* (*7 Days*, 2010), and both films serve as morally-degrading updates on Wes Craven's *The Last House on the Left* (1972). *The Tortured*, in particular, is a mostly vile piece of work; 'torture porn' in every sense of the term, in which the viewers and protagonists alike get to indulge in the most heinous acts of barbarity whilst retaining a sense of 'justice' with a good conscience throughout.

Tourist Trap (1979)
Dir: David Schmoeller /USA
An impressive, atypical effort from the slasher movie heyday, *Tourist Trap* sees a group of teens arrive at a mannequin museum whose kooky owner uses telekenesis to puppeteer the dolls to kill. Similar to *Psycho* (1960) in many ways; the insane Mr. Slausen (Chuck Connors) shares a similar, Ed Gein-like psychosis as Norman Bates in the way he channels split personalities to commit the deadly deeds. And just like the Bates Motel, the museum is located in a backwoods area that has been cut off from the rest of civilisation by a newly constructed

motorway nearby, causing the tourist trade to bypass the museum. Includes an eccentric score by Pino Donaggio.

Trick Or Treat (1986)
Dir: Charles Martin Smith /USA
Everything that sucked about 80s rock music is rubbed in your face for 98-minutes in this horrendous time-capsule of a movie hailing from the decade that taste forgot. The spirit of a devil-worshipping rock star comes back from the dead to empower a victimised school kid into getting even with bullies. *Trick Or Treat* is a lukewarm, non-eventful 'revenge of the nerd' movie in the vein of *Evil Speak* (1982), *Christine* (1983) and *976-Evil* (1988). Includes an amusing cameo by Ozzy Osbourne as a Reverend campaigning on TV against 'rock pornography.'

2001 Maniacs (2005)
Dir: Tim Sullivan /USA
Remake of Herschell Gordon Lewis' *Two Thousand Maniacs!* (1964), in which Pleasant Valley is re-imagined as a *Deliverance*-esque hick town run by the crooked Mayor, Robert Englund. Three separate groups of teens arrive by car to the strange town, and the familiar story unfolds. This time the filmmakers openly mock the southerners by portraying them as backward hillbillies, and yet the tourists, who are supposedly superior, are nothing but a bunch of pubescent piss-babies whose gruesome deaths you can't wait to revel in. However, there's very little imagination here; the killings are almost identical to the ones in the original; limbs torn off by horses, axe dismemberment, death by crushing, etc. Other murders include death by acid drinking and human shish kebab, but none of them are impressive. There is great story potential here, as Lewis demonstrated in the original, but this time it's squandered with a predictable yarn about obnoxious youngsters getting offed in the wilderness. Also, this time the townsfolk aren't just vengeful spirits but cannibals too. And this alteration of the original has no bearing on the story whatsoever. It was followed by by Tim Sullivan's *2001 Maniacs: Beverly Hillbillys* (2010).

Undead (2005)
Dir: Michael & Peter Spierig /Australia
A tranquil fishing village in Australia is bombarded with meteorites which somehow bring the dead back to life. A group of survivors – consisting of cops, weirdos and other loudmouths – find themselves stranded in the basement of a nearby house. Sort of a spoof on George Romero's *Night of the Living Dead* (1968) with not a decent gag to be found. The Spierig brothers financed the film themselves with the help of their friends. And though the film is competently made in terms of lighting and editing, etc, the 'dialogue' is atrocious. The film's best scenes stray into early Peter Jackson splatter territory, but overall, this dud will only find favour with those who are easily amused.

The Unseen (1980)
Dir: Peter Foleg [Danny Steinmann] /USA
A TV reporter and her two assistants find themselves stranded in a town with no motel. So they spend a few nights at a house owned by a local museum owner, whose sister is severely withdrawn. On day two of their stay, one of the unlucky girls discovers that in the basement dwells a bloodthirsty being out to kill them all... This film plods along familiar territory up until the last half hour when the heroine gets locked in the basement. Things pick up immediately from there on in, with a blackly comic revelation as to the identity of the Sloth-like killer, which astute viewers will suspect long before the reveal. Director Steinmann was so disappointed with the final cut of the film that he had his name removed from the credits, but *The Unseen*, for all its faults, is worth a watch just for the crackpot ending. The film also pre-dates Wes Craven's *The People Under the Stairs* by more than a decade.

Vacancy (2007)
Dir: Nimrod Antal /USA
A couple break down on the road and end up checking in to a creepy motel for the night. For entertainment they have a few movies which the couple soon realise are actually real murders that took place in the very room they're staying in. To make matters worse, they discover they

have been locked in the room and are being recorded by hidden cameras, and some very bad people are out to get them. This is middle-of-the-road fair all the way; plodding, routine and unwilling to take any risks, despite its compelling premise. The script (by Mark L. Smith) has some good ideas and moments where tension and suspense could have worked wonders, but the execution is handled very badly and it was clearly directed by a nimrod (Nimrod Antal) who clearly has no warmth towards the genre. The snuff movies are bloodless and unimaginative, and the way the digital footage is artificially 'scratched' to make it look like battered old film is laughable.

Vacancy 2: The First Cut (2009)
Dir: Eric Bross /USA
"Just make sure you get it on camera!" A prequel set in the same Meadow View motel in which the gang of deviants allows a psychopath to murder the guests on camera, with the aim of selling the tapes on the 'booming' snuff movie market. *Vacancy 2* is better than the crappy original – it wasn't difficult to beat - even though the entire scenario beggars belief. But, having said that, the story is kept nicely compact with just a handful of characters in a limited location.

Vampires: Los Muertos (2002)
Dir: Tommy Lee Wallace /USA
Jon Bon Jovi stands in as a poor James Woods substitute in this direct-to-DVD sequel to *John Carpenter's Vampires* (1998). A formulaic but quickly paced movie, *Los Muertos* sets up Bon Jovi as a semi-pro vampire hunter who teams up with the already bitten heroine, Natasha Gregson Wagner, and a group of cardboard characters to follow an undead princess into picturesque Mexico.

The Velvet Vampire (1971)
Dir: Stephanie Rothman /USA
Just as the hippy dream had turned sour, filmmakers were keen to examine the fallout of the flower power movement. And though *The Velvet Vampire* does have its contemporaries in Harry Kumel's

Daughters of Darkness (1971) and Jose Larraz's *Vampyres* (1974), this film – which sees a bisexual vampire riding through the Californian desert in a dune buggy, picking up couples to feast on their blood – was a definite break from the norm at the time. *The Velvet Vampire* takes its time to bring the audience down from its hippy high and confront them with the base, animal instincts of human nature: the need for chaos, violence, control and domination. The vampire, Diane LeFanu (played by Celeste Yarnall) is obviously named in tribute to the author of the classic vampire story, *Carmilla*. She is calm and seductive and lays on the heavy innuendo, she perhaps represents the modern-day feminist female, in contrast to her female victim (Sherry Miles), a sexually-repressed, pre-feminist screamer.

V/H/S (2012)
Dir: -Various- /USA
A disappointing anthology horror shot on video. A vampiric demon wipes out a motel room full of arseholes; a dull couple on a road trip are targeted by a masked intruder; a vicious knife killer in the woods picks off another group of cretins. We're constantly reminded in horror movies that dicks with video cameras are no fun, and *V/H/S* is no exception. A man witnesses his girlfriend being terrorised by 'evil spirits' via skype; more idiots show up at a Halloween party, but the house is empty – They encounter some kind of exorcism going on in the attic. We also get dialogue that doesn't reach far beyond "Fuck, dude. What the fuck?" Brad Miska of Bloody Disgusting.com came up with the concept of the film. BD is the most popular horror site on the web, and this gave the filmmakers the opportunity to promote their film on their own site, with everyone queuing up to give this trash a collective blowjob. Of course, many declared it a masterpiece, so there goes their credibility.

V/H/S 2 (2013)
Dir: -Various- /USA /Canada /Indonesia
If, like me, you felt that the original *V/H/S* was an over-hyped dog turd of a movie, you may be pleasantly surprised by this follow-up as, for

me, this is easily one of the all-time great horror anthologies. The wraparound segment sees a private investigator on the search for a missing son. He and his glamorous assistant enter a house and find the usual stack of TV screens and a sinister looking video tape collection. The girl begins watching the tapes, and there looks to be a hooded figure closing in behind her... The first tape is about a man who has been fitted with a bionic eye, and is spooked by a child ghost and a fat 'dude' in his underwear. The second tape sees a cyclist capture a zombie outbreak in the woods via helmet cam (and this story is perhaps the one that best utilises the 'found footage' format). This exceptional zombie tale flicks through George Romero's evolving mythos in a rapid ten-minute sequence in which the cyclist is first bitten, then transforms in super-quick time, attacks a birthday party celebration nearby, becomes self-conscious (like 'Bub' in *Day of the Dead*), becomes adept at firearms, and blows its brains out with a shotgun. The next tape is even better: A documentary crew enter a religious cult in Indonesia to interview the 'father' of the group. But not long after their arrival a mass suicide breaks out. And if that isn't freaky enough, something else very sinister happens which I won't spoil here. This is easily the best segment in the film, recorded in a genuinely creepy location – an abandoned, derelict school building. We get very little background information on the cult or the other creatures; the chaos just unfolds right there on screen with a real-life scrappiness which makes viewers feel just as lost and horrified as the characters are. If you enjoyed *[Rec]* and *Cloverfield*, then *V/H/S 2* is worth watching just for this sequence alone. In the final tape, child pranks are interrupted by the arrival of home-invading evil extraterrestrials. This segment even borrows the loud, brass-like drone effect on the soundtrack that was put to good use in Spielberg's *War of the Worlds* (2006). My my, what a turnaround. I repeat: This is one of the finest, creepiest anthology horrors ever made.

Victim of the Haunt (1996)
Dir: Larry Shaw /USA
A nice middle-class family moves into a dream suburban home. Trouble is, the house was built on a burial ground, and also harbours a

dark past; 75 years earlier, a man drowned his own daughter in the bathtub. The house is also haunted, and puts on pretty light shows as spirits wander across the bedroom walls. However, the spirits soon become increasingly threatening. And before you can say 'Zelda Rubinstein,' along comes the eccentric psychic to battle against the smoke and lights while urging the spirits to "go into the light," and save the day. *Victim of the Haunt* is basically a lightweight TV remake of *Poltergeist* (1982) which brings nothing new to the fold. The film is supposedly based on 'real events,' but it's about as real as Pamela Anderson's fake plastic udders.

Video Violence (1987)
Dir: Gary Cohen /USA

A husband and wife open a video store in a small town where everyone seems to be obsessed with murder and violence. And when snuff videos are discovered to be in circulation, the couple begin to suspect that they could be potential targets. It's a surprisingly competent and even-paced effort (unlike many other SOV 80s movies) which offers lots of blood and death, and is even quite creepy in places. It sure beats other cheese-fests like *They Don't Cut the Grass Anymore* and *Horror House On Highway 5* (remember that one?) Writer/director Gary Cohen formed the idea for the project when a customer at the video store he worked at enquired about a film called *I Dismember Mama*. She wanted to know if it contained any sex scenes. Cohen told her that he hadn't actually seen it but knew that it contained scenes of strong bloody violence. And with that, the mother deemed it to be acceptable viewing material for her kids and promptly rented the tape. A fictional re-enactment of that bizarre encounter actually made it into the film.

Video Violence 2 (1987)
Dir: Gary Cohen /USA

Later that same year, Cohen returned with *Video Violence 2*, in which Howard and Eli host their own pirate cable TV show where they invite the viewing public to send in their favourite home-brewed snuff movies. This time the plot is replaced by skits and bloody clips, but that sense of old skool video nostalgia is still in place.

Violence Jack (1986)
(aka *Violence Jack: Slum King)*
(Orig title: *Baiorensu Jakku: haremu bonba-hen*)
Dir: Ichiro Itano /Japan
Set in the future after a series of natural disasters have destroyed civilisation, *Violence Jack* depicts the chaos of life on earth as roaming gangs of sub-humans enslave and rape young women. Violence Jack, a ten foot tall badass, serves as a lone vigilante dishing out street justice on the scumbags, and who also loses an arm and an eye for his troubles. Banned in Australia for its graphic depictions of rape, this 37-minute video stood out from the usual anime fare due to its extreme violence, and became a cult item on home video in the early 90s.

Violence Jack 2: Evil Town (1988)
(aka *Violence Jack Part 2: Hell City*; aka *Hell Wind)*
(Orig title: *Baiorensu Jakku: jigoku-gai-hen*)
Dir: Takuya Wada /Japan
Based on another of Go Nagai's manga comics that ran from the mid-70s until the early 90s, here Violence Jack seems to have miraculously grown back a new arm. This time, the giant breaks out of concrete and takes on a predatory gang leader called 'Mad' while earthquakes ravage the lawless town. This sequel is a little less action-packed than the original, and takes a while to reach full throttle. But once it gets going, the violence is just as extreme, and includes a graphic massacre of innocent children, pixelated sex scenes, cannibalism, and a bloody showdown between Jack and his nemesis.

Violence Jack 3: Hell's Wind (1990)
(Orig title: *Baiornsu Jakku: herusuuindo hen*)
Dir: Takaya Wada /Japan
A ruthless motorcycle gang, Hell's Wind, lays waste to a peaceful community, terrorizing the locals and cutting them to pieces with chainsaws and raping the women., until Jack shows up and unleashes

his now familiar brand of brutal justice. At just short of an hour, this third and final entry in the series reveals its influence as a future western set in a post-apocalyptic Tokyo.

Visiting Hours (1982)
Dir Jean Claude Lord /Canada
Michael Ironside plays a misogynistic psychopath who targets a women's rights campaigner. And when he learns that she has survived the vicious attack, he heads to the hospital where she's recovering to finish what he started... *Visiting Hours* is an above-average slasher movie with lots of suspense and impressive set-pieces, the most memorable of which is the initial attack sequence in which the victim tries to hide in the laundry chute.

The Walking Dead (2010-)
Dir: -Various- /USA
You'll notice that this mini-review is very vague, but I really don't want to give anything away. If you haven't seen this then I suggest you go away, grab the box sets and get stuck in because this is really as good as TV gets – yes, right up there with *The Wire* and *Breaking Bad*! I was a late comer to this show. I hadn't watched it. I'd always dismissed it as "*Lost* with a few zombies in the background". I couldn't have been more wrong. So when I eventually settled down to play catch-up during the mid-season 4 break, I was completely blown away by what I saw: excellent, well-drawn characters, stunning performances, truly ghoulish imaginative touches, and an emotional engagement you only usually get with epic novels. I am rightly ashamed of myself for dismissing this show so easily.

Based on the series of graphic novels by Robert Kirkman, Tony Moore and Charlie Adlard, Season 1 kicks off with local Sheriff's Deputy, Rick (Andrew Lincoln) getting shot during a routine pursuit of criminals. Weeks, or months (or 28 days) later, he awakens from a coma in hospital and walks out to meet the zombie apocalypse. He collapses in the street due to weakness brought on by hunger and dehydration, and is rescued by Morgan and his boy Duane, a couple of survivors and perhaps the only living humans left in town. They later raid the gun cabinets in the Sheriff's office and go their separate ways. Rick heads out to Atlanta to find his wife and son, and when he reaches the city, he finds it overrun with zombies who are so hungry they could literally eat a horse. Rick is rescued once again, this time by a band of survivors who have a camp out in the woods. This sequence is memorable for the role of Michael Rooker who plays a drug-fuelled, trigger-happy redneck called Merle whom they handcuff to a pipe on the roof of a building, and end up having to leave to his fate when their stronghold is broken. When they get to the camp, Rick is reunited with his loved ones, Lori and Carl. It turns out that Lori has been sleeping with Shane, the Sheriff who is Rick's best buddy (but, to be fair, they *did* think he was long dead). Hence a love triangle becomes apparent. And this is when I thought things would slip into soap opera territory with the zombies becoming a background abstraction, but thankfully, that never happens.

By the way, the description above covers only the first couple of episodes. A group heads back for the city on a rescue mission for Merle, but he isn't there. It appears he has cut off his own hand with a hacksaw and cauterized the wound on a hot plate. The series continues until the group reaches a secure scientific research silo. Season 2 expands to 13 episodes, and gets off to a suspenseful hoot on the highway before the survivors hold out at a nearby ranch to nurse an injured member of their group. This is where we meet new characters, including the stubborn but wise Hershel and his daughters, Maggie and Beth. If there are any faults with Season 2, for me it would be that it feels overstretched in places to meet the designated 13 episode duration; as a consequence, the drama is sometimes spread dangerously thin, and teeters on becoming like '*Little House On the Prairie* with Zombies,' or something. The 'romance' between Glen and Maggie is also badly developed, and we're supposed to accept the fact that they're in love after what feels like five minutes of awkward moodiness and silly games. It just feels so phony and loveless, there are probably zombies out in the woods who have a more convincing romance going on (I should say though that these love birds did grow on me eventually). Fortunately, things do pick up, and interesting themes are explored, such as the changes in people's perspectives and beliefs when faced with such existential horror of corpses walking around trying to eat you. And also the dilemmas of the values of civilization versus the zero-tolerance and zero-sum games of group survival. If you're kind and helpful to others, you're in danger of falling victim, but if you're cold and brutal and unsympathetic to others you have a greater chance of survival, but you lose your humanity and sense of civilization in the process. So what's it to be? Season 2 is the first to address the Cold War-like tactical agendas of survivors, and the fact that trust – or the lack of it – among the people becomes just as big a danger as the shambling ghouls.

Season 3 sees the ever-dwindling group stumble upon a secure prison while Andrea teams up with a sword wielding survivor, and they find themselves inculcated into a small fortress town called Woodbury headed by the quietly unstable 'Governor,' a kind of cross between Howard Hughes and Jim Jones. We're witness to some real ghoulish ideas in this season, including the scene where one character is tied to a chair while another is murdered and left to 'turn' and chew the flesh of the helpless victim. Season 3 also drags out the plot to an excruciating degree, especially during the last few episodes, but my my, I was well and truly hooked by this point. It's riveting stuff. Also, I find it amusing that scenes of gruesome bloody violence are given a big thumbs up, while F-words and tiddies are forbidden on screen. That's American network TV for you.

Season 4 is the most emotionally engaging (and devastating) season yet, though, as of this writing, Season 5 is in the works. And if you can't relate to the Governor on even the most basic level, you're inhuman. Or a 'liar.' Season 4 sees life in the prison becoming increasingly desperate as a deadly flu ravages the refugees, unleashing hordes of zombies in their hideout. None of the characters are safe here; any one of them can be taken out at any time. And with this life-or-death balance hanging over these characters we have grown to like, it's all the more heart breaking when things fall apart. My favourite character is Daryl; the evolution of his character development has been the most impressive, the way he has emerged from his brother Merle's shadow and found his sense of self, which is to say that he's basically a decent person. With his trusty crossbow and no-questions-asked approach to dealing with the awful situation, his loyalty to the group is perhaps down to him having found his 'family' at last.

Maybe I've been caught up in all the hype, but *The Walking Dead* is really fucking good! In fact, it makes most of the other films and TV shows in this book look like garbage. I understand that the emotional manipulation of viewers is perhaps this show's strongest asset overall, but I don't care. It works! The Canadian comedy series *The Trailer Park Boys*, has a knack of finding humour in the tiniest of details – the look of an eye, the almost unconscious facial expressions, the almost inaudible throwaway lines of dialogue, etc – and it works because we know the characters so well. Similarly, in *The Walking Dead* we're plunged into a nightmarish world which rings true even in the smallest details – the psychological angle, the end of the world feeling, the words that go unsaid speak volumes. I had always held film to be superior to television, and 99% of the time it probably is. But this show has made me think otherwise. Do yourself a favour and catch up with this incredible show if you haven't already. You won't regret it.

The War Zone (1998)
Dir: Tim Roth /UK /Italy
Tim Roth's depressing film is about a teenage boy who learns that his father is having an incestuous relationship with his sister . This is a downbeat - and very British - kitchen sink bore-fest. Described in the Guardian as "a soft-core child abuse drama reeking of good intentions and middle brow arthouse good taste." The difficult theme of child abuse is rendered more palatable to viewers by giving it a heartfelt, family-friendly sheen. Jesus Christ, what next? Rick Moranis in *Honey, I Brown-Dicked The Kids*?

Wheels of Terror (1990)
Dir: Christopher Cain /USA
Better than average TV movie in which a filthy black Sudan is driven

around the desert roads of Arizona, and its driver is abducting and murdering young girls. And when school bus driver, Joanna Cassidy, witnesses her own daughter taken, she pursues the vehicle along a lonely stretch of road. Like the villain in *Duel,* viewers never get to see the driver. He enjoys toying with his victims, and the car is seemingly indestructible and demonic, just like the sinister vehicle in *The Car* (1977). Miles better than other similarly-themed TV movies like *Road Rage* (1999) and *Death Car on the Freeway* (1979).

When a Killer Calls (2006)
Dir: Peter Mervis /USA
"Have you checked the girl?" A loose remake of Fred Walton's classic, *When a Stranger Calls* (1978).This film revamps and updates the familiar old tale by making it fit into the 00s 'torture porn' trend. Thus, the babysitter is pestered not only by phone calls, but text messages too. The killer also sends pictures to her phone which serve to illustrate his grisly crimes, and the girl initially thinks they're fake. And – gasp! - the calls are actually coming from inside the house! She is also trussed up and tortured for a while until she re-distributes the maniac's brains by blasting a massive hole in his head. For newcomers – which this film is probably aimed at – this may be good enough to pass a slow evening, but for the rest of us, there's really nothing of interest here.

When a Stranger Calls Back (1993)
Dir: Fred Walton /USA
This official sequel to *When a Stranger Calls* (1978) delivers much of the same as the original, minus the all-important surprise factor. Babysitter Julia (Jill Schoelen) is pestered by a stranger who knocks on the door one night and complains that his car has broken down. Julia refuses to open the door but agrees to call the auto-club. However, the phone lines are down, and rather than telling him to go away, she stupidly tells him that she has made the call. As time passes and the stranger becomes increasingly restless, she struggles to keep up the lies for much longer... Cut to five years later, and Julia is a paranoid recluse who is convinced that someone is entering her apartment and re-

arranging her belongings. She gets help from a retired ten-bellied cop and a college psychiatrist to track down her stalker. *When a Stranger Calls Back* is a lacklustre attempt to out-do the original but fails badly. Rather than escalating the terror, the filmmakers instead settle into an inept social drama about women doing it for themselves. However, the film is worth a watch if only for the creepy scene in which the maniac shows up at a hospital late at night.

While the Children Sleep (2007)
(aka *The Sitter*)
Dir: Russell Mulcahy /USA
A young woman with an unhealthy obsession with a district attorney lands the job of in-house nanny for his and his wife's kids. And no sooner has she ingratiated herself into the household when she reveals herself to be a dangerous psychopath. This is an adequate interloper movie with a great performance by Mariana Klaveno. It's basically a remake of *The Babysitter* (1980).

Who is the Black Dahlia? (1975)
Dir: Joseph Pevney /USA
TV movie mystery based on the true – and still unsolved – case of Elizabeth Short, a young woman whose bisected body was discovered under shrub growth in California in 1947. The story of her life is then told in a series of flashbacks. Turns out that Elizabeth was an aspiring actress from Maine who picked up the moniker 'The Black Dahlia' because of the dresses she wore. The filmmakers portray her in a good light while acknowledging her flaws; i.e. that she was a fantasist and a compulsive liar. Disappointingly, the filmmakers are less than faithful when it comes to portraying the disgusting behaviour of journalists swarming the police over the case, as a reporter for the *Los Angeles Daily News*, Gerry Ramlow later stated: "If the murder was never solved it was because of the reporters... They were all over, trampling evidence, withholding information." It took several years for the police to take full control of the investigation, during which time reporters roamed freely throughout the department's offices, sat at officer's desks,

and answered their phones. Many tips from the public were not passed on to the police, as the reporters who received them rushed out to the get the 'scoops.' *True Confessions* (1981), starring Robert De Niro and Robert Duvall, is loosely based on the same case, as is Brian DePalma's *The Black Dahlia* (2006).

Wicked City (1987)
(Orig title: *Yoju toshi*)
Dir: Yoshiaki kawajiri /Japan

A man is picked up in a bar by a hot female. They go back to a hotel room and have sex. And afterwards, she transforms into some kind of demonic, humanoid spider with a toothy vagina... And so begins this lurid tale of sex, death and monsters as a peaceful pact between the worlds of the mortal and the supernatural is put under strain by the arrival of a group of bloodthirsty demons. It's up to a government bodyguard and a female demon to protect a sex-crazed scientist whose job it is to sign a peace treaty between the two worlds. *Wicked City* is more of a laid back effort than the usual anime monster mayhem from Japan. This time the Lovecraft-inflected material is given a deliberately ponderous pace with poetic flourishes. See also *Monster City* (1991).

The Willies (1989)
Dir: Brian Peck /USA

Kids out camping exchange tales that are 'grosser than gross.' Both stories involve schoolboys – one catches a demon taking a shit in the toilets, and the other is a twisted fat kid who is tricked into using a super fertilizer for a bug farm, which causes horribly mutated giant flies to come after him at night. The film also contains a trio of short vignettes before the title credits, in which a woman tucks into something grosser than gross at a fried chicken restaurant, a old man gets trapped on a ghost train ride, and a senile old lady puts her pet poodle in the microwave. Fans of *Weird Tales* and *Tales From the Crypt* should enjoy.

Witchboard (1986)

Dir: Kevin S. Tenney /UK /USA

House party revellers break out a ouija board and unleash the angry spirit of a young boy. The spirit then engineers a series of brutal 'mishaps' on the party goers, one by one. A collapsed roof, some tossed beer cans, and a dead psychic later, the remaining ones soon learn that a much more powerful spirit, Malfeitor, is actually responsible for the murders. *Witchboard* is your typical 80s teen horror flick which borrows elements from *The Omen* (1976), 80s slasher movies, and even *The Exorcist* (1973). Silly at times, but also watchable if you're in the right mood, this film also went on to influence the *Final Destination* series years later.

Witchboard 2: The Devil's Doorway (1993)

(aka *Witchboard: The Return*)

Dir: Kevin S. Tenney /USA

A young woman, Paige (Ami Dolenz), rents an apartment and discovers a ouija board among the leftover belongings of the previous tenant. Of course, it isn't long before curiosity gets the better of her, and she has a dabble out of boredom. She contacts a spirit called Susan, and learns that she was the previous tenant who was murdered. Paige then attempts to solve the murder mystery while something evil takes out a couple of characters by way of faulty car breaks and a wrecking ball. Slightly better than the original. It was followed by *Witchboard III: The Possession* (1995).

The Wizard of Gore (1970)

Dir: Herschell Gordon Lewis /USA

Perhaps the most bizarre film of HG Lewis's career. With self-parody taking centre stage, we're introduced to Montag The Magnificent (Ray Sager), a hammy stage magician who performs tricks whereby audience members are sawn in half with a chainsaw or forced to shallow a sword. After the grisly 'illusions' have taken place, the volunteers seem to be okay at first until hours later when they turn up dead with their sloppy innards strewn across the floor. The master of *grand guignol* later finds himself on a live television show demonstrating an existential stigmata sequence. And if this film doesn't leave you questioning your sanity then nothing will.

The World Beyond (1978)
Dir: Noel Black /USA

The second of two pilot TV shows (the other is *The World of Darkness*) about a sports writer who has a near death experience, and returns with the power to hear the voices of spirits. The spirits guide him to solve supernatural crimes. In this episode (titled on screen as '*Monster*'), he is sent to deal with a Golem-like creature made of mud that has been terrorising a small fishing community in Maine. The show lacks energy and interest, the protagonist lacks personality, and the monster – though noisy enough – looks like Godzilla ate the Swamp Thing and shat it out whole. No wonder the shit-caked wailing bum is so pissed off. Unsurprisingly, the networks passed on it and consigned this nonsense to oblivion.

The Year After Infection (2012)
Dir: Antonio E. Greco /USA

A rare thing; a horror anthology based exclusively on the zombie mythos. It's just a shame that this is such a plodding, amateur bore-fest. As the title makes clear, these stories are set a year after the outbreak of the zombie virus. The first story concerns a 'dear diary' type girl with a bland sense of humour who has taken refuge in a barn. She talks to herself while carrying out the daily chores, and keeps a pet zombie called 'Roy' for amusement. The tranquility is disrupted, however, when three armed men show up... In the second story, a handful of survivors stranded in the wilderness set off down river in rowing boats. But, perhaps inevitably, they are attacked by zombies while trying to paddle under a bridge that is swarming with them. In the third, another band of survivors – this time stranded in a town building – have to deal with the consequences of having killed one of their own who had become infected. And finally, the fourth story sees a black man befriend a young white boy who has been left alone in the family home for five months. Ah, life is too short for this shit. *The Year After Infection* is a chore to get through; anyone but the hardiest of zombie freaks will struggle to make it to the end (the ending is, however, the most impressive moment in the film in the way it brings the stories full circle with shocking abruptness). But before the ending, viewers have to make do with dull characters who barely stand apart from the ghouls, nevermind their fellow humans. And with a running time of more than two hours, it's way overlong.

Young Poisoner's Handbook (1995)
Dir: Benjamin Ross /UK /Germany

A boy fascinated by the power of poisons tests them out on his stepmother and uncle, and is sent to an institution for the criminally insane. He is later declared to be sound of mind and is released, whereupon he continues poisoning others. Told in the style of a black farcical comedy, this film will probably appeal more to audiences who aren't looking for factual details. The story is based on the life of Graham Young, known as 'The St Albans Poisoner', who was sent to Broadmoor in 1962 at the age of 14 for giving poison to his father, sister and friend. He was released as "no longer a danger" in 1971 when he killed two more people with poison and injured six others. He died in prison in 1990.

Zipperface (1992)
Dir: Mansour Pourmand /USA

Florida's first female detective (Donna Adams) squares up to the title character, a leather-clad, S&M sadist who wears a gimp mask and enjoys murdering prostitutes. This is routine, police procedural nonsense that has nothing on Friedkin's *Cruising* (1980). It's a fairly slick and professional-looking production but is cast entirely with planks of wood. And this spoils things. The heroine is so plain she may as well be a glass of water on legs.

Zombie Wars: War of the Living Dead (2007)
Dir: David A. Prior /USA

Set decades after the zombie apocalypse, the living dead have had 50 years to evolve, and have reached the stage where they have enslaved humans and farm them for food. The last resistance comes in the form of a ragtag band of soldiers who use guerilla warfare tactics against the 'puss-bags.' *Zombie Wars* has its moments – it works best during the fleeting battle sequences – but too much time is wasted on characters sitting around and talking about their pasts (i.e. poor character development), and earnestly blowing smoke up each other's bottoms. Low on narrative drive but high on entrail-ripping, this film is basically a remake of the VHS anti-classic, *Blood Rush* (1983), with zombies standing in for the evil, post-apocalyptic slave-drivers.

Zombio (1999)
Dir: Peter Baiestorf /Brazil
A man drags his girlfriend through the Brazilian zombie wilderness and fondles her tits while fending off the occasional rotter that comes by. *Zombio* is empty-headed non-entertainment used as a way of promoting local punk and metal bands by having their music constantly swamping up on the soundtrack. This is beyond 'bottom of the barrel,' beyond *Hunting Creatures*, *Redneck Zombies* and *Automation Transfusion*, beyond the worst movies ever made, and out to some far-flung dimension that sucks all the life and colour out of you. If there is a hell, it will probably entail being strapped to a chair and being forced to watch this video over and over again for eternity. The U.S. Military should screen this at Guantanamo Bay; believe me, the terrorists will tell them all they want to know so long as they promise to switch it off.